Red Sauce

Red Sauce

How Italian Food Became American

Ian MacAllen

ROWMAN & LITTLEFIELD
Lanham • Boulder • New York • London

Published by Rowman & Littlefield
An imprint of The Rowman & Littlefield Publishing Group, Inc.
4501 Forbes Boulevard, Suite 200, Lanham, Maryland 20706
www.rowman.com

86-90 Paul Street, London EC2A 4NE, United Kingdom

British Library Cataloguing in Publication Information Available

Library of Congress Cataloging-in-Publication Data

Names: MacAllen, Ian, 1981– author.
Title: Red sauce : how Italian food became American / Ian MacAllen.
Description: Lanham : Rowman & Littlefield, [2022] | Includes
  bibliographical references and index. | Summary: "A narrative social
  history tracing the evolution of traditional Italian American cuisine
  from its origins in Italy and its transformation in America into a
  distinct new cuisine"— Provided by publisher.
Identifiers: LCCN 2021042830 (print) | LCCN 2021042831 (ebook) | ISBN
  9781538162347 (cloth) | ISBN 9781538162354 (epub)
Subjects: LCSH: Tomato sauces—United States—History. | Italian
  Americans—Foods—History. | Cooking, Italian—History. | Cooking,
  American—History. | Food habits—Italy—History. | Food habits—United
  States—History.
Classification: LCC TX819.T65 M33 2022 (print) | LCC TX819.T65 (ebook) |
  DDC 641.81/4—dc23/eng/20211004
LC record available at https://lccn.loc.gov/2021042830
LC ebook record available at https://lccn.loc.gov/2021042831

For Annmarie, who wanted to read a book.

Contents

Acknowledgments

Writing a book begins as a solitary endeavor, but it never concludes that way. I am so grateful to the numerous people who have helped over the years of research and writing.

First, I need to thank my writing and workshopping group: Jonathan Corcoran, Max Gray, and Mark Labowskie for their support with craft and literary gossip. I am also grateful to Marisa Siegel and everyone at *The Rumpus*, who have all supported my growth as a writer, and Catherine LaSota and the Cabana Club, who have been essential for kvetching about the pandemic and supportive through the final phases of preparing the book.

I am forever grateful to Clayton Lamar, who is always willing to be my first reader, and to Kristen Majewski, Heather Pharo, Cyriaque Lamar, Annick Lamar, and Peter Geller, who have put up with hearing about many obscure macaroni and tomato sauce facts.

Thank you to Brian Gresko for his guidance preparing the book proposal. Thank you to Jonathan Agin and O'Connor Literary for believing in the project and guiding me through this process, as well as Suzanne Staszak-Silva and everyone else at Rowman & Littlefield for trusting me. Thank you to Sabrina Cartan for your insights to publicize the book and to Emily Epstein for connecting me to the right people. I am, of course, indebted to the New York Public Library for maintaining many rare and expensive books and online database access. Thank you also to my parents, Arlene and Tom Mac Allen, and my in-laws, Joe and Judy Pisano, for serving many varieties of red sauce through the years and, of course, for keeping tabs on Bruno.

And, finally, an especially big thank you to Annmarie Pisano, who put up with many piles of research books stacked around the living room and endless talk of sauce. I would promise it won't happen again, but we know that's not true.

Introduction

My mother enjoys telling the story of the night she met her future mother-in-law. My grandmother cooked spaghetti that night as an acknowledgment of my mother's Italian ancestry. It was the mid-1970s, and my blue-blooded grandmother was better at mixing martinis than cooking spaghetti. As my mother tells the story, my grandmother threw a strand of spaghetti against the tiled backsplash before turning to my mother and asking, "That's how you know it's cooked, right?" In some retellings, depending on my mother's audience, my grandmother declares this more matter-of-factly, and other times she asks somewhat humbly. But in all versions of the story, my mother replies smugly, "No, we taste it."

My mother's parents arrived in the United States as part of the great wave of Italian immigration in the decades straddling the turn of the twentieth century. My grandfather was born in Bagnoli del Trigno, in what is now the Molise region. My maternal grandmother's family descended from Naples and Sicily. They were, as was typical of prewar Italian immigrants, from the south of the country. They settled in immigrant enclaves surrounded by the friends and neighbors who left Italy alongside them.

My wife, like me, is descended from mix of Italian and northern Europeans. Her sprawling Italian American family has red sauce deeply entrenched in their traditions. When we first started dating, she introduced me to a trattoria in the West Village. She called it Italian Home Cooking, although the sign on the awning said Trattoria Spaghetto. She and

1

her family had been eating there since the restaurant opened in the early 1980s. Trattoria Spaghetto was everything a red sauce joint should be: red checkered tablecloths, spaghetti and meatballs, squat bottles of Chianti, and crunchy breadsticks. These became not just symbols of Italian American restaurants but also, for a generation, the image of the entire nation. Where Italian Americans settled, they opened restaurants modeled on this nostalgic fantasy.

I was eating a plate of rigatoni alla vodka and halfway through a carafe of house red wine when I posed the question: *Where did all of this come from?* My wife and I both knew spaghetti and meatballs were not Italian from Italy, and veal parmigiana was likely some American invention. We'd both traveled through Italy. We had eaten authentic Italian food in Rome and Milan and across the countryside. But this question left me wondering about the origins of Italian American food. Who invented it? Where? Why?

For most of the twentieth century, in the United States, red sauce has been synonymous with Italy and Italian cuisine. It expanded from an ethnic food into a widespread cultural phenomenon. Yet, more recently, red sauce has been displaced by "northern" Italian food. Television personalities, contemporary cookbooks, and eventually social media have reinforced the importance of seeking out authentic Italian recipes. Red sauce has fallen out of favor, even as pizza, lasagna, and spaghetti and meatballs have grown into American staples.

I set out to out to discover the stories surrounding the origins of red sauce recipes and offer a narrative history of how and why red sauce came into existence. What I found was the story of poor immigrants working hard, integrating into their new nation, sharing their cultural and culinary traditions, and eventually becoming a seamlessly accepted part of the broader American culture. I had found the story of the American dream.

1

❖ ❖

Salty Like the Sea

In an early episode of the television series *The Sopranos*, Paulie Walnuts and Sal "Big Pussy" Bonpensiero saunter into a chain coffee shop as the barista calls out drink orders. The corrupted Italian drink names the barista shouts mirror the grande, venti, and trenta drinks from the corporate lexicon of Starbucks. As they wait for their coffee, Paulie bemoans how Italian Americans missed out on their opportunity to exploit coffee. He looks around the busy establishment. Customers are everywhere. He launches into a rant about how Italians invented coffee culture while providing some choice expletives on the people profiting from it.

In some respects, Paulie is correct. The modern espresso machine, with high pressure applied to ground beans, was invented by the Italian Achille Gaggia in 1945, and even the founder of Starbucks has pointed to his own travels to Italy as the inspiration behind the chain.[1] Although early Italian espresso machine patents date as far back as 1884 in Italy,[2] coffee remained largely an unattainable luxury product. Italians living in Italy during the period of immigration had at most only one espresso per week.[3] Only in later decades, when Italian brands began marketing their products to those immigrants, a natural client base, did these former subsistence farmers and laborers enjoy Italian luxuries like espresso. Marketing linked the products of the Old World to the immigrants in America, even though most of those people had been too poor to enjoy those products while in Italy.

Paulie continues ranting about the commodification of Italian foods like pizza, cheese, and olive oil. Indignant over the corporate appropriation of foods he perceives as part of his heritage, his anger is in response to the shift in the perception of Italian American cuisine from a cheap, low-quality ethnic food into a commodity product, mass marketed, and often symbolizing American imperialism. Yet he fails to comprehend how so much of his own understanding of Italian culture has been crafted by these corporations.

This disconnect is best illustrated by Paulie's experience abroad when Tony Soprano and his crew travel to Sicily. The Italian mobsters treat Tony's entourage to elaborate restaurant meals. Paulie feels a deep, personal connection to the country even though he had never visited before, speaks only a few words of an antiquated dialect, and struggles to fit in. He even finds the food unfamiliar. At one point he demands the waiter bring him a plate of macaroni with gravy. This request stumps the Italians, who don't understand until he clarifies, with a look of annoyance, that he means a tomato sauce. For Paulie, Italian food is a tomato-based cuisine, but he is mistaking the tradition of Italian American red sauce for contemporary Italian food. His conception of Italian-ness aligns with concepts constructed by the very restaurant chains he maligns as having appropriated and commodified his heritage.

The perception of Italian food in America has evolved alongside the perception of Italian Americans. Today, Italian American foods like pizza or spaghetti and meatballs are synonymous with Americans and American food, available in every state at a variety of price points. Yet when Italian immigrants first arrived in the United States, Americans of northern European ancestry viewed the food eaten by Italian immigrants as too foreign and ethnic, the strong spice of garlic off-putting and foods like pizza and lasagna unpronounceable.

But during the course of the twentieth century, Italian American food traditions expanded from catering to immigrants residing in ethnic enclaves to Americans of all sorts, of all races, and of all ethnicities. Red sauce cuisine, the tradition of foods closely linked with tomato-based sauces, grew in popularity, first as an acceptable ethnic food before eventually losing the connotation of ethnicity altogether. Fast-food restaurants like Pizza Hut and sit-down restaurants like Olive Garden have brought Italian American food to every corner of the country, from suburban strip malls to Times Square.

Pizza Hut, the earliest of the big fast-food pizza chains, had almost 7,500 restaurants serving in-store meals and takeout[4] before the pandemic-related economic slowdown. Little Caesars, Domino's, Papa John's, and other chains have tens of thousands of pizzerias serving up Italian-influenced products from pizzas with pineapple to irreverent pasta combinations. The expansion of mass-market Italian American cuisine was not limited to fast-food chains. The sit-down, casual restaurants that defined the wealth and abundance of middle-class lifestyles in the 1990s included concepts themed around Italian ethnicity as well. Brands like Romano's Macaroni Grill, Johnny Carino's, Carraba's, Bertucci's, and Buca di Beppo sell Italian-influenced cuisine nationwide. The largest of these chains, Olive Garden, boasted 840 restaurants serving 391 combinations of Italian-inspired pasta dishes in 2018.[5] These chains helped make Italian American food available in every corner of the United States. Paulie Walnuts may not agree, but it is now safe to say Italian American food has become simply American food.

To see how entrenched Olive Garden has become in American culture, we only need to consider its breadsticks. Every Olive Garden serves un-limited breadsticks—warm, puffy bread seasoned by a proprietary blend of garlic, salt, and butter, and a hallmark of the chain since it opened in 1982. The breadsticks are not especially Italian, although the garlic flavor had been synonymous with Italian immigrants—the strong odor has been referred to, in a diminutive way, as Italian perfume.[6] Yet these breadsticks featured prominently in news headlines in September 2014 when the American hedge fund Starboard Value published an epic three-hundred-page PowerPoint presentation criticizing the popular eatery. For one thing, the breadsticks had become a costly liability. Servers brought baskets with too many breadsticks to each table. The bread grew cold, becoming ined-ible, and diners would ask for more, leading to waste.

The investment group assembled the report in an effort to outline its strategy for revitalizing the chain. Starboard Value was engaged in a proxy fight with the company's management team, and it intended the presenta-tion to win over stockholders. The analysts hardly expected to attract the attention of the mainstream media and internet meme makers, much less to achieve viral fame. The popularity of the presentation spoke to a hard truth facing Olive Garden at the time: America loved Italian food, so why didn't America still love Olive Garden?

At busy times, it was not unheard for families to spend upward of two hours waiting for a table at the Olive Garden. Yet, by 2014, Darden Restau-rants' empire saw declining customers in nine out of fourteen years.[7] Casual dining restaurants were losing the shrinking middle-class, with wealthier customers dining elsewhere and poorer customers dining less often. The great wealth of previous years had given way to declining sales across the board, but Olive Garden had been hit by particularly difficult times.

Starboard Value's presentation outlined a number of strategies the investors believed could improve the outlook of Darden Restaurants generally, but Olive Garden captured the attention of the media with clickbait headlines detailing the fall of the once-mighty terra-cotta-tiled empire. "Transforming Darden Restaurants" was the PowerPoint presentation heard around the world. *BuzzFeed* turned the report into a series of memes highlighting the worst offenses, and *Slate*'s article "Olive Garden Has Been Committing a Culinary Crime against Humanity" highlighted the short-sightedness of not salting pasta water.[8] And two years after publishing the analysis, *Vanity Fair* credited the hedge fund report with saving Olive Garden from financial ruin by highlighting its many failures.[9] It isn't every day that an obscure financial analyst ends up making headlines with a PowerPoint presentation, but Starboard Value had struck a chord. While plenty of articles discussed the chain's signature breadsticks, the most damning elements of the report highlighted food quality: Olive Garden wasn't even salting the pasta water.

Adding salt to the boiling water used to cook pasta provides flavor and reduces the pasta's starchy stickiness. Celebrity chefs have instructed home cooks on the method for three decades through avenues like Food Network and competitive cooking shows on numerous networks, as well as glossy magazines and food blogs, with "salty like the sea" becoming a popular adage. By 2014, even the most rudimentary home cook had been well educated and was familiar with the technique. Salting the water, however, voided the warranty on the restaurant's cookware, and yet Italian-influenced pasta dishes were Olive Garden's signature food. Consumers noticed.

Unsalted pasta water wasn't the only problem identified, with an analysis finding other issues with the overall food quality. Pasta came out of the kitchen overcooked. Sauces were simply ladled over the pasta rather than tossed together. Specialty dishes had been replaced with less appetizing choices. Yet it wasn't just the sloppy, low-quality preparations damaging the restaurant. The report declared Olive Garden's most dire concern had been the shift away from authentic food. The report used the word *authentic* or *authenticity* on twenty-six pages before concluding that turning the restaurant around would require updating the menu, notably to include, as might be guessed, more authentic dishes. Although Starboard Value even went as far as suggesting several new items such as a vegetable Bolognese sauce, it never actually defined a metric of authenticity.

In the same way Paulie Walnuts had come to link himself to Italy, the marketing around Olive Garden had also always hinted at a loose connection to old-world Europe. The first iteration of the theme included stores designed to look like Mediterranean villas. The chain also launched a series of television commercials claiming to send its chefs to a Tuscan culinary institute housed in a similar villa. The commercials depicted a mountaintop Italian town, with chefs-in-training diligently standing over a stove, introducing audiences to Chef Neri, a kind of cross between an Italian grandmother and a stern but wise culinary master. And yet their signature menu items like spaghetti with meatballs, chicken alfredo, and chicken *parmigiana* have far less connection to Tuscany than the cuisine of Italian Americans arriving during the great wave of immigration. Adding a vegetable Bolognese sauce may have expanded the restaurant's appeal for vegetarians, but authentic vegetable Bolognese is impossible. It can be authentic, or it can be vegetarian, but not both. What the Starboard Value report authors wanted to say is Olive Garden had strayed too far from the Italian American traditions that the casual restaurant had been built on. They employed the term *authentic* not to mean authentically Italian, but rather authentically Italian American, a variation of the cuisine arriving with Italian immigrants over a century earlier.

Olive Garden had come to represent a certain kind of authentic America. The heyday of the chain had been during the great economic boom of the 1990s, a period that corresponded with the heyday of the American middle class. Italians in America by then had become a well-established group—so much so that they weren't really all that ethnic anymore. The swell of Italian immigrants had been staunched two generations before, with the vast majority of Italian Americans now in their second and third generation and having accumulated wealth and political and cultural influence. They had an all-American mythology too, as mobsters in movies like *The Godfather*, baseball heroes like Joe DiMaggio, or entertainment legends like Frank Sinatra. Italian American food had lost its ethnic connotations and simply became American food.

Red sauce has not always been such a widely available, widely accepted, widely eaten cuisine. Spaghetti confused early adopters. Pizza was unpronounceable. Garlic was feared. A little more than a hundred years before viral outrage over Olive Garden's refusal to salt its pasta water, Italian American red sauce was a frightening ethnic food consumed by a maligned immigrant group in crowded urban ghettos in cities like New York, Boston, Chicago, New Haven, and Baltimore. The evolution from peasant food to icon of the middle class transpired over the course of the twentieth century, bolstered by a war, reinterpreted by the Midwest, and reinvented over and over again right up until and including the Olive Garden's Fried Lasagna Fritta, a dish that earned the scorn of Starboard Value's analysts.

American red sauce cuisine is influenced by the traditions of Italian immigrants, but it is not Italian food. Tomatoes, pasta, and cheese all play a vital role in red sauce cuisine; there are, of course, exceptions, with a few dishes lacking tomatoes entirely. The cuisine is largely (although not exclusively) drawn from southern Italian recipes, though often these are not necessarily the domestic recipes Italian immigrants had cooked in their homes. In this regard, red sauce cuisine is as much an invention of Americans as of Italians. The evolution of these recipes can be traced across multiple decades beginning in the first years of the twentieth century. Many earlier Italian American dishes have since faded from the forefront of menus and cookbooks, giving way to the midcentury recipes that dominate the remaining Italian American restaurants.

In the latter half of the twentieth century, red sauce began to adapt again in response to the changing expectations of a more cultured world. As Americans, particularly those in the middle class, learned how to eat such exotic dishes like spaghetti and meatballs, the red sauce restaurants of old found themselves competing with new, modern imported recipes. Restaurants employed terms like *authentic* and *northern* to distinguish their menus from red sauce dishes, and embracing modern international style of Italian cuisine.

As of the 2012 census data, there are more than 21,000 Italian restaurants generating over $25 billion in annual sales in the United States.[10] There are more than 35,000 restaurants where the principal menu item is pizza. Although the census does not distinguish between restaurants serving traditional red sauce menus and "northern Italian" or "authentic" Italian, the love of Italian-influenced cuisine began with the red sauce traditions of immigrants, and even when modern Italian restaurants market themselves as genuinely Italian, they often include a few classic Italian American dishes to appease customer expectations.

The evolution of Italian American cuisine is the story of immigrants finding acceptance, evolving from ethnic foreigners into mainstream Americans, and serving up in fast-casual mall restaurants across the nation. Red sauce is a distinct cuisine invented through the confluence of Italian immigration, the bounty of the expanding American economy, and the unique cultural interactions between disparate ethnic groups in early twentieth-century American cities. It is also the story of impoverished peasants improvising and reinventing to imitate lifestyles they could have only dreamed of in their native country, and in the process, they created these beloved foods, while integrating into mainstream society. This is the story of red sauce.

2

❖ ❖

The Great Arrival

Italians first arrived in North America with the Spanish, before English settlers or the establishment of the colonies that eventually would become the United States. These Italians came from regions of Italy and Sicily ruled by the Spanish king. The Spanish treated Italians as equals,[1] but they represented only the tiniest fraction of Europeans arriving in North America. They trickled in as tradesmen, skilled artisans, and occasionally as merchants. Most of these Italians did not even consider themselves Italian since they lived under the rule of independent principalities, republics, or kingdoms. Their identity was tied to these regions rather than Italy as a whole. They formed small communities in places like New Orleans and as far west as California, serving as gateways to imported Italian products and trade with counterparts in Europe. In New Orleans, Italian merchants would eventually create trading pathways to exchange the grain of the American heartland with products like Sicilian oranges, a practice proving profitable for both parties. Californian settlers benefited from a climate similar to Italy and thrived by farming domestic agricultural products to sell to Italian immigrants. By the nineteenth century, California produced high-quality olive oil[2] and later became a major tomato producer, as well as wine and garlic.

These early Italian groups did not contribute substantially to the red sauce culinary tradition, a movement that began much later and mainly originated in East Coast cities. Italian merchants did rely on macaroni—

dried pasta—to feed sailors at sea. They created a pathway to introducing macaroni to America, and quite possibly a link to early macaroni and cheese dishes. Early American macaroni and cheese recipes were widely distributed and varied, particularly across the southern states, and appeared long before tomato sauce and pasta.

Italians in New Orleans did create the muffuletta sandwich, contributing to the Italian American culinary tradition. Filled with Italian meats and named for Sicilian bread, Italian merchants made the sandwiches, often from scraps, in the nineteenth century, with Central Grocery selling the sandwich around the dawn of the twentieth century. A layer of olive tapenade distinguishes the muffuletta from other sandwiches containing Italian meats. The specific meat varies by sandwich maker but usually includes preserved pork and salted ham or cured sausages or both. The muffuletta sandwich draws on creole traditions as well as Italian and is distinctly part of a New Orleans culinary tradition.

The muffuletta is not the only sandwich featuring Italian meats. Cured meats had been an important part of the upper-class culinary tradition on the Italian peninsula since the sixteenth century. Shops known as salumeria sold smoked and cured meat. Their popularity grew because Pope Gregory XIII had adopted new austerity policies in 1572 banning bishops and cardinals from employing more than one household chef. The sudden culling of their household staff created two problems: excess staff trained in culinary arts and too few staff to prepare elaborate meals. The surplus chefs opened the shops to cater to these and other upper-class Italian households.[3] Salumeria allowed wealthy households to supplement their tables without additional staff by outsourcing food preparation, but the meats remained a luxury product. A few centuries later, in the United States, meat grew more accessible to poorer households. Immigrants imitated the lifestyles of the wealthy, and cured meats were sometimes offered as an antipasto (the appetizer course) at restaurants to mimic these luxuries. Early antipasto were simple affairs. The legendarily grand experience now common at Italian American weddings, as depicted in *The Sopranos*, or available at red sauce restaurants, did not come into being until much later when Leone's, the Times Square spaghetti palace, turned the humble antipasto into a grandiose, twelve-item extravaganza.[4]

Cured Italian meats also commingled with other ethnic foods in places like New York City, where German immigrants brought a tradition of delicatessen, specialty shops providing luxury foods or delicacies. Jewish Germans in particular embraced delicatessen, adding prepared foods alongside kosher butchered meat. Early delicatessens appeared in New York in the 1870s, and Jewish and German immigrants were not immune to the great abundance offered in America. The shops displayed their goods in the window to show off this bounty.[5] New York's delicatessens helped encourage a sandwich culture, and by the 1920s, New York had grown into a city of sandwich eaters. A survey undertaken by George Jean Nathan found 946 unique sandwich varieties, including one made with spaghetti.[6] Italian cured meats were no exception to the sandwich trend, with the evolution of the "Italian hero" describing sandwiches made from long loaves of Italian bread, along with hot variations featuring meatballs and veal. The term *Italian hero* entered the lexicon in the 1930s in New York, with other regional variations like "hoagie" in Philadelphia, "grinder" in New England, and "submarine" after the submarines at the Groton, Connecticut, naval base,[7] and in Chicago, an Italian beef was sliced meat with hot peppers.[8]

The intermingling of food between immigrant groups was common, especially in crowded cities like New York. Jewish and Italian immigrants lived in close proximity in the Lower East Side neighborhood. "Deli" grew into a popular food across ethnic groups by the postwar period, and Italian dried sausages and cured hams fit alongside pastrami and brisket in nonkosher providers. Pizzerias can function as de facto Italian delicatessens, selling more than the signature pizza pie by offering prepared Italian dishes, cured meats, deli meat sandwiches, and hot sandwiches such as veal parmigiana.

In California, Italian Americans contributed cioppino, a seafood soup, to the American culinary heritage. The soup consists of whole fish, clams, and crab or other shellfish, cooked with tomatoes and onions. Although the soup does contain tomatoes, its limited regionality implies it is outside a national red sauce cuisine. Cioppino is better classified as part of regional California recipe tradition rather than associated with Italian Americans more broadly. Although its origins in San Francisco are tied to Italian American immigrants, it originates with people from the northern regions who arrived with the Spanish, further distinguishing it from recipes of the red sauce tradition.

Italian-born immigrants remained a small fraction of the total immigrant population in the United States until the end of the nineteenth century. During the early years of the American republic, the few Italian arrivals tended to come from northern regions and principalities. Almost all were skilled artisans, such as stone masons, and recruited for specific projects. Thomas Jefferson, naturally inquisitive and enriched by slave labor, had the luxury of time and money, and he played an outsized role in the Italian American narrative. As a farmer, he promoted the tomato. As an industrialist, he acquired a pasta-making machine. And as a statesman, he invited Italian sculptors to work the marble on the House of Representatives. Skilled sculptors and painters from Italy helped build many of the monuments in Washington and nearby Baltimore.[9]

In addition to skilled artisans, merchants from Genoa and surrounding provinces made up a significant number of these earliest arrivals,[10] working as traders connecting to networks in the Mediterranean and setting up the pathways that would support larger populations of Italians purchasing imported goods later. Merchants and artisans tended to possess in-demand skills and, as a result, accumulated wealth. Nevertheless, the total number of immigrants remained miniscule up until the 1880s. In 1860, the census counted less than twelve thousand Italian-born immigrants, out of 5.5 million foreign born.[11]

Beginning in the early 1880s, immigration from Italy began to change dramatically, primarily by rapidly accelerating. Between 1876 and the First World War, more than half a million Italians left,[12] and by the start of the Second World War, more than nine million Italians had arrived in the United States.[13] Italians also settled in other countries in the Americas. Of immigrants coming to the United States, Italians made up a huge percentage of the total number during these decades, while previously they represented only a very small fraction of foreign arrivals.

Conditions on the peninsula had changed when the nation of Italy formed as a politically united entity in 1871. The people remained culturally distinct, including linguistically and culinarily. The political unification also exaggerated an important reality: northern Italy possessed a lot more wealth than southern Italy. This wealth disparity had a big influence on the second change in immigration patterns: southerners left. Unlike the artisans and merchants recruited to the United States, southern immigrants were predominantly peasant farmers. America promised higher wages, social advancement, and the opportunity to accumulate wealth. Red sauce cuisine evolved directly as a result of the confluence of this shift in immigration patterns as this new wave of immigrants arrived in America, confronted American abundance, and flourished.

Southern Italian immigrants departed from the *mezzogiorno*, the area encompassing the south of Italy, Sicily and Sardinia, with Rome generally considered part of this area. The southern Italians settled first along the Atlantic seaboard in cities like New York before spreading westward to Chicago and eventually California, constructing Little Italy neighborhoods throughout the country. In these enclaves, imported Italian goods became available, along with shops, restaurants, and community organizations. But even within these enclaves, the residents clung to their regional and local identities. Micro enclaves within immigrant neighborhoods formed with people from specific cities clustering together.

These neighborhoods catering to the hodgepodge of "Italians" would germinate a new kind of cuisine with broad-stroke representation of a myriad of local tastes, combined with the abundance made possible by American industry. The resulting recipes emerging from these interactions is what we think of as red sauce cuisine, evolving in both restaurants and domestic kitchens. Red sauce recipes are dominated by tomato-based sauces, but as a broader cultural concept, restaurants included tropes like Chianti wine bottles wrapped in straw and red gingham tablecloths, constructs curated by the immigrants to represent a sense of nostalgia for their homeland.

The southern Italians did not come to the United States intending to invent a new cuisine. Many intended to return to Italy, and some did. They sought wealth and opportunity, a chance to rise above the nothingness Italy offered them. In the southern regions, control of the land fell to a few wealthy, landed *padroni*[14] (the bosses). The workers who farmed the land never had control of it. A labor surplus kept wages low, and farmers maintained their subsistence but had few other opportunities. Their living conditions were far from the bucolic countryside captured by Hollywood. These farmers did not live on stunning Tuscan villas. Instead, they resided in (even by European standards of the time) low-quality housing that was small, without flooring, with unplastered walls, and often the door served as the only opening for light and venting chimney smoke.[15] These people left Italy because conditions were bad and there was no hope of those conditions improving, while America promised a significantly better quality of life. Many intended to work in the United States for a time and return to Italy with wealth to buy access to land, and many sent wages home in the interim.

The immigrants also wrote home with news of the abundance available to them.[16] Sometimes they embellished, but, in general, the standard of living for those who came to America was unimaginably better, with greater access to food and the promise of one day owning land or having access to their own small patches of land for growing food, even in cities. With this abundance came a greater variety of food choices. The food and life made available to immigrants became known as the *abbondanza* (the abundance). This concept fundamentally shaped the way Italian American recipes evolved. American variations celebrate bounty and quantity, where more is always better.

Even though arriving in America meant more wealth and better access to food, the abbondanza was imperfect. Italian immigrants earned low wages compared to other immigrant groups. Italians were generally considered cheap laborers for employers.[17] The "self-made" Italians didn't necessarily fare any better. One common business Italians launched was selling fruit and vegetables from pushcarts, but these were not always lucrative. Many peddlers ate the bruised and moldy fruit from their cart rather than buying fresh goods for themselves.[18] From pushcarts, successful entrepreneurs eventually set up more permanent stores. Italians worked as grocers and butchers, with more than ten thousand Italian-owned grocery stores operating by the 1930s in New York City alone.[19]

Another common income source included boarding fellow immigrants, and families would host lodgers in some rooms of their tenement while living in the main part of the house. Men often arrived ahead of their families, or never intended to bring their families with them, creating a natural customer for boarding houses. Some of the industrious would also make and sell pasta, suspending the drying product from the ceiling above where the family slept.[20]

Despite these challenges, life in America was generally considered more plentiful than back at home. The abbondanza meant people who had lived a primarily vegetarian lifestyle could suddenly consume meat with much more frequency, as often as once or even several times a week. This abundance came from not just better wages but also cheaper food. In Italy, peasant families paid nearly 10 percent of their annual income just toward the taxes on food[21] and even owed taxes on the produce they grew in vegetable patches.[22] American food, in part because of rapid industrialization, expansion of railroads, and innovations in production, was far cheaper.

As food-canning industries matured, canned foods evolved from a luxury item for the wealthy into a readily accessible product providing low-cost, high-quality food. Early canned foods were expensive, a means of preserving fruits and vegetables that would spoil a few weeks after harvest. But as production ramped up and techniques were perfected, canned products provided a variety of foods year-round. Tomatoes especially benefited from canning operations, and railroads expanded markets for fresh produce over the same period, allowing fruits and vegetables like tomatoes grown in the south and eventually places like California to reach markets where immigrant communities settled.

The Italians arriving in this period ate in the style of *cucina povera*, the poor kitchen, a way of cooking invented out of necessity: increasing calories mattered, vegetables dominated, meat was a rare treat, and waste nonexistent. Cucina povera meant not just recipes that immigrants reproduced in their domestic kitchens but also an entire philosophy of cooking, a style the immigrants retained even as they grew their personal wealth in America.

Cucina povera contrasted with *cucina ricci* (the rich kitchen), a style of cooking associated with French chefs and aristocrats, who preferred pale-colored foods.[23] The peasant farmers of the mezzogiorno rarely (if ever) had access to these foods, including the meat common in the cucina ricci. Especially rare for peasants were whole cuts of meat. If and when they could afford to buy meat, they usually bought sausages made from scraps or offal. As laborers left southern Italy, wages did rise. Yet, even with this increase, southerners consumed only half the meat of northern Italians in 1901.[24]

Red sauce cuisine owes a great deal of its richness to the fact that the immigrant groups never actually consumed foods produced in the cucina ricci style. Only once immigrants arrived in the United States and earned better wages could they afford better foods, but they lacked the experience of eating the expensive foods of their homeland. The recipes invented or augmented in America often have sumptuous properties because peasants were imitating what they believed the rich ate. The resulting recipes are merely interpretations of food they never had actually eaten. Italian travelers often found American restaurants lacking familiar or identifiable food.

A third style of Italian cooking, *le cucini dei conventi*, existed in the monasteries and nunneries. Monastic cooking, with access to dedicated gardens, often was rich with fruits and vegetables.[25] These cooking traditions are more likely to thrive today as cooks seek out some version of authenticity, but, like cucina ricci, monastic diets were not really obtainable for the average southern peasant. Even in places like New York, when immigrants had better access to those foods, monastic cooking was not aspirational in the way kitchens of the rich appealed to the newly wealthy.

In the United States, ingredients like meat found their way into the ordinary diet of Italian Americans. Red sauce cuisine evolved as a tradition created by poor eaters' understanding of wealthy cooking combined with their own familiar recipes.

The Italian-born immigrants spent a high proportion of their income on food. Despite sending wages back to Italy, many paid a premium for imported products like Italian olive oil and Italian cheese and even Italian macaroni.[26] Food often superseded other desires. In some cases, families struggling to pay for essentials like heating oil would pay the premium prices for genuine imported cheese and olive oil rather than concede to American products.[27]

The established Genoese merchants facilitated trade. They provided links to food from home, creating direct conduits between Italian-produced goods and the immigrants settling in the United States. These merchants proved essential. Italians in America grew their small street pushcart fruit stands into grocery stores with imported goods and even early pizzerias. Eventually some of these stores evolved into specialty, luxury shops serving descendants of immigrants who had grown wealthier and no longer even lived in the traditional ethnic ghettos. Shops like Di Palo's in New York thrive today because the goods they sell have high value and target consumers beyond the small ethnic groups they once served.

Di Palo's exemplifies the evolution of Italian American food culture over the last century. Savino di Palo immigrated around 1903[28] and opened the first iteration of the grocery store, selling fresh-made cheese in 1910.[29] His daughter, Concetta, opened a second business, a grocery store, in 1925.[30] Grocery stores serving the local ethnic communities were a common profession among Italian immigrants, but eventually, as the ethnic community left the neighborhood, the shop evolved into a specialty store focused on high-quality imported goods. The shop is still run by Savino's descendants, who have expanded the operation to include a café.[31] Yet Lou Di Palo, one of Savino's great-grandsons, who heads the store, had only first visited Italy on his honeymoon.[32] In many ways, their family narrative is typical of the evolution of Italian immigrants who worked hard, built a business, and established themselves successfully in America.

In the early twentieth century, connecting immigrants to the foods they left behind generated big profits. Although the United States already produced huge quantities of wheat, Italian durum wheat was harder and produced better dried pasta, an easily exported good. Olive oil also continued to be hugely important as an Italian export, with California only just beginning to experiment with olive production.

The Italian government, especially the fascist government in the 1920s and 1930s, relied on exporting food to raise cash to support the regime. Even as the fascists pushed an ascetic diet and limited pasta consumption at home, they continued exporting products to America. Domestic American producers would eventually produce comparable products, but it would require disruptions in global trade created by the world wars and protectionist tariffs. The immigrant communities remained slow to accept alternatives even when they had become well established as Americans. The tariffs slapped on Italian products in the lead-up to World War II made many imported products too expensive, especially during the Depression years. Until then, immigrant groups largely ignored domestic versions of products, and the tariffs saved the California tomato-canning industry.

Consumer culture, particularly of food, helped forge the Italian American identity, with substitute American products perceived (often correctly) as inferior. America's breadbasket produced large quantities of wheat, but it was softer, lower-quality wheat. Immigrants, who now had a greater buying power as laborers in America than they did as peasants in Italy, wanted to pay for the best. Immigrants attempted to replicate Italian recipes, but the abundance of certain ingredients or the shortage of others dictated what they cooked.[33] Although ingredients influenced how Italian American cuisine evolved, at the time these people still largely thought of themselves not as Italian but by their regional identity. Sicilians, Neapolitans, Calebresans—the provincial identities remained. Italy had only just been politically united when the mass migration started. But what was united were the exported products. The marketing of Italian products lost regional identity and instead were advertised as Italian.[34] The branding helped invent the idea of a unified Italian cuisine even when the country itself was not culturally unified.

Food played a major role in Italian American culture, and that significance is in large part the reason so many of the red sauce dishes emerged as standard, everyday fare. First, food linked the immigrants with a homeland many planned on returning to. They dreamed of returning wealthier than the bosses they had escaped. Splurging on imported food kept that connection and that dream alive, a reminder of why they had separated from their families.

Another important factor was in holding together the family units that had been separated by time and space. The evening meal became ritual, "a tangible expression of family solidarity, loyalty and love."[35] The crowding of tenement buildings did not prevent Italian families from squeezing together for a meal. Multiple generations and extended families often lived in the same building or within a few blocks, and meals were regularly part of maintaining these bonds. Moreover, as the children of immigrants began to grow up in the United States and started adopting American values, the family meal became a method of control. Parents accepted their children's participation in American mores so long as they continued to appear at and participate in family meals at home.[36]

Italian American culture, as a result of these demands, embraced celebratory foods. Family meals meant celebrating family itself. Often a meal meant the reunion of family after long periods separated. The sumptuous nature of red sauce is linked with the desire to express the joy of family.

The cultural link of food also made Italians the target of social reformers. Looking to see greater integration of ethnic communities, reformers started with school lunches, where they hoped to assimilate immigrant children through their stomachs and made clear distinctions between American food and Italian food in places like school lunchrooms.[37] It is with some irony that years later, government social workers attempted to integrate Puerto Rican communities into New York City by teaching them about Italian American–style spaghetti.[38] For all of these reasons, daily and weekly meals became intertwined with celebration.

Many of the dishes in red sauce cuisine evolved from foods of festival and celebration in response to these factors. The richer the food, the more love was expressed. The new wealth allowed immigrant Italians to eat well all the time, and the distinctions between celebration and regular meals faded over time.

3

❖ ❖

A Macaroni by Any Other Name

Pasta—macaroni, vermicelli, spaghetti, lasagna, tortellini, ravioli, fusilli, ziti, and any of hundreds of shapes—is elemental to red sauce cuisine. The term *pasta* refers to both fresh noodles and dried macaroni, although southern Italian immigrants often use *macaroni* interchangeably for all pasta. A meal without pasta is no meal at all for many Italian Americans, and both fresh-made and dried macaroni have been an indispensable component of Italian and Italian American cuisine for centuries. Macaroni sailed with Italian merchants from cities like Genoa and Venice, and immigrants imported high-quality macaroni when it remained unavailable in the United States. Many families also manufactured their own, both for personal use and to sell. Sauced pasta dishes evolved in America to become more sumptuous, heartier meals and are served as an entrée rather than an intermediary dinner course. Most important, pasta's affordability, adaptability, and versatility aided in the transformation of pasta dishes from an ethnic food into a mass-marketed, mainstream American food.

Italian pasta did not originate, as myth would hold, with the return from China of Marco Polo. This well-known legend appeared in *The Macaroni Journal*, a trade publication intent on selling ever-greater quantities of pasta. The magazine often published tall tales surrounding Italian American food to assist its subscribers—mainly pasta manufacturers, grocers, and manufacturers of pasta equipment—in attracting new customers. The publication suggested Marco Polo obtained spaghetti on his adventures with a story sponsored by the Keystone Macaroni Company of Lebanon, Pennsylvania.[1] The adventure narrative added a bit of intrigue to the basic pantry item. Although Marco Polo may have returned to Italy with dried rice-based noodles, Italians had been eating some form of pasta since at least the era of the Roman empire and compared the noodles he came across to their own existing lasagna.[2]

The earliest pasta appears on the Italian peninsula in the ancient period of history. The simplest forms started as sheets of dough, *sfoglia*,[3] which are cut into a variety of sizes. Who invented pasta remains the subject of debate. In one account, the earliest proof of pasta-making appears on the tombs of ancient Etruscans, the people who lived in central Italy before the Romans settled the area. The Etruscans are known to have decorated their tombs with scenes of domestic life, and some scenes contain tools that might be the grooved rolling pins used for cutting sheets of pasta and a wheel for shaping the dough.[4] For many historians, these images are not enough evidence to conclusively declare Etruscans the earliest pasta eaters. If correctly interpreted, the tools depicted in the Etruscan tombs indicate they had developed pasta that could be shaped and cut and, by definition, contained the gluten formed in wheat dough through the process of kneading. The elasticity, firmness, and consistency of gluten distinguishes pasta from other wheat products. Not everyone agrees the illustrations actually depict pasta tools, but if so, they predate Roman pasta consumption.

In the areas of Magna Graecia, the extreme south of the Italian peninsula along the heel and sole of the boot, fresh-made sheets of pasta definitively emerged. The Greeks called these *lagana*,[5] *laganon*,[6] *laganono*, or *lasanon*,[7] depending on the source and the translation and dialect. A direct ancestor of modern pasta sheets better known today as lasagna, these dough sheets could also be cut into smaller strips. Lagana could be made from soft wheat and contained less gluten than modern, dried lasagna noodles, but otherwise was a flat pasta, similar to *tagliatelle* found in Bologna and *maltagliati*, a wider version of tagliatelle. Both are essentially modern names for the various lagana that had been served since ancient Rome.[8]

The Romans also relied on a recipe combining wheat and water to form an early ancestor of pasta, a paste-like dough or mushy gruel known as *pultes*[9] that fed the Roman legions. The critical factor in the success of the dish was the ability to transport the ingredients long distances and feed the army as it marched. Pultes persisted in the culinary legacy of Italy for two millennia, and centuries later, after the discovery of maize during the Columbian Exchange, pultes became a dish recognized today as polenta, a more flavorful and nutrient-rich food than the original wheat paste. Early pultes would be seasoned with the ingredients on hand, mostly salt and cheese and perhaps some dried meat, not unlike the condiments for future pasta recipes. While the paste-like pultes is not a food we would think of as pasta today, it was a very close and a direct predecessor. Unlike pultes, pasta requires not just mixing wheat and water with the correct ratio but also adding the right amount of force to develop gluten. Pultes was not shaped or as structured as lagana, but it was widely consumed.

Whether Romans developed pasta dough themselves or inherited the tradition from the Greeks or Etruscans remains disputed. Both lagana and pultes were present during the era of the Roman empire, but these were fresh products made from soft wheat for immediate consumption. Once the flour became lagana and pultes, the food products quickly degraded. Even worse, before mixed for a meal, wheat flour could easily spoil. Macaroni, a dried pasta product, would dramatically change consumption patterns because, after processing, it became a shelf-stable food. Once dried, macaroni is nearly impossible to spoil and resists pest infestations. The advantage of lagana and pultes is that both can be made with soft, low-gluten wheats that are easier to cultivate and mill. Macaroni works best with higher-gluten flours, and centuries would pass before the dried-pasta revolution.

The turbulent years following the end of the Roman empire disrupted many existing food patterns, particularly agriculture. The Romans had distributed food to their citizens, including bread and pultes, but after the government's collapse, these systems broke down. The stability of the empire allowed for intensive agriculture, but even this diminished. Commercial bread-makers closed. Even staples like olive oil became hard to come by largely because of the time and resources required to produce olives.

Political stability returned in the thirteenth century. Cities grew, trade and commerce flourished, and agriculture expanded. Swamps were drained. Wheat was planted. Agriculture expanded around urban centers, and surplus wheat induced demand. The urban land-reclamation projects led to increased yields, leading to greater consumption of bread and pasta. This era also saw the expansion of dairy milk production in the north and introduction of water buffalo in the south. Both developments would profoundly impact the cuisine over the next few centuries with butter, cheese, and other dairy products growing in importance, especially in northern Italian cuisine. During these years, wheat grew in importance to the economies of the Italian city-states, with places like Venice and Florence creating new regulations and central warehouses for flour and grain provisioning.[10] Soft wheat became widely available and was used in the production of lagana, now starting to take on properties similar to modern lasagna. The medieval era saw lasagna noodles develop a variety of new shapes and sizes.[11] Broad, narrow, long, short, hollow, and filled pasta all emerged. It is likely during this period too that lasagna was first boiled in water rather than cooked in an oven with liquid as lagana had been.[12]

The origins of dried pasta, macaroni, begin in the Mediterranean basin. Dried pasta requires dehydration, and in the ancient world that meant relying on a hot, dry climate with a lot of sun. Sicily in particular, but the southern portion of Italy generally, proved to have the right combination of heat, low humidity, intense sun, and arable land for growing the high-protein durum wheat. Still, the development of macaroni in Italy would not have been possible without the influence of Arab invaders and neighbors from the Mediterranean basin.

In the centuries after the Roman Empire, Sicily was ruled as a Byzantine province and an Arab emirate. Many of the culinary traditions on the island exist because of these interactions, and because of the constant shift in ruling forces. In some accounts, Arab merchants developed dried pasta to feed their caravans transiting the desert,[13] with Sicilians adopting macaroni from them. Long travel periods required portable, shelf-stable foods and products that survive in high heat without refrigeration. Dried pasta is ideal for this purpose, as it doesn't spoil in the heat and can resist pests better than raw grain. Arab populations did consume dried vermicelli—long, string-shaped noodles—as an ingredient in stews, and yet production of dried pasta presumes proximity to farmers and millers, as well as devotion of energy to the drying of pasta, all of which contradict nomadic lifestyles.[14] Although they consumed dried pasta and disseminated it across the Mediterranean basin, they alone are unlikely to have committed the resources to production. By the middle of the twelfth century, the interaction of Arab and medieval Italian cultures brought macaroni noodles as we think of today into existence.[15] Yet it was not just the Arab tribes spreading macaroni. Dried pasta is also an ideal food for sailors on long sea voyages. The city-state of Genoa, a merchant culture dependent on ships, helped spread dried pasta across the Mediterranean and Europe.[16]

During this period in China, vermicelli developed independently. The Chinese often produced their pasta with rice or other grains, and if they did use wheat, it had a lower protein than the durum wheat used in Italy. In either case, Italians were manufacturing and consuming vermicelli-shaped pasta long before Marco Polo's trading expeditions, and the main Chinese contribution to pasta was in the inventiveness of flours and starches in producing it. The critical ingredient in Italian and Sicilian dried pasta was the durum wheat, a darker grain with more protein. Higher protein levels allowed greater rigidity, and durum wheat was readily available in Sicily and the south of Italy.

Dried pasta quickly grew in importance as both a trading commodity and a portable calorie source.[17] These early dried pastas were called *tri, trii,*[18] or *tria.* The terms originate from the Syrian word *itriyya* or *itriyah,* meaning "string"[19] and the Greek word *itrion,* used in medical texts.[20] Tria evolved into the more common term *vermicelli,* meaning "little worms," with the terms *macaroni* and *vermicelli* popular by the fourteenth century.[21] Since then, *macaroni* has come to be used generically for dried pasta, interchangeably regardless of the shape and including extruded pasta shapes, while *vermicelli* now serves as an umbrella term for dried, string-shaped pastas. *Vermicelli* often includes dried noodles made with other starches, commonly rice in Asian cuisine. The word *spaghetti,* a specific kind of macaroni, would not appear in print until the early nineteenth century,[22] just before the start of the great wave of Italian immigration. The spaghetti shape most likely was created around Naples in the early nineteenth century with the construction of machines to make the pasta.[23]

Sicily became a primary producer of dried pasta because of the natural climate of the island and availability of durum wheat. The long, dry summers were ideal conditions for producing macaroni naturally—and cheaply. Sicily also endured regular regime changes with Arab, Norman, German, French, and Spanish kingdoms all having conquered the island. These repeated conquests created an interchange of culinary traditions, both introducing dried pasta to Sicily and creating customers for trade. Arab merchants were the first to involve themselves in the dried-pasta production on the island, with their nomadic livelihoods making them ideal consumers. Macaroni production continued even after the end of the Arab reign, and as early as 1295, the house of Anjou, a French dynasty, began manufacturing pasta on the island.[24] The dried pasta was produced near Palermo, and from there shiploads were exported.[25]

Pasta in the thirteenth century began to look more like simple versions of dishes we would recognize today. Cheese, butter, and exotic spices became common condiments,[26] including cinnamon. At first, cinnamon accompanied cheese, resulting in a savory dish. Then Arab merchants introduced cane sugar to Sicily.[27] Sugar spread across the peninsula, and by the Renaissance, even Florentines enjoyed cinnamon and sugar on their pasta as a dessert course.[28] In Calabria, honey was used,[29] revealing the north-south wealth disparity even then, although condiments generally remained expensive and the purview of the wealthy.

It wasn't until the fifteenth century that pasta's industrial production reduced the cost enough for common people to eat it, eventually becoming a staple food for the poor in places like Naples and Sicily, minus the flourishes of cheese and other accoutrements. As dried pasta grew in popularity, the demand for the product necessitated industrialization. Making macaroni by hand is a costly, labor-intensive method. By moving to mechanical processes, production scaled up quickly, reducing costs and allowing a food consumed primarily by the rich to evolve into a food for the masses. By the era of the great migration to America, macaroni was a staple alongside fresh pasta.

Commercial pasta manufacture during the Renaissance lead to the creation of guilds protecting the trade. These guilds created, for the first time, standards to define *pasta*.[30] Cooks and lasagna makers in Florence teamed up, forming the Arte dei Cuochi e Lasagnari. The *lasagnari* (as the lasagna makers were called) eventually split to form their own guild.[31] In Naples, the registry of guilds distinguished between *maccaruni*—pasta that was pierced like *bucatini*—and vermicelli.[32] Bucatini and spaghetti are similar in shape, but bucatini has a narrow hole down the middle of the strand, while spaghetti is a solid string. The distinction became important as the industry mechanized. The vermicelli guild eventually required members to own an extrusion press,[33] an expensive piece of equipment used to force dough through dies. The guild cited quality assurance, but the expense of the press also served as a gatekeeping device to protect existing members.

Mechanization proved an essential development in making modern pasta. In the sixteenth century, the first *ingegni* machine used for pressing pasta sheets appeared in the area around Naples.[34] Mechanization reduced the costs of producing pasta, allowing it to become a basic essential.[35] Kneading the dough to produce gluten was labor intensive, and machines reproducing this labor hastened the spread of consumption. By the eighteenth century, Naples became known as a city of "macaroni eaters," the *mangiamacaroni*, a slur, and a title previously held by Sicilians, because of the mass production of pasta.[36] The poor in Naples could buy hot pasta from stalls, and street beggars bought pasta with a few coins tossed to them by tourists on the grand tour. These urchins became known as *lazzarone*, with bourgeois American magazines like *Good Housekeeping* reporting on how the lazzarone made a sport of attempting to swallow the longest spaghetti string without it breaking.[37] The depictions were unflattering and no doubt tainted the perception of spaghetti-eating immigrants.

Industrialization also meant finding new ways of drying pasta. Dried pasta produced through the classic natural Neapolitan system—a method used throughout southern Italy and Sicily—was slow, inefficient, and weather-dependent, all conditions counter to mass-market production. The Neapolitan system involved three stages: *incartamento*, a preliminary stiffening when the surface dried in direct sunlight; *rinvenimento*, a resting period in which the pasta was stored in a cool place; and the *essicazione definitiva*, a second and final drying sheltered from direct sun and protected from varying temperature.[38] The last stage would sometimes require several repeat cycles. This natural method, while highly productive in the dry southern Italian climate and especially Sicily, eventually gave way to oven drying, where the process could be controlled. French pasta-makers attempted to naturally dry pasta indoors[39] but despite producing pasta with hard durum wheat, it was considered inferior to Italian pasta.[40] Immigrants in the United States preferred importing Italian brands.

The evolution of pasta from a handmade food into one pressed by machine also changed the shape of pasta in a literal way. The force leveraged by the presses allowed for the creation of new shapes and styles. Early presses focused on replicating the center hole, as in bucatini. The earliest holes had been created by manually pressing a noodle string through wooden rods. The first machines used wood cylinders lined with copper, pushing dough through the die to create a centered hole.[41] Then dies of bronze and nickel emerged, both stronger materials that were stiffer and created the possibility for the extrusion of other shapes, and the relatively small number of pasta shapes began to multiply.[42] Today there are at least 1,300 factory-made shapes.[43] The romantic notion of every small village producing a unique variety of macaroni shape is merely a quaint fiction. Pasta manufacturers developed shapes of their own design to distinguish themselves as a marketing ploy. By the eighteenth century, Italian pasta had grown so popular that Thomas Jefferson wanted to make his own using a genuine Italian machine. He sent a friend to purchase a press in Italy, but, either by accident or by intent, the machine he acquired was relatively small and designed mainly for home use rather than industrial production.[44] Although Jefferson is known to have enjoyed fresh pasta, produced by his household slaves, he never ended up producing any on a factory scale.

Despite never pursuing it commercially, Thomas Jefferson had stumbled onto a viable product. Pasta manufacturing and consumption in the United States predated large-scale Italian immigration. Italian sailors often stocked macaroni on their ships and exchanged goods for American agricultural products and may have been a vector for introducing macaroni. A popular early nineteenth-century American dish was macaroni and cheese. The first recipes included baking pasta, milk, and cheese into a kind of casserole.

The dish did not rely on the elbow pasta commonly used today, and spaghetti remained a foreign food.[45] Fresh-made pasta or macaroni made from softer American wheat would work in this style of recipes, not unlike early Roman lagana, with the cheese adding structure. The United States was not yet growing durum wheat used in making higher-quality dried pasta, but early demand for macaroni did allow a nascent industrial macaroni sector to develop prior to the arrival of Italian immigrants and create a domestic demand for products they produced.

Growth of industrial manufacturing of pasta exploded in the nineteenth century, starting with Italian macaroni factories. Factories grew beyond natural drying processes and were made possible by oven-drying the macaroni. In Italy, familiar names like De Cecco, Buitoni, and Barilla began churning out pasta for both domestic consumption and export.[46] These pasta-manufacturing facilities started small, but by reducing labor costs, they induced greater demand, and the operations expanded rapidly. Barilla, for instance, operated at an artisanal level at first,[47] before expanding into an international exporter. By the turn of the century, Italian pasta factories would employ tens of thousands, like that of Torre Amunziata, owners of Napoli Bella and Vesuvio brands, who operated fifty-four plants and employed ten thousand workers by 1880.[48] Pasta had grown into big business by the era of Italian immigration.

American factories were competing with these Italian companies. The first pasta factory in the United States was founded in 1848 by a French immigrant, Antoine Zerega, who started by drying pasta on the rooftops in Brooklyn.[49] Zerega powered his dough-kneading device with horses at his Brooklyn waterfront factory.[50] Although he was first, Zerega was soon joined by numerous American competitors. In 1865, a Philadelphia pasta factory was opened by a baker named Goodman, and Frederick Mueller opened another factory in Jersey City in 1867.[51] These producers competed with Italian firms but continued using softer wheat because it was less expensive. As a result, American dried macaroni did not feed the Italian immigrants, who often chose to pay extra for the imported goods. Italians were accustomed to high food prices anyway. The merchant class in places like New York originated in regions responsible for producing high-quality pasta, first from Genoa, and then Naples and Sicily, further cementing the demand for imports.[52] Although other regions produced macaroni, Genoa and Naples became well known as macaroni producers outside of the Italian peninsula, while other pasta regions remained virtually unknown.[53]

Macaroni wasn't just an industrial product. Small-scale production of pasta continued and also became a significant industry for immigrant families. Their main challenge was access to durum wheat, and they, too, primarily used softer American varieties unsuitable for high-quality macaroni. These small-scale producers dried pasta indoors, hanging the spaghetti strings from the ceiling of their flats and shops, as well as windows and in doorways.[54] However, they also merged work and living space so that racks of drying macaroni often hung from the ceiling above where their families slept. With large families filling tenements, and many renting rooms to boarders, usually other immigrants, these artisanal manufacturing facilities were seen as unclean and unsanitary. The cottage industry became the target of anti-immigrant, anti-Italian regulators, and previous immigrant groups also saw an opportunity to undermine Italians and targeted immigrants seen as overly ethnic. Reform-minded organizations worked to prohibit these conditions. Closing immigrant businesses proved a popular policy, and small-scale bakeries and pasta manufacturers were forced out of basements with regulations requiring minimum floor dimensions, ceilings, and windows.[55] The new laws terminated not just Italian immigrant pasta businesses but also bakeries producing ethnic breads.

Larger businesses also saw a marketing opportunity. They began advertising campaigns touting the benefits of factory production, emphasizing cleanliness and purity. By the early twentieth century, the United States was obsessed with food quality and purity. The new laws and the consumer preference created by these ad campaigns, for instance, helped destroy the ethnic breads so valued by artisan bread-makers today, and with the rise of factory-made white bread came ad copy promising foods that never touched human hands.[56] These cleanliness campaigns helped ensure the success of big-business manufacturing. Factories of the twentieth century came to represent cleanliness and modernity, and large-scale production allowed the growth of pasta as big business. The era of the immigrant-family pasta shop had come to an end. Shutting down cottage industries encouraged immigrants to find other sources of income, like restaurants, and explains why many early red sauce joints opened in the parlor rooms of immigrant families.

One example of the growth and evolution of American industrial pasta manufacturing can be seen in the Ronzoni Macaroni Company, eventually sold to General Foods in 1984 for $60 million. At the time Ronzoni produced seventy varieties of pasta.[57] Emanuele Ronzoni departed from San Fruttuoso, a small city outside of Genoa,[58] in 1881, and arrived in the United States, where he took a job working in a Manhattan pasta factory as a child laborer.[59] He set up his own business in 1892 with the Genoese immigrant Frenceso Zunino.[60] In 1895, they named the business the Atlantic Macaroni

Company, and operations moved from Manhattan to Long Island City, Queens.[61] For twenty years, Ronzoni oversaw operations, and the Atlantic Macaroni Company grew into a major pasta manufacturer. They were selling four thousand boxes of macaroni per day and using five hundred barrels of flour.[62] By 1915, Ronzoni had saved enough to open his own factory. Meanwhile, the Atlantic Macaroni Company was also in financial trouble and eventually was sued by an investor for misrepresenting their finances.[63] Emanuele founded Ronzoni Macaroni Co. in 1918, and by the 1930s, Ronzoni had 250 workers and was chasing a national consumer market.[64]

Ronzoni oversaw the company before passing away in Flushing, Queens, in 1956 at the age of eighty-six.[65] His son, Emanuel Ronzoni Jr., took control of the company, serving as chairman of the board. The company grew rapidly during the 1950s, with pasta becoming a major part of the American diet. Italians had begun losing their foreign otherness by then. Following Ronzoni Jr.'s death, the family sold the company, and by the 1990s, the factories in Long Island City were closed.[66] The Ronzoni brand continues to produce macaroni today as part of a larger conglomerate.

Emanuele Ronzoni's early company, like many American pasta factories, almost certainly benefited from the wars and political unrest of the early twentieth century. Trade with Italy was disrupted, and tariffs were implemented. World War I raised the cost of foreign production, and it was then the domestic pasta producers finally began to steal market share from Italian imports. Improved quality in the domestic pasta helped bolster sales as well. By 1919, the National Macaroni Manufacturers Association began publishing *The Macaroni Journal*,[67] a business-oriented trade publication. The journal promoted best practices and created many modern consumer expectations. For instance, in the nineteenth and early twentieth centuries, pasta was often sold in bulk to grocers. Grocers would spoon out macaroni from a large barrel or bag in the desired quantity. But the journal promoted factory packaging, including boxes and boxes with plastic window panes, as well as other, less exciting modern innovations. *The Macaroni Journal* was published until 1984, when the name was changed to reflect the new trade organization, *The Pasta Journal*. By that final issue, 80.3 percent of the U.S. population used dry packaged pasta, and a quarter of them were classified as "heavy users."[68]

Pasta gained more momentum as a major consumer product in the United States between the First and Second World War. By 1929, more than 550 factories were producing pasta, and 377 of those were on a large industrial scale.[69] As the Great Depression rolled through the American economy, pasta proved itself an economic food for the value conscious, providing large quantities of calories at an affordable price. Indeed, Italian American cuisine generally, owing to its origins as a cuisine of the poor, proved popular in Depression kitchens. American pasta manufacturers invested in aggressive marketing to show consumers how spaghetti was "healthful and economical."[70]

During this period, the reform-minded, progressive public health officials who had spent the previous decades impugning immigrant communities as dirty and unhealthy reversed course. The policymakers had at one time gone so far as to turn public schools into Americanization propaganda machines to convert children of immigrants into Americans through their palates. Schools served American lunches in attempts to convince immigrant children they had to eat American food to become American,[71] but the Depression changed attitudes. Italian food traditions, especially pasta, offered great value. Spaghetti offered an inexpensive food on the "advised" list of approved foods, and eventually social workers even attempted to foist spaghetti onto Puerto Ricans.[72] Pasta produced in America continued to include soft, American-grown wheats, further lowering the price. The *other*ing of Italian Americans had started to erode, as new immigrant groups displaced them and Italian American foods and traditions slowly became Americanized.

Meanwhile, in Italy, the rise of fascism threatened pasta consumption. The fascists sought a self-sufficient economy; wheat was in short supply, and exporting pasta brought in a revenue stream providing foreign currency. The durum wheat required for Italian pasta could not be produced in sufficient quantities to satisfy both domestic and export demands, and the government wanted consumers to move away from pasta toward bread.[73] Since bread could be produced with soft wheat, managing consumption of wheat became a priority.[74]

The government also envisioned a bold, bright Italian future, including an entirely new cuisine. They embraced futurism, an art and political movement that included a dedicated cookbook. Filippo Tommaso Marinetti, the founder of Italian futurism, published *The Futurist Cookbook* in 1932, presenting this new vision for Italian cuisine.[75] Pasta was out. Food cubes were in. The old traditions of the peninsula's cuisine were to be displaced by this new ideological diet. The cookbook is as much a manifesto as an actual cookbook and included conceptual ways of eating and neologisms to replace common words.[76]

Marinetti, a writer and political thinker, had been an eager fascist. In addition to the cookbook, he wrote the *Futurist Manifesto*, an artistic thesis outlining the futurist art movement. Futurism rejected the past and celebrated modernity, violence, and streamlined design for speed, themes reiterated in *The Futurist Cookbook*. He founded a futurist political party but quickly merged it with Mussolini's Italian Fascist Party. Marinetti's obsession with the destruction of past traditions, particularly in food, dovetailed with the fascist goal of food independence.

Mussolini's attempts to exert influence over food consumption in Italy went as far as encouraging revisions in popular cookbooks to reflect those needs. Ironically, Mussolini himself was a fussy eater owing to ulcers, and his distaste for elaborate foods probably didn't help protect food culture. The futurist expectations of foods come across now as unrealistic or satire, but Mussolini's government did actively discourage pasta consumption.

Embracing pasta at the time, but following a similar ascetic approach to food, was the 1930 cookbook by Duke Enrico Alliata di Salaparuta, *Cucina vegetariana: Manueale di gastrosofia naturaista* (*Vegetarian Cuisine: A Manual of Natural Gastronomy*). The collection was based on vegetarianism as a philosophy rather than a fascist ideology, and pasta was very much part of the book. Born in 1879 in Sicily, Enrico Alliata's family operated a wine business that he eventually ran.[77] Alliata explored spirituality and philosophy. He saw vegetarianism as an ethical imperative and a means of finding balance and a link to the natural world.[78] There is some irony, then, that he lost an eye during a hunting accident.[79] The collection was the first vegetarian cookbook published in Italy, and the large number of pasta dishes created a stark contrast to the official state policy of rejecting pasta in the national diet. The duke includes in his sparse recipe collection eggs and dairy products, but at one point he advocated for raw food diets.

Despite Mussolini's efforts, Italians continued eating pasta, and with the fall of the fascist government and conclusion of the Second World War, the love of pasta returned. The propaganda that had worked its way into Ada Boni's *Il talismano* during the fascist period was removed.[80] Balance was restored to Italian cuisine.

In the United States, the 1930s brought a food revolution as well. Canned foods, once a luxury product providing out-of-season fruits and vegetables, became a conduit for prepared foods entering the mass market, such as a line of products by Chef Ettore Boiardi, better known by the commercial name, Chef Boyardee. Boiardi opened a processing plant in 1928 for canning spaghetti and sauce and achieved a national market by the 1930s with the chain A&P.[81] While Boiardi achieved great financial success, his story is, on a larger scale, similar to those of many Italian immigrants of the time. Boiardi immigrated from Piacenza, a town in Emilia-Romagna, where he had worked in a hotel starting at the age of eleven.[82] Following his brother, also a maître d',[83] he arrived in New York in 1917 and worked in a number of restaurants in New York before settling in Cleveland,[84] where he eventually opened his own popular establishment in 1926.[85] Boiardi began selling jarred sauce after restaurant patrons requested to take it home. He used old glass milk jars at first[86] before founding the American Home Foods company in 1928.[87] The first three sauces they sold were tomato sauce, mushroom sauce, and spicy Neapolitan sauce.[88] By the 1930s, Boiardi sold ready-made packages including cheese and pasta, and he had national distribution, first through A&P, and then competitors, consuming twenty thousand tons of tomatoes per season.[89] He changed the name from Boiardi to Boyardee after salesmen complained about the difficulty of pronouncing the Italian.

Boyardee contracted with the U.S. Army to provide canned foods for the Second World War. The decision helped further fuel demand for his product as returning GIs longed for the comforting taste of spaghetti.[90] The canned product meant by the postwar period, Italian American spaghetti products were common household items. Boyardee would sell the company but continued consulting with the brand through the 1970s. He died in 1985.

But it wasn't just Boyardee and canned spaghetti that benefited from the war. Italian American cuisine in general benefited, and the postwar period might very well be the golden age of red sauce cuisine. If Americans hadn't tasted Italian American food before the war, they almost certainly did during the conflict. Spaghetti and meatballs, along with chop suey and chow mein, was one of the few ethnic recipes to make it into the 1942 edition of the U.S. Army cookbook.[91]

The American soldiers loved spaghetti. They loved it so much they even exported it to Japan. Following the Japanese surrender after World War II, American soldiers occupying the country took up residence in the New Grand Hotel in Yokohama. The hotel served as a temporary headquarters of the allies and then housing for officers. The hotel's head chef, Shigetada Irie, invented a recipe for *Spaghetti Napolitan,* a tomato-based sauce served over spaghetti. Irie's original sauce probably used tomato paste, but other restaurants began copying the dish, and by the 1950s it had become a domestic Japanese staple. Postwar Japan suffered from food shortages, and ketchup proved an accessible and easily cooked ingredient for the dish. Today, Spaghetti Napolitan is readily available and a popular dish at *yoshoku*—Japanese restaurants serving Western-style food. Pre-made Japanese-style spaghetti is so common that it's even readily available in convenience stores alongside rice onigiri and sushi. In the decades that followed the war, pasta—particularly spaghetti, but also other shapes—evolved from a foreign, exotic ethnic food into a mainstream American export, something the American empire was disseminating through its sphere of influence.

By the 1960s, spaghetti had penetrated deeply into the American consciousness, but consumers were tiring of red sauce stalwarts like spaghetti and meatballs. American consumers lusted for newer and fancier Italian fare, and by the 1970s, "northern" Italian food had started to whet the appetites of diners. For pasta, this development meant the introduction of new styles, like gnocchi, not just new preparations and sauces. Gnocchi are more aptly categorized as dumplings than pasta and consist of ingredients like ricotta cheese, potato, and squash rather than the simple flour doughs of pasta, although Italian American menus regularly interchange gnocchi with pasta.

Pasta consumption continues to grow. In 2005, the International Pasta Organization was formed, a nonprofit organization based in Rome with the mission to promote pasta globally. The organization invented World Pasta Day, selecting a city each year to host the event. There is also the *Associazione delle Industrie del Dolce e della Pasta Italiane* (Italian Association of Confectionery and Pasta Industries), representing the culture for Italian tradition and promoting the consumption of pasta around the world, and the *Accademia Italiana della Cucina* (Italian Kitchen Academy), intended to protect the cuisine and traditions of Italy. The Barilla company also hosts Academia Barilla, an international center dedicated to promotion and diffusion of Italian cuisine, with a particular emphasis on the pasta produced by the Barilla company. In the United States, the National Macaroni Manufacturers Association became the National Pasta Association in 1981.[92]

Despite these organizations, there is no unified system for cataloging and identifying the many possible variations of pasta shapes available.[93] Associazione delle Industrie del Dolce e della Pasta Italiane has identified about two hundred shapes circulating in the Italian consumer market.[94] Most of these shapes are named for identifying features or because of their resemblance to other objects: *capelli d'angelo* (angel hair); penne (pens); vermicelli (little worms); *pisarei* (baby penises).[95] Pasta continues to be a major source of calories for Americans, Italians, and Italian Americans, even as the taste for newer recipes has come to replace the twentieth century's tomato-sauce-based pasta dishes.

4

❖ ❖

We Are What We Read

Tracing the history of red sauce is made difficult in part because Italian cooking traditions lack the formality of cuisines like those coming from French kitchens. The same recipe prepared by different cooks will vary widely in preparation and ingredients, and even the same recipe prepared by the same chef may vary, too. This style contrasts with French cuisine, with its standard methods and narrowly defined preparations, with precise recipes any French chef can assemble in the same way with the same result. The informality of Italian cooking allows cooks to easily adapt to available ingredients, weather, climate, and the immediacy of the situation. This quality allowed Italian Americans to alter their cooking traditions to adapt to the ingredients and plentitude of the United States.

The adaptability of immigrant cooks defined the evolution of red sauce cuisine, rooted in the cucina povera but reinterpreted in the new world. Immigrants often ended up merging known recipes with the foods they perceived wealthy Italians eating, or foods they normally reserved for festivals and celebrations. The peasants brought with them experiential knowledge but were less likely to possess formal recipes. The wealthy did have cookbooks, and as early as the nineteenth century, commercial cookbooks became a viable, profit-generating enterprise. But even after the invention of moveable type, the cost remained high, and cookbooks required literacy among domestic cooks.

The lineage of red sauce cuisine has origins in early Italian cookbooks dating to the Middle Ages, although these are distant cousins of the foods eaten in the United States. The *Liber de Coquina*, a Latin-language cookbook, appeared in Naples in the fourteenth century. This book documents dried pasta and recipes from across what would become Italy, and similar books in local dialects began to appear shortly after, with Tuscany becoming a center for cookbook production.[1]

The tomato, of course, had not yet arrived in Europe. The earliest documented tomato sauce in Italy comes in the 1690s from Antonio Latini, author of *Lo scalco alla moderna* (*The Modern Steward*), a two-volume collection published in Naples. Latini, an orphan on the streets of Rome, eventually found himself working in the kitchen of Cardinal Antonio Barberini.[2] Latini proved a success in the kitchen. He cooked for the cardinal's wealthy and politically powerful guests, including Barberini's uncle, Pope Urban VIII. He eventually went on to serve as steward to the Spanish governor of Naples,[3] where he was knighted. It was during this time that he encountered a wide variety of new-world ingredients imported by the Spanish empire and wrote *Lo scalco alla moderna*. Writing in the seventeenth century, his recipes are a bit primitive and mostly unrecognizable to contemporary chefs and diners alike. His collection does include recipes for Italian ice flavors like lemon, cherry, and chocolate,[4] the same flavors still sold at Italian festivals and pushcart street venders.

In the manuscript *Lo scalco alla moderna*, Latini provides a recipe for Spanish tomato sauce, a versatile condiment for meat and fish. He does not suggest serving it on pasta. Latini also mentions basic preparations for foods like eggplant with olive oil, offering a glimpse at the early use of vegetables from the Columbian Exchange in Europe. Cookbooks of this era provided only basic instructions "to boil, fry, stew, and roast" without a duration or expressions such as when a dish was "ready" or "cooked."[5] Cooking methods well into the nineteenth century, especially in peasant households, remained rudimentary. Domestic cooks often worked over open fires, relying on high, irregular heat, and even with the invention of stoves, wood-fueled stoves lacked the precision of modern gas and electric stovetops.

Only in the nineteenth century do modern-style cookbooks with more precise instructions appear. *Il cuoco gallante* by Vincenzo Corrado, first published in 1773, but widely distributed in subsequent printings in the nineteenth century, includes early tomato recipes alongside other new-world foods. In the middle of the century, the first recipes presenting early red sauce dishes were published. Italy was then still a divided collection of principalities.

In 1837, Ippolito Cavalcanti published *Cucina teorico-practica*, or *The Theory and Practice of Cooking*, a volume of recipes designed for aristocratic households. The second volume, *Cucina casareccia in dialetto napoletano* (*Home Cooking in the Neapolitan Dialect*), focused on food for modest households. He provides what very well may be the earliest documented recipe for pasta and tomato sauce. He also has recipes for *raviolo* (pasta stuffed with cheese and meat),[6] a dish that would become popular as ravioli in American red sauce cuisine. Raviolo were eaten as far back as Latini, when he considered them widely consumed.[7] Cavalcanti's books were first published in Neapolitan dialect, limiting their audience, but offering an early example of basic red sauce dishes. Tomato sauce grew in popularity in Naples during the nineteenth century as the lazzarone population became dependent on low-cost street pasta.

Another notable and relatively modern collection of Italian recipes was written by Pellegrino Artusi in 1891. *La scienza in cucina e l'arte di mangiar bene* (*Science in the Kitchen and the Art of Eating Well*) combined recipes from across the united Italian peninsula, although the book favors Emilia-Romagna and Tuscany.[8] Artusi included the foundation for much of contemporary Italian cooking. In the book's 475 recipes,[9] Artusi attempts to formalize Italian cooking, and he focuses mainly on the food of the elite. The book does showcase underlying fundamentals of the cuisine of Italy during the period of unification.

Although the collection would eventually become a bestseller, Artusi had to self-publish the first edition. Publishers at the time were more interested in the platform of authors than with the content of the book, and despite offering a unique subject, Artusi's career as literary critic and academic rather than a famous chef or notable restaurant owner meant his book was undesirable for publishers. Chefs and restauranteurs had been highly sought after for producing cookbooks in the period, but Artusi could not convince a publisher to back the manuscript.[10] When he did publish it, he dedicated the book to his cats. By the time of his death, he had sold 52,000 copies.[11] The collection had grown by then, too, and the fourteenth edition included more than 790 recipes[12] and spoke to an Italy that had only just been invented by the unification process. Many of the potential readers still spoke only in local dialects, and yet his recipes show a direct link to many modern Italian recipes and the recipes brought to the United States by the wave of immigrants that would become red sauce cuisine. Artusi's recipes continue to be published in Italian and in translation, and they represent a collection of recipes we would recognize in contemporary times.

In the United States at the time, many domestic cookbooks were being published featuring regional foods and cuisines from northern Europe. Macaroni and cheese already had become a popular American dish. Italian pasta dishes, especially spaghetti and tomato sauce, were still seen as ethnic foods and did not appear in an American recipe book until 1912. In that year, Antonia Isola published *Simple Italian Cookery*, offering the first Italian recipes in English for Americans. The collection "shows that Italian cookery is far from being all 'garlic and macaroni,'"[13] according to a widely syndicated review of the collection. The review assures us Isola collected the recipes during her time living in Rome, as to suggest they are authentically Italian. Isola, however, was a pseudonym for Miss Mabel Earl McGinnis.[14] McGinnis was born in New York, although she did live in Rome for a time and included Italianized names for the recipes; publishing under a pseudonym shows consumer preference for the idea of authenticity, not unlike the hedge-fund managers reporting on Olive Garden a century later.

To Isola's credit, many of the recipes are recognizable as Italian. Only a few recipes fit what is now stereotypical Italian American dishes. Pasta plays a prominent role in the collection, including a variety with olive oil, butter, and cheese. Recipes like *polpettone* (small meatballs) and tomato sauce are qualified with "alla Napolitana" or "alla Siciliana" indicating a provenance or regionality, a distinction that would disappear from Italian American red sauce cuisine over the next decades. Isola's "meatballs" are also far from the spaghetti and meatballs we now associate with red sauce. Instead of ground meat bound together with egg and breadcrumbs, these polpettone are slices of meat stuffed with more meat and tied together.

Another early Italian cookbook published in English was Maria Gentile's *The Italian Cook Book: The Art of Eating Well*, from 1919. Gentile has almost certainly copied and translated a number of Artusi's recipes. Portions of the book follow *La scienza in cucina*'s recipe order exactly. Pirating recipe collections was not uncommon at the time. All the recipes in the collection are presented with English names and Italian in parentheses, so tomato sauce is also listed as *salsa di pomidoro* and macaroni Napolitaine is *Maccheroni alla Napoletana*. By this period, though, these recipes are beginning to lose their ethnicity and regionalization, as the Italianized titles are reduced to the secondary name. Despite Gentile also winnowing down many of Artusi's recipes, the collection remains primarily Italian rather than Italian American. Spaghetti and meatballs, veal parmigiana, and manicotti are not part of the cuisine.

Many domestic recipes during this period were being published in magazines. *The Macaroni Journal* regularly published "tried and true" recipes to promote the sale of pasta. These included various preparations for Italian-style spaghetti with tomato sauce and baked pasta dishes with Italian influence. But they also ran alongside Mexican Spaghetti and other concoctions like spaghetti in aspic. These recipes are recognizable as American for their fusion of cuisine, economy of ingredients, and abundance of meat, but not necessarily as Italian.

In 1939, Diane Ashley published a combination restaurant guide and recipe collection featuring recipes from New York City's restaurants and chefs. The book is framed as a response to constant requests for restaurant recommendations from friends looking to dine out in the city. The restaurants featured in the collection catered to the upper and middle class in New York City, including steakhouses, French bistros, and other haute cuisine, alongside Italian restaurants. *Where to Dine in Thirty-Nine* is a snapshot of prewar restaurant dining and is regularly cited for its look at not only Italian restaurants but also all cuisines available in New York City in the era. Red sauce cuisine had entered a golden age—no longer served exclusively in ethnic ghettos, but catering to respectable middle-class people. Of the two hundred restaurants, thirteen were Italian or Italian American and included recipes like meatballs, veal parmigiana, lasagna, lobster fra diavolo, and minestrone soup. Since Ashley was writing as much about the restaurants as she was about particular cuisine, the book provides a broad spectrum of popular foods. The inclusion of so many Italian restaurants demonstrates how significant red sauce cuisine had become to American diners by then.

Restaurants served as incubators for many red sauce recipes that we know today, and likewise, cookbooks related to restaurants serve as archives documenting the progress of Italian American favorites. *Vittles and Vice* by Patricia Bronte contains recipes of Chicago restaurants and America's earliest carbonara recipe; George Rector, a restaurant owner and food writer, published *The Rector Cook Book*, featuring alfredo sauce; Knickerbocker Hotel chef Louis DeGouy published a variation on spaghetti Caruso.

Few restaurants better represent the red sauce traditions than the famed Leone's, a midtown Manhattan eatery serving red sauce cuisine for nearly a century. The conglomerate Restaurant Associates bought out Leone's in 1959, but recipes from the restaurant were collected and published in 1967 as *Leone's Italian Cookbook*. The book includes the restaurant's version of favorites like lasagna, manicotti, marinara, Bolognese, veal and eggplant parmigiana, and lobster fra diavolo. In a way, the sale of Leone's to Restaurant Associates marked the arrival of red sauce as American food and helped pave the way for national Italian-style chains in the 1980s. Restaurant Associates worked to turn Leone's and Italian-inspired food into a mass-consumer product. Red sauce cuisine came under assault by a new wave of cookbooks, celebrity chefs, and a whole new way of thinking about Italian cuisine.

Postwar America saw more contemporary Italian-style cookbooks mixing Americanized recipes alongside more traditional continental Italian such as the 1948 collection *The Art of Italian Cooking* by Maria Lo Pinto. Lo Pinto was a New Yorker with Italian heritage, living in Bay Ridge, Brooklyn,[15] but also visiting her grandmother's kitchen outside of Palermo. The postwar recipe book was published as pizza and lasagna were being introduced to American consumers in popular magazines. Lo Pinto also goes to great length to educate her readers on basics like olive oil, Italian cheese, and rudimentary pasta shapes before laying out Italian and Italian American recipes. Like Ashley's celebrity chef recipes, Lo Pinto offers up a number of red sauce recipes but has attempted to make them more Italian sounding, mashing together Italian and English names, like *aragosta* fra diavolo instead of lobster fra diavolo. The book represents an odd moment—when red sauce wasn't quite ethnic enough on its own that it had to be artificially Italianized; lobster fra diavolo was an American invention, though she uses an Italianized name.

Matilde La Rosa published in 1950 a translation of Ada Boni's *Il talismano della felicità*, although some of the original recipes were removed and several Americanized recipes added in. *Il talismano della felicità*, first published in 1929, contains 882 recipes compiled by Ada Boni.[16] Boni, an upper-class Roman, served as editor of *Preziosa*,[17] a food magazine. She asked readers to send in recipes from around the nation, creating the first truly unified Italian cookbook. Many recipes didn't make the cut for the first edition and were added to subsequent printings and printed in the magazine. During the rise of fascism, Boni's book was modified to reduce the emphasis on pasta, and editions of Boni's book were censored until after the war.

The current edition of the *Talisman* has more than two thousand recipes and is continually updated. The massive book remains wildly popular, the sort of book gifted at weddings. Boni presents a collection more representative of ordinary household dining than previous works, such as Artusi's emphasizing the meals of wealthier households. The English-language version first appeared in the postwar period but remains adulterated by the translator, who abridged Italian recipes and added American ones.

In 1955, Maria Luisa Taglienti published *The Italian Cookbook*, a collection of recipes introducing "420 authentic Italian recipes"[18] from Italy. Alongside American recipes like chicken Tetrazzini and spaghetti and meatballs, Taglienti introduces Americans to several pasta dishes that have ultimately ended up in the red sauce repertoire. As early as the 1950s, two competing concepts of Italian food had begun to foment—Americanized red sauce versus European Italian cuisine.

Beginning in the 1970s, traditional red sauce Italian food began to lose out in favor of a new wave of Italian cuisine. The release in 1973 of Marcella Hazan's *The Classic Italian Cook Book: The Art of Italian Cooking and the Italian Art of Eating*, a title no doubt paying homage to Artusi's collection, altered the way Americans thought about Italian food. Hazan followed up with a sequel, *More Classic Italian Cooking*, five years later, and eventually the two volumes were combined into *Essentials of Classic Italian Cooking*. Hazan's books were marketed as authentic, "northern" Italian food and set off a new rush for alternatives to what had become traditional red sauce cuisine. She is often compared to Julia Child, and her books are credited with bringing Italian cooking into America's domestic kitchens in the same way *Mastering the Art of French Cooking* introduced conventional French cuisine.

Italian-born, Marcella Hazan married her husband Victor in 1955 before moving to New York City.[19] She held two doctorates and worked as a biochemist researching gum disease.[20] Eventually she and Victor had a son, Giuliano, and she quit the lab research position while pregnant.[21] She rarely cooked before coming to New York, but cooking became a way to connect to her native Italy.[22] Through cooking for her family, she mastered Italian recipes. Her curiosity and love of Chinese food inspired her to enroll in a class, and the experience led her to launch her own Italian cooking class from her apartment. Victor wrote to the *New York Times* to have the class listed.[23] Craig Claiborne, the long-time food editor, responded personally. After having lunch with Hazan, he became her champion, writing about her food and classes and eventually leading to the publication of her cookbook. She continued teaching out of her Manhattan apartment and later hosted classes for Americans in Bologna, Italy.

American supermarkets weren't always up to the challenge of meeting Hazan's exacting standards, and much in the same way Julia Child had to teach Americans how to imitate *crème fraiche*, many of the ingredients Hazan cooked with were available only in Italian specialty stores. Despite the emphasis on Italian ingredients, one of the most impactful elements of Hazan's legacy is the simplest of her recipes: a tomato sauce made with only onion, butter, and tomatoes.

Hazan opened the floodgates to Italian food with a closer connection to Italy than the food reproduced by the early twentieth-century immigrants from the south. Hazan's popularity lead many restaurants and chefs to brand their offerings as northern Italian food in order to appeal to modern consumers, even when those recipes originated in southern Italy. Chefs like Lidia Bastianich and Mario Batali, known as northern chefs cooking in the style of Istria and Tuscany, include recipes with southern Italian roots on their menus and in cookbooks. The "authentic" variations of these dishes tended to be lighter and less meat-centric than the food in the United States, thus providing the air of northern cooking despite having a common, southern lineage with red sauce recipes.

Coinciding with the renewed interest in authentic Italian food, the ingredients and food products required to prepare these recipes started becoming available in the United States. Although today seemingly every large-format national grocery chain carries high-quality Italian products, this revolutionary availability of ingredients is a new phenomenon. Italian imported products were primarily the domain of ethnic grocers like Di Palo's in New York and other local sellers in Little Italy neighborhoods around the country. Eventually gourmet grocery markets like Dean & DeLuca and kitchenware purveyor Williams-Sonoma made products accessible,[24] and only in the most recent years have these products become widely available. Consumers sought out imported products and paid for higher quality. Simultaneously, third- and fourth-generation immigrants now had more money to spend on authentic foods but also had a more distant connection to their ancestral homelands. Red sauce restaurants began losing ground to newer-style Italian cuisine, especially as home cooks gained access to the recipes and ingredients to make them.

The consumer desire for "authentic" food can be seen in the popularity of cookbooks targeting these recipes. Efrem Funghi Calingaert and Jacquelyn Days Serwer, the wives of American State Department workers, published a collection of recipes in 1983 titled *Pasta and Rice Italian Style*. The recipes were collected while the women's husbands were stationed in Rome in the late 1970s.[25] Much like the more notable *Where to Dine in Thirty-Nine*, the collection offers a snapshot into zeitgeist dining culture just as red sauce restaurants began to lose favor among restaurant goers and domestic cooks.

While the latter half the twentieth century did see increasing interest in authentic Italian cuisine over American red sauce, defining just what that was remains a challenge. Besides Ada Boni's ever-evolving *Il talismano della felicità*, the other keeper of the faith is *Il cucchiaio d'argento* (*The Silver Spoon*). First published in 1950 by the design firm Dumus, the massive collection of recipes, like Boni, attempts to represent the collective wisdom of Italian cooks. Boni had amassed many domestic recipes from prewar Italy, but *Il cucchiaio d'argento* was modern Italy. Italy and Italians suffered tremendously during the war, especially in terms of access to food. The postwar period brought with it a new prosperity. By the end of the1950s, an economic boom had swept the country, and *The Silver Spoon* represented a rich culinary tradition contrasting the scarcities created by the war and the fascist government. Mussolini's desire for food independence had pressed on the public an ascetic approach to food, but the postwar prosperity fueled a renewed interest in cooking and meals. It has become the ultimate collection of postwar Italian recipes and is translated into numerous languages.

An English translation of *The Silver Spoon* was not published until 2005 and is often criticized for failing to adapt the recipes for American readers. Americans require more handholding when it comes to cooking instruction than Italian cooks, and many of the recipes offer limited technical information. The 2005 edition contained two thousand recipes and included contributions from celebrity chefs.[26] Despite these shortcomings, it became a *New York Times* bestseller, highlighting the interest in more diverse Italian dishes.

Perhaps, though, the more powerful influence on the concept of authentic Italian food came with the arrival of the Food Network. Launched in 1993, the network bolstered personalities like Mario Batali and Giada De Laurentiis, celebrity chefs who helped make famous Italian food marketed as authentic or northern. Notwithstanding his history of sexual harassment, Batali did help popularize Italian cooking in America, and if not for him, the Starboard Value critique of Olive Garden's failure to salt pasta water would not have resonated. The power of television amplified Batali, so when he told audiences pasta water should be salty like the sea, people listened. He and his business partner Joe Bastianich also helped with the resurgence of traditional southern foods like *cacio e pepe*, as much as convincing Americans of the superiority of Italian food.

These changes happened as the price of jet travel fell rapidly, allowing more Americans to travel to Europe and experience Italian food in Italy. Meanwhile, gentrification of cities began to push out the traditional ethnic enclaves that remained. With the immigrant populations now in the third, fourth, and fifth generation, many had left those enclaves for suburban tract homes. The shifting interest in northern-style Italian food further accelerated the end of the red sauce era and amplified the desire for an authentic experience.

5

Red Sauce Fundamentals

The initial wave of Italian immigration consisted primarily of men arriving as laborers. Food remained an important connection to the lives they left behind. Many workers cooked for themselves, and because the merchants from regions like Genoa had already established trade networks, they had access to Italian goods. Meals prepared by working men remained simple, in part because the domestic labor—wives, daughters, and sisters—remained in Italy. This first wave of immigrants had always intended to return with the riches earned in the United States, and transporting their whole households didn't make economic sense.

Restaurants serving Italian food began to appear in cities once a sizable population had arrived. By the 1880s, Italian American restaurants opened in cities such as New York, where more than twenty thousand Italians had already settled, thus providing enough customers to support ethnic restaurants.[1] Southern Italians significantly outnumbered immigrants from the north and, as a result, had the greatest influence on cooking. In addition, because the arrivals had not eaten in restaurants or hotels in Italy, their concept of the foods served in such establishments existed only in their imagination, even as they now earned higher wages, allowing them to eat in the fashion of wealthy people.

As the population of immigrants from the mezzogiorno increased in number, restaurants targeting them as customers opened in the neighborhoods where they lived. These were not glamorous banquet halls, but rather low-cost dining rooms. Many opened in basements,[2] intentionally seeking the lower-priced spaces. Many early establishments consisted of just a few tables in the living rooms of the houses the proprietors lived in. These restaurants essentially served the food of domestic kitchens, the cucina povera immigrants had been accustomed to. The cooks and the customers alike had simply not experienced food from a professional kitchen before arriving in America. When they opened restaurants in the United States, they focused on variations of foods they were familiar with.[3] Tomatoes and macaroni provided the major part of Neapolitan and Sicilian cooking, and since southern peasant cooking generally tended to be vegetarian, these menus reflected those traditions. Dried macaroni served as a mainstay of Italian American cooking even as Italians gained the wealth to add meat and other luxuries to their diets.

Red sauce cuisine evolved in the United States as a result of a unique combination of these historic links to southern Italian food, the availability of goods in the cities like New York where immigrants settled, and the conditions the immigrants lived in. Central to these culinary traditions is the tomato, and the resulting red sauce that serves as a base to many of the recipes. Although sauces the world over include the tomato, it has come to define the Italian American culinary experience in a way no other food tradition has. Red sauce cuisine exists as a discrete variation on historic Italian recipes, with the majority including tomatoes. Tomato sauces of the cuisine vary in style, from thick to thin, simple to complex, and can be used as a base for compound recipes. Early immigrants, especially from Sicily where there was a tradition of turning tomatoes into paste to preserve the summer crop, employed tomato-based sauces because they were instrumental in their domestic recipes.

The most basic tomato sauce preparations combine raw tomatoes tossed with hot pasta and starch-filled water left behind after cooking pasta. The starchy water thickens the tomato juices, and only the heat from the hot water and pasta lightly cook the tomatoes. Early pizza employs a similarly simple sauce—raw, crushed tomatoes poured over the dough as it goes into a hot oven. The most complex tomato sauces cook over a long period of time and combine vegetables, meat or seafood, spices, and additional ingredients for flavor. A longer cooking duration creates a thicker sauce. Light, thin sauces like marinara and *puttanesca* are cooked quickly, while thicker sauces like Neapolitan ragù or ragù alla Bolognese require longer cooking times to reduce the liquid volume and combine the complex flavors. Although localized and regional in Italy, these different styles came together in the United States, merging into a monolithic red sauce cuisine.

In modern Italian, *sauce* translates from both *sagu* and *salsa*, and influential cookbooks intermix the terms, although *sagu* tends to traditionally be reserved for sauced pasta. Both *sugo di pomodoro* and *salsa di pomodoro* have historically been valid terms for *tomato sauce*, although *sugo* more directly translates as a stewed fruit, while *salsa di pomodoro* refers to a general tomato sauce.[4] Italian dialects include variations of sagu, *sucu*, and *saghu*; these variations mainly refer to similar, slow-cooked, meatless tomato sauces. Despite lacking meat, sagu can take on the hearty savory flavor of meat sauces, and in some places it is referred to as a false ragù (*sucu fintu*).[5] Sagu sauces contain either fresh or preserved tomato along with onion and garlic, and are cooked down for a long period of time. What gives sagu the fullness and richness of flavor is the prolonged cooking time. As water evaporates, it leaves behind a thicker, condensed sauce enriched with flavor. Tomato paste can imitate this concentrated tomato flavor, but fast-cooked sauces, such as marinara, will never have the time to merge the flavors of ingredients.

Sagu was the everyday sauce of the Italian American household. The term has grown obsolete in America as the term ragù grew synonymous with most thick, slow-cooked tomato sauces even when it does not include meat. Italians refer to pasta boiled in water, drained, and then served with an accompanying sauce as *pastasciutta*, distinguishing it from pasta served in broth, known as pasta *en brodo*. Broth-based pastas are commonly reinterpreted in American restaurants as simply a soup.

The distinction between soup with pasta and pasta in a broth reveals a conflict between Italian and American restaurant dining. Italian meals often are broken into several smaller portions, usually two principal courses.[6] Pasta dishes are considered a *primi piatti*, a first course of a meal. The *secondi*, usually the meat or protein of the meal, is akin to the entrée. This meal structure was common enough to warrant mention in Gentile's 1919 *The Italian Cookbook*. A formal meal begins with an antipasti, akin to an appetizer course, followed by the pasta and then the meat. Vegetables and salads are served as *contorno*, a side dish. Southern Italian immigrants, if they had access to meat, reserved it for celebration and holiday meals. A pasta dish might have been the only dish at a meal while in Italy, but the abundance of America allowed for more regular consumption of meat. Sunday dinners, where family gathered and meat was most often served, would be an opportunity to separate out pasta and meat with formal courses. Meat would cook in tomato sauce but be served separately.

Italian American restaurants, however, complicate this meal structure. Many of the soups offered in restaurants include pasta. For instance, a pasta *e fagioli* (beans and pasta) is often offered on menus as a starter portion of soup, available almost everywhere, from the corner red sauce joint to the Olive Garden. Another popular soup, minestrone, when served in America, also often includes a small pasta. There are too many variations of minestrone to point to a definitive version, but common ingredients include carrots and celery, potatoes, beans, broth, and sometimes pasta. Yet rarely does ordering a pasta-laced soup prevent diners in America from eating pasta as an entrée course, and entrée portions of proteins will often come with a small side dish of pasta lightly sauced with marinara or garlic and oil, similar to a northern European meat accompanied by potatoes or rice. In effect, diners end up eating two primi piatti pasta dishes in addition to their secondi piatti. Sometimes traditional Italian American restaurants will provide a smaller portion of a pasta entrée as a primi piatti as an off-menu request, but more likely an American restaurant simply serves twice as much pasta.

The sauces served with pastaciutta are known as *condimenti*, translated as "condiment," and here language illustrates another difference in preparations between Italian and American cuisine. Italians will often decry Americans for using too much sauce with pasta, drowning the noodles rather than complementing them. For Italians, sauce should behave like a condiment, enhancing the flavor of the pasta rather than overwhelming and dominating it. Americans embrace the abundance available to them in the United States.

One of the earliest condiments for pasta was a basic combination of butter and cheese. Even the Roman legions likely ate a variation of this with olive oil and cheese, staples of the legion. Another similar form of this was the French-style spaghetti *l'Italienne.* Spaghetti l'Italienne, a French vermicelli dish sauced with brown butter, was commonly available in American restaurants in the nineteenth century. The arrival of Italian immigrants and vermicelli served with tomato sauce profoundly changed customer expectations, and over time the brown butter was replaced with a tomato sauce. The condimenti most familiar to Americans is marinara sauce, a thin, quickly cooked tomato sauce often used on pizza, accompanying fried foods, or tossed over pasta. Marinara, or tomato sagu, is often the base for other recipes requiring tomato sauce, and many twentieth-century cookbooks call for prepared tomato sauce rather than fresh or canned tomatoes.

An early ancestor of sagu is likely Latini's "salsa di pomadoro alla Spagnola," from *Lo scalco alla moderna.* His sauce contains ripe tomatoes, onions, and peppers, another new-world fruit, as well as salt, oil, pepper, and thyme for seasoning. Latini doesn't suggest serving it with pasta, but otherwise the sauce appears as a modern tomato sauce. At the time of Latini's writing, tomatoes were rarely used ingredients, and the Spanish sauce is the only tomato-based sauce included in the book. Latini served as a steward for a noble Spanish family in Naples, meaning his recipes served the wealthy of the era rather than peasants. In other words, the food Latini was dealing with was not the cucina povera, but rather the cucina ricci, the food of the rich. Since peasant domestic cooking rarely was recorded, it is possible other tomato sauces were more common at the time and since forgotten. Tomatoes in the seventeenth and early eighteenth centuries were still considered foods better suited for the poor or people who occupied low positions in society.

Tomato sauce met with pasta as early as the 1820s,[7] with documentation showing pasta and tomato sauce appearing when Ippolito Cavalcanti published two collections of recipes in 1837 and 1839. Vermicelli pasta, cooked al dente and served with tomato sauce, is included in his books, about forty years before immigrants started arriving in American cities. The combination of pasta and tomato sauce proved popular in the nineteenth century. Sicily and Naples had become producers of both ingredients, and the street vendors included tomato sauce as one of the more luxurious condimenti. Neapolitan pizzas at the time used fresh tomatoes rather than sauce. Pellegrino Artusi's 1891 *The Science and Art of Eating Well* presents a unifying Italian cuisine; salsa di pomodoro is not just a common condiment but also an ingredient to be added to many other recipes. Artusi ends the recipe by stipulating that it has many uses and is good with meat but excellent for pasta along with cheese and butter. By the 1880s immigration, pasta and tomato sauce had a strong foundation in southern Italian recipes.

Although nineteenth-century America did grow tomatoes, the primary use of the fruits before the arrival of Italians had been for catsups, an ancestor of modern ketchup.[8] These vinegar-based condiments included tomatoes among many other ingredients, and derived from interpretations of Asian sauces that had become common in England and trading colonies along the Pacific. *The Carolina Housewife* does contain two recipes for "tomato catsup," as well as a variation made from mushroom and walnut. Catsup also proved popular as a way of preserving the foods, essential in era before refrigeration. The catsup recipes are worth noting, as they demonstrate the availability of tomatoes in the southern United States, especially since the collection is presented as domestic cooking collected from a housekeeper and home cooks, dishes "made in our own homes."[9] The cookbook focuses on southern American domestic recipes but does include a tomato sauce recipe, a "macaroni a la Napolitana," as early as 1847,[10] three decades before the start of the mass migration. The sauce also includes breadcrumbs and eggs as thickening agents. Southern Italian recipes do include bread-crumbs in dishes as an inexpensive way to add calories; however, southern marinara sauces tended to be simpler. Italian merchants from Genoa were connecting the southern United States with Italy, perhaps explaining this outlier of macaroni and tomato sauce.

When the Italians arrived in the United States, they found a bounty of tomatoes, in part because American innovation had created inexpensive canned tomatoes and new methods for supplying fresh tomatoes to urban markets, and immigrants took advantage of the availability. They then combined tomatoes with a variety of other foods they previously did not have access to, such as meat and fish, even though these were foods of the aristocratic landowners, of urban restaurants and hotels, and of celebrations and holidays. Red sauce recipes are heavy, calorie-rich foods because the immigrants were replicating foods they had eaten rarely (if ever) in Italy but suddenly could afford to acquire. By the early twentieth century, tomato sauce recipes were being published for English-speaking cooks and also paired with pasta following the southern Italian traditions. *Simple Italian Cookery* (1912) and *The Italian Cook Book* (1919) both have tomato sauce recipes that resemble *sugo di pomodoro*, with instructions calling for the sauces to thicken. The thickening of sagu distinguishes it from marinara, which should be thinner and lighter. These recipes though are distinctly influenced by two factors. First, American cooks unfamiliar with Italian cuisine required simplified recipes. And second, these early recipes look more like early Spanish tomato sauce, the first iteration of tomato sauce in Italy, rather than of Italian American red sauces that became common in American trattorias.

Marinara sauce is elemental to red sauce cuisine and is one of the light-est and thinnest of the common sauces. Marinara is cooked quickly with fresh tomatoes, although canned tomatoes can be used when tomatoes are out of season, with herbs like parsley, basil, and oregano adjusted to taste. In some variations, *alla marinara* means simply scalding the tomatoes.[11] The least-cooked variation of this sauce is sometimes referred to as salsa *all'insalata* (the salad sauce).[12] All'insalata sauce is built by tossing hot pasta with diced tomatoes and olive oil with only the heat from the pasta cooking the sauce. The heat brings out the juice of fresh tomatoes, but there is little cohesion or "sauciness."

Marinara has not always been a simple tomato sauce. In some regions of Italy, marinara also includes anchovies, tuna, or other fish, and even in the United States, marinara sometimes indicates a tomato and fish sauce over pasta. Over time, the term *marinara* sauce in America became more standardized, especially with the advent of the chain pizzeria in the postwar period. In the context of a pizzeria, marinara sauce is often fortified with sugar to sweeten it, especially because large-scale tomato production can reduce the natural sugars. Otherwise, modern American marinara sauces primarily consist of fresh tomatoes, olive oil, and garlic, heated rapidly and briefly. The resulting sauce is often chunky because the tomatoes do not have time to break down and the natural liquid of the tomatoes remains. With sagu and ragù sauces, the moisture of the tomatoes evaporates, concentrating the flavor even as extra liquid is added. Marinara will only just start to come together as a cohesive mixture.

Many recipes, especially early in the twentieth century, call for adding marinara as the base to complex sauces instead of raw tomatoes. Sauces like *arrabbiata*, *puttanesca*, and *amatriciana* can be built using marinara as an ingredient. Using prepared sauce is common in cookbooks for domestic cooks, especially those adapted for Americans, while Italian recipes are more likely to call for fresh tomatoes, canned tomatoes, or tomato paste. Red sauce restaurants now also serve marinara as a condiment to fried foods, including fish, like squid, or zucchini, including the flowers. American marinara can also be slightly sweet, and if the fresh tomatoes are not sweet enough, the secret ingredient is a pinch or two of plain white sugar.

The origins of marinara sauce come from the south of Italy, but even here there are disputes over the constitution of the sauce. Sicilian fisherman cooked a noodle dish topped with a simple tomato, garlic, and oil sauce known as marinara, usually serving it over linguine and topped with grated cheese.[13] Marinara sauce provided a quick meal while in port or offered a simple sauce they could prepare while at sea. Although the linguine is regularly swapped out with a variety of macaroni types, this Sicilian pasta, marinara, and cheese represents a standard, basic pasta dish served in both Italian and Italian American communities.

Sometimes Italian American dishes serve linguine with clams in tomato sauce, and menus refer to this dish as marinara or linguine alla marinara. This variation has given rise to the myth that marinara sauce included fish because it was a fisherman's pasta, but fisherman are not financially incentivized to eat the catch they intend to sell.[14] More likely, the discrepancy in what constitutes marinara sauce stems from regional differences, with Neapolitans historically more likely to include fish in marinara sauce. Nineteenth-century Neapolitan pizza varieties include a pizza alla marinara topped with tomato, garlic, and small fish, usually anchovies, and in Campania, the region around Naples, *marinara* refers to a slightly more complex tomato sauce, including ingredients such as fish and olives, resulting in a marinara similar to spaghetti alla puttanesca, although the fish used for a Campania marinara was either tuna or anchovies.[15] In these regions, a simple marinara sauce of tomatoes, garlic, oil, and oregano is referred to as *pizzaiola* sauce.[16] The inclusion of oregano is significant, with the herb often known in mid-century America as the pizza spice, since the flavor was common in sauces used in American pizza. Over the course of the century, these variations faded in the United States as a more standardized red sauce lexicon emerged.

Italian immigrants often segregated themselves not just by region but also by city of origin, creating micro-enclaves within a Little Italy ghetto. They did not come from a monolithic culture and often spoke mutually incomprehensible dialects. Although today the distinction between Neapolitan and Sicilian variations of marinara have been blurred, when the immigrant groups first arrived, they continued to maintain their hyperlocal traditions, including language and terminology. *Pizzaiola sauce* is a much less common term today, while *marinara* has come to refer to simple tomato sauce served over spaghetti, topping pizza, or as a condiment to fried food.

The evolution occurred in the United States at the time Italian restaurants were beginning to grow in popularity with mainstream American diners, while simultaneously second- and third-generation Italians were becoming Americans with Italian heritage. Identity began to shift from the hyperlocal to the national, and the individualized variations homogenized. At the same time, the introduction of Italian terminology to mainstream American consumers was slow. Generic terms like *spaghetti* and *macaroni* were the norm, in part because diners were already familiar with French spaghetti a l'Italienne. Tomato sauce, if it had a specific term at all, was referred to as *a la Napolitaine,* but more often was simply a tomato sauce.

Marinara began to enter into the national American zeitgeist in the 1930s. In the 1930 film *Rain or Shine*, a character asks for spaghetti with marinara sauce.[17] But a guide to New York City restaurants from 1931 refers to a "marinari" sauce served with chicken and "spaghetti Napolitano,"[18] indicating that in this period, marinara sauce is not yet exclusively a pasta condiment. Newspapers also often swapped around vowels, adding to the discordance on a standard spelling. By the 1950s, pizza pies started becoming a nationalized, mainstream American food. The sauce on top of these pizzas, often referred to as marinara sauce, started becoming standard as chain pizzerias popped up across the nation. Thin, sweet, and with a hint of oregano and garlic, marinara is today the workhorse of Italian American cooking.

6

❖ ❖

One Fruit to Rule Them All

The tomato is now synonymous with Italian Americans and functions as the foundation for red sauce cuisine. Italian Americans viewed tomatoes as vital, with many immigrants planting tomatoes in home gardens, even in tiny city lots. Yet the tomato is not native to Italy, nor was it an agricultural product in Italy until relatively recently. Although pasta can be traced more than two millennia, the rise of the importance of the tomato in southern Italian cuisine dates back only about two centuries. Although now a symbol of Italian American food, and even Italy itself, the fruit did not arrive in Europe until the Columbian Exchange.

During the fifteenth and sixteenth centuries, European explorers, led by the Spanish, began exchanging plants, animals, and diseases with indigenous people in the Americas. Europeans warmed to the tomato slowly but eventually cultivated useful varieties before exporting the new strains back to the Americas as they colonized the continent. Tomatoes proved a temperamental crop since they ripen during the bounty of the summer months, quickly rot, and are difficult to preserve—all undesirable qualities. In areas around Naples and Sicily, tomatoes saw increased consumption because of favorable growing conditions. Tomato-based recipes surged in popularity among immigrants in the United States in part because of links to these regions, as well as nineteenth-century innovations in growing, shipping, and preservation. Canning helped make the fruit readily available in American markets year-round, and investment in railroads expanded the fresh tomato season. The combination of familiarity and availability led the immigrant chefs to embrace the tomato as a signature ingredient.

The tomato's immediate predecessor is likely the species *solanum pimpinellifoium*, and it still grows wild in Ecuador and Peru, producing fruits "the size of large garden peas."[1] Researchers seek out these primitive tomatoes today hoping to find desirable genetic material to breed into commercial tomatoes. Other than serving as a bank of genetic material, these small fruits are not particularly useful, although they do taste like tomatoes.[2] They are too small to gather in any quantity, but fortunately the Mesoamericans began selectively breeding the fruit to resemble a size we recognize today. The Aztecs cultivated these early tomatoes, and several different fruits evolved from their work[3] with similar names.

These earliest tomatoes were cultivated in central America long before the arrival of Europeans. Mesoamerican farmers domesticated the plants more than a thousand miles from the tomato's native ancestors.[4] Aztecs consumed these plants as food and medicines. The medicinal uses have largely been lost due to the inability of Europeans to follow the indigenous recipes.[5] Sauces prepared with tomatoes and multicolored chili peppers were sold in the prepared foods marketplace in Tenochtitlan, the capital of the Aztec empire.[6] As with corn, potatoes, and syphilis, Europeans were slow to grasp the significance of the tomato.

The word *tomato* comes from Nahuatl, the Aztec language. The English phonetic translation of the Nahuatl, *tomatl*, meaning "firm and swollen,"[7] gives us the word *tomato* and, in Spanish, *tomate*.[8] Although many European languages like German and French adopted a variation of *tomatl/tomato/tomate* to refer to the newly discovered fruit, modern Italians use the word *pomodoro*. There are several possible explanations. Until the 1800s, the French for *tomato* was *pomme d'amour*, meaning "love apple," and it was thought at the time the fruit might have aphrodisiac qualities.[9] However, the connection between *pomme d'amour* and *pomodoro* may be simply coincidental, or perhaps even a case of mistaken identity. French and Italian culinary arts do have many shared elements, and this lineage could have led early Italian cooks to adopt a word similar to *pomme d'amour*. Yet tomatoes and tomato sauce arrived in Sicily by way of Spain, not France, and it's more likely the Italians would have been introduced to the Spanish *tomate* rather than *pomme d'amour*. Some dialects of Italian, like those around Genoa, use a term more similar to the Spanish and Nahuatl rather than the Italian *pomodoro*.[10] So then where does the Italian *pomodoro* come from? The earliest printed recipe with tomatoes in Italian comes from Antonio Latini, who includes Spanish tomato sauce (salsa di pomadoro) in his collection *Lo scalco alla moderna*.[11]

One theory is that the Italian word comes from *pomo del moro*, meaning the "apple of the Moors," who traded off with Spain as rulers of Sicily.[12] Another phonetic variation of the linguistic play is *pomo d'oro*, meaning "golden apple." The idea of a golden apple makes sense when considering many or most of the early tomatoes were yellow rather than red. These variations all play on the belief they had some kind of apple growing in their gardens, and no doubt the belief that the Columbus expedition had landed in the Garden of Eden further fueled the idea of the tomato as the forbidden fruit of the creation myth.[13] By the time tomatoes regularly began appearing as sauces for pasta and meats in the nineteenth century, the issue had been settled in Italy; tomatoes were known as *pomodoro*.

The tomatoes arriving in Europe during the Columbian Exchange were not yet the bright red spheres so commonly available in supermarkets today. Tomatoes began as a weed-like plant[14] and at the time of their arrival in Europe were more bitter[15] and mostly yellow.[16] They evolved in the gardens of Europe before achieving the sweet succulence we expect today. Gardeners at first planted them primarily as decorations[17] rather than to eat. The tomatillo, also cultivated by the Aztecs, was initially seen as more useful as a food. Tomatillos progressed at least as far as Bologna in Italy but then disappeared from Italian cuisine. The fruit still does not have an Italianized name.[18]

Although the tomato was not at first a popular food, it was embraced as a potential medicine. The European conquerors slaughtered the Aztecs before seeking to understand how they employed tomatoes for medicinal purposes. The conquistadors did observe them using tomatoes for healing[19] but simply never bothered to learn the methods. A popular myth today is that fifteenth-century Europeans refused to eat tomatoes because they were members of the nightshade family. But even if they believed tomatoes poisonous, they knew nightshade plants as useful medicinal ingredients, like, for instance, mandrakes. The mandrake root was used as surgical anesthetic by the ancient Greeks and, perhaps more mythically, as a fertility aid to boost conception.[20] The mandrake contains an alkaloid, with the ability to cause "hallucinations, delirium, and in larger doses coma,"[21] and these same alkaloids are found, in lesser quantities, in the leaves of tomato plants. These hallucinations are likely why the Spanish believed nightshades to be, as Wolf D. Storl notes, "associated with witches and their wicked brews and salves that led to licentiousness, whoring and other damnable activity."[22] Even if they had bothered to understand the Aztec medicine, the conquering Europeans likely would have dismissed the tomato medicines as witchcraft.

The folklore surrounding nightshades also may have been enough to prevent commoners from experimenting with the new fruits, fearing the association with wizardry. The tomato was sometimes known as a "love apple," and it earned a reputation as an aphrodisiac affiliated with love potions. Puritans in northern Europe, fearing both witches and love, even went as far as declaring the tomato poisonous.[23] This period was a dangerous one for witches. Somewhere between 200,000 and 500,000 Europeans were executed for witchcraft[24] over the three centuries during which the tomato and other new world nightshades were introduced to the continent. Considering how rarely people accused of witchcraft met with a peaceful end, the hesitation to consume tomatoes seems a logical decision.

The elites at the time may have had more practical reason to avoid the tomato than fearing the dark arts. In that era, the wealthy often had dishes made from pewter, a metal that can leach lead into high-acid foods like tomatoes, causing people to feel sick and die (or simply go crazy).[25] Certainly, such results could have been interpreted as the result of witchcraft. However, peasants who could not afford pewter plates would have avoided these problems simply by not having access to fancier dishware. The absence of early tomato recipes can easily be explained, then, because rarely in history have peasant recipes been recorded.

Early adopters of the tomato might very well have included Jewish populations, who were often marginalized and frequently maligned as witches regardless. In England, it was observed Jewish families ate tomatoes with cucumbers or stewed in soups as early as 1753,[26] and Jewish cuisine often included foods outside the mainstream culture, like eggplants,[27] another nightshade. In times of shortages in Italy, Jewish residents were often restricted by local governments on what they could eat or sell, leaving them the undesirable foods like tomatoes. For instance, Jews at one point were prohibited from selling macaroni or lasagna and faced sumptuary laws targeting household food consumption.[28] Jewish families expelled from Sicily during the Spanish Inquisition also ended up on the Italian peninsula. The earliest consumption of tomatoes in the south of Italy prepared the fruits like eggplant—fried with salt and pepper, but this was merely peasant food.[29] All of these factors suggest the tomato may have traveled to and through Italy by way of Jewish communities before enjoying wider acceptance and consumption.

Adoption of the tomato moved slowly over the sixteenth and seventeenth centuries. Early documentation of tomatoes includes a still life from the first decade of the seventeenth century, *Flowers, Fruit, Vegetables and Two Lizards*, an oil painting in the Galleria Borghese.[30] The image appears to include other new-world vegetables as well, including peppers and squash.[31] Latini's early tomato sauce recipe suggests the fruit did begin to appear on even the plates of elites, albeit in rare instances and as a foreign food. The tipping point for the tomato came in the eighteenth century when famines in 1745 and 1771[32] encouraged commoners to eat whatever could be grown. In Sicily, with plenty of sun and a dry climate, the tomato thrived and became a common source of calories. The tomato in places like Sicily has been compared to the potato in Ireland: a workhorse of calories for a peasant class.

Tomatoes became an increasingly important part of southern Italian diets in the eighteenth century, but documented sources of tomatoes and pasta don't occur until the nineteenth. The combination of vermicelli pasta and salsa di pomodoro appears an 1844 Neapolitan cookbook using *estratto* (a tomato concentrate) and pork fat.[33] Tomato sauce dishes begin appearing in taverns the following decade.[34] The use of tomato sauce likely has as much to do with the availability of tomatoes as market crops than the presence of Italian immigrants.

The heat of southern Italy, especially on the island of Sicily, proved particularly important in the evolution of the consumption of tomato, not just in Italy but also globally. The Sicilian sun solved one of the major problems of relying on tomatoes: preservation of a fickle fruit. On the rooftops of Sicily, tomatoes were preserved first for domestic consumption and then commercially into a thick, dark paste. The original paste, known as estratto[35] or *astrato*,[36] was produced by crushing tomatoes on sheets and allowing the tomatoes to dry in the sun for several days. Immigrants to the United States mimicked this process by stretching bedsheets over wooden frames to preserve tomatoes for winter.[37] Winters in America proved a particular challenge for immigrants from the south because American winters reduced the number of growing seasons for fresh tomatoes from the accustomed two or three[38] to only one—requiring Italians in America to preserve the summer tomatoes for use all year. Estratto is a concentrated tomato paste; add water, and the thick, brownish material turns into tomato sauce. What Sicilians accomplished through roof-drying in the sun eventually became a big business. Commercial production in places like Fidenza started more than a century ago, and eventually estratto produced on rooftops gave way to industrial-scale production of paste called *concentrato*.[39] Tomato paste is now a commodity produced on a massive scale, in both Italy and California, as well as upstart markets like China. Italians today fear imports of paste from China, both because it undermines their valuable agricultural product and because of contamination from industrial waste or corrupt oversight of regulations.

In the United States, canned tomatoes and paste products are some of the few tomatoes that are ever allowed to ripen fully while on the vine. Today, most American-grown tomatoes are picked green. They turn red when gassed with ethylene. Sometimes gassed, unripe tomatoes turn red but are not mature enough to fully ripen. The tough green skin allows them to be harvested mechanically and shipped across the country without bruising. By contrast, processing plants making paste want the freshest, ripest tomatoes. The factories worry less about bruising because within a few hours of harvest, the tomatoes are crushed and turned into paste or canned. For canning operations, the critical element in modern agriculture is scheduling. Canners want fruits harvested during peak ripeness, but also at a time when the factory can process them immediately to avoid delays.

The development of Italian American cuisine around the tomato also depended on the reintroduction of the fruit to the Americas. It returned during the period of colonization, having evolved into a sweeter fruit in European gardens. Although the British initially saw the tomato as ornamental, they recognized that it was often consumed in southern Europe and North Africa, boiled with "vinegar, pepper and salt."[40] And as British colonists began to settle in the United States, they found tomatoes already growing in the Carolinas, although these probably came from Spanish settlers depositing cultivated plants.[41] The Spanish had also grown the plants in Florida,[42] a feat that would prove prescient later in the industrial cultivation of the tomato. These scattered plantings left behind by the Spanish may explain the early documentation of a tomato sauce recipe in the United States. *The Carolina Housewife* proved well ahead of its time with a pasta and tomato recipe, including it along with other American dishes, but tomatoes were not initially cultivated inland until the middle of the nineteenth century.

The primary use of tomatoes in the early United States had been in British-style catsups, inspired by fish sauces encountered in Asia, and these are the most common tomato recipes circulating domestic kitchens through the nineteenth century. The original source recipes are modeled on spicy sauces from the British empire in the far east, such as Malay and China, and usually made from pickled fish, oysters, or walnuts combined with vinegar, sugar, and spices. These condiments complement all sorts of bland British foods. Tomatoes offered a perfect substitute ingredient because of their acidity and bright red color.[43] The Americans also used tomatoes for producing imitation soy sauce.[44] Using tomatoes in Asian-influenced fish sauces and as a substitute for soy sauce made sense because of the high levels of umami flavor, the savory flavor of glutamate. These sauces also served as methods of preserving tomatoes, and demand for these products spread tomato agriculture across the United States.

Tomatoes spread northward. Thomas Jefferson noted their availability in markets in Washington, DC,[45] and tomato recipes beginning to appear in magazines.[46] The primary mode of consumption was through preserved methods rather than eating fresh tomatoes. Americans remained skeptical of fresh tomatoes based on their unfounded reputation for causing cancers and tumors[47] and general digestive discomfort. Luckily for the tomato, a number of people hoped to profit from the fruit, and their marketing efforts turned the tide. One stunt in New Jersey helped popularize it in the southern region of the state. Robert Gibbon Johnson, a New Jersey farmer, set out to eat a whole basket of tomatoes to prove they were not deleterious to his health in any way. Johnson presented the challenge as spectacle, not unlike Edison electrocuting an elephant a century later, with less shocking results. The ploy worked. Johnson stood on the steps of the courthouse in Salem, New Jersey, and ate an entire bushel. Salem locals, in need of a local celebrity, have celebrated Robert Gibbon Johnson Day since 1987, nearly 150 years since.[48] Johnson wasn't the first to try this stunt. Thomas Jefferson pulled off a similar spectacle in Lynchburg, Virginia, supposedly plucking a fruit from a garden and eating it, to the amazement of onlookers.[49]

In addition to the attempts to popularize fresh tomatoes, other hucksters promised not only that the tomato was safe but also that it offered health benefits. Archibald Miles marketed a tomato-extract pill promising relief from a variety of diseases,[50] including common colds. Miles invested heavily in advertising, and newspapers and magazines often ran flattering stories about the benefits of tomato pills.[51] Miles's success selling his supplement led to knock-off competitors and ultimately a tomato-pill war. Not only did the competing companies advertise heavily in newspapers, but each also made claims of slander and corporate espionage while filing lawsuits and counter-claims. The only winner of all this was the tomato, a fruit that emerged from the fracas with an increase in demand.

With consumers finally seeking out tomatoes, including fresh tomatoes, American agriculture invested heavily in ensuring its availability. The American industrial complex focused on two ways of providing tomatoes—canning and developing techniques to sell fresh tomatoes in all twelve months of the year. Both developments contributed to the abundant availability just as the waves of southern Italian immigrants arrived.

Although today the mass-market American winter tomato is bland, tough, and flavorless, even having a fresh tomato in the dead of winter a century ago would have seemed a miracle. Tomato crops as a commercial enterprise present a specifically unique challenge because they spoil quickly. American innovators created low-cost, year-round products available in northern cities even in winter, and the agricultural industrial complex found ways to turn the challenging fruit into cash. New England began growing tomatoes in greenhouses as early as 1837,[52] but these remained an expensive novelty. Another tactic involved selectively breeding plants to grow earlier in the season.[53] The initial goal had been extending the season by growing fruit both earlier and later, eventually manipulating tomatoes to grow well outside of the normal growing period. But the real innovations in winter tomatoes arrived with the railroad.

The growth of railroads in the nineteenth century shrunk the expansive nation. The transcontinental railroad linked New York and San Francisco in three and half days, opening up vast stretches of agricultural land to markets along the East Coast. More important, these trains traversed a variety of climates, linking the urban centers in the north with warm growing regions throughout the country. Trains allowed for commercial development of Florida-grown tomatoes whisked north on railroads to markets in the dead of winter. Beginning in the 1890s, high-value winter tomatoes in cities like New York lead to a rapid expansion of the industry in Florida.[54] In the first year, a few crates of Florida tomatoes sold at a huge premium in New York, and the profits set off a race to expand Florida's winter tomato acreage. Consumers never looked back. They began expecting fresh tomatoes available in markets and grocery stores all year long. The Florida tomatoes, along with other warm-weather crops, would end up in the pushcarts of Italian American grocers, one of the occupations many new immigrants ended up with.

The expansion of Florida's tomato industry is one reason why fresh tomatoes in modern grocery stores have so little flavor. The state now accounts for a third of tomatoes grown in the United States and dominate grocery stores from October to June.[55] The Florida climate, while warm enough to grow tomatoes in winter, is too wet and requires the use of fungicides and pesticides to keep the fruits from rotting on the vine. Florida tomatoes also have to travel hundreds of miles before reaching consumers in a complex delivery network. Transporting them often led to bruising, until farmers realized the tomatoes could be picked green. By harvesting green tomatoes, the fruit can be ripened later with exposure to ethylene gas in warehouses closer to consumers. The process helped reduce the costs of those tomatoes since green tomatoes are sturdier and hold up better during transport, and it is used as a method to reduce waste. There are drawbacks. Green tomatoes are less flavorful than those grown until red on the vine, and some early green-picked tomatoes will never ripen even when exposed to the gas.[56] But at the turn of the century, connecting those fresh tomatoes with consumers was a model of innovation.

The second major contribution made by American innovation, and a real turning point for tomato consumption, was the perfection of canning and the rise of a new food-processing industry. Tomatoes were first canned in Jamesburg, New Jersey, and the practice was sustained by army contracts during the Civil War. As a result, New Jersey developed into a major tomato-growing state,[57] Trenton and Camden, major food-processing centers, and Rutgers, the State University of New Jersey, invested in tomato research. By 1900, New Jersey and nearby Maryland had come to dominate tomato canning.[58]

Developing new tomato varieties became a major industry on its own. The most famous of the Rutgers research was an eponymous variety that became standard for fresh tomatoes for many years. Since the Rutgers tomato could not be mechanically harvested, sometimes had imperfections, and didn't hold up during long-haul shipping, farmers eventually relegated it to heirloom status. The rise and fall of the Rutgers tomato epitomizes the best and worst in American innovation. Although they had succeeded in producing a delicious tomato, the qualities desired by the consumer ran counter to the desires of the tomato industry. Big business wanted tomatoes with tougher skins to withstand shipping and avoid blemishes, and many of the cultivating decisions valued qualities other than taste. New Jersey and Maryland remain highly productive tomato-growing states even today,[59] although they have since ceded the crown of canned tomatoes to California.

California developed a canning industry for "Italian" tomatoes, intending to compete with imported products, but they barely survived against their foreign competitors until tariffs protected the industry in 1930.[60] Canned foods remained luxury products at first, but by 1874, overproduction had created a glut.[61] The Italian immigrants arrived in America at a time when tomato prices began to rapidly fall, further contributing to the idea of an abbondanza. Eventually canned vegetables were available to them in a way they couldn't have expected in Italy. Despite southern Italy having longer growing seasons, the cost of food remained high, while American industrial farming cut costs.

Although the United States took the lead on canning technology (and not just of tomatoes), Italy launched a canning industry focused on tomatoes in the middle of the nineteenth century. Francesco Cirio set up a modern canning factory as early as 1856, expanding to San Giovanni around Naples in 1900.[62] Canning tomatoes also became big business in Italy after unification,[63] and Italian immigrants helped fund the industry, preferring to pay to import known brands of food over domestically produced American tomatoes. The Italian state encouraged these immigrants in order to create export markets for their products.

Canning tomatoes is a very different industry than whole fresh tomatoes. Consumers want fresh tomatoes without imperfections and of uniform shape, size, and color. Farmers selecting for these qualities end up producing fruits that look beautiful, have a long shelf life, and taste like cardboard. Canned tomatoes, by contrast, disfigured by the canning process and hidden behind the opaque tin, can only be judged by their name brand printed on the label and the taste of fruit after the can is opened. As canned tomatoes became a mainstay of the pantry, a marketing decision solidified the red tomato as the ideal aesthetic variety.[64] The image of the perfect round, red tomato was created by marketing departments at food-processing companies, and today it should be a symbol of mass-market, Florida-grown imitations of tomatoes rather than the sweet, delicious fruit.

Another more recent development has been the use of mechanical pickers for tomato crops. Developed in the 1960s, the harvesting equipment requires slightly sturdier tomatoes to avoid crushing the product, as well as fruits that will ripen at the same time. But canned tomatoes can be picked by machine because within a few hours they will end up processed, stripped of their skins or crushed into sauce, paste, and soup. Canned tomatoes are also picked at their peak ripeness. Odd shapes or imperfections in color and skin don't matter for canned products because no consumer will see these attributes once the tomato is processed, and damage caused by machines that turns consumers off fresh, whole tomatoes simply doesn't matter. The one thing mechanical harvesters are incapable of is distinguishing between vines with mixed green and red fruit, so the qualities most desirable in canning tomato varieties are crops that ripen simultaneously. Sorting machines in the canning factory can prevent unripe fruit from ending up in the canned product, but these green fruits are wasted. Corporations dependent on tomatoes for their products like Heinz and Campbell's cultivated varieties with simultaneous ripening in mind. Some of these are even available to farmers, though companies like Heinz often reserve a few varieties for their own product lines to ensure consistency and competitor exclusion.

A large variety of tomatoes can ultimately end up in red sauce, but not all tomatoes are created equal in this regard. One of the most prized today is the San Marzano. The rise in popularity (and price) of San Marzano tomatoes is in part due to celebrity chefs promoting it, but also because Italy has sought European Union protections for the cultivar. The origins of the San Marzano remain disputed. It may have evolved naturally as the result of a spontaneous mutation of genes around the turn of the century in fields on the volcanic hillside of Mount Vesuvius. Another account claims the original variation was a gift to Naples from a mythical king of Peru.[65] A pear-shaped tomato, possibly a predecessor to the San Marzano variety, was described by Italian abbots,[66] pointing to a lineage that would explain the hybridization process through monastic gardens. When sliced open, the tomato reveals an elongated pericarp (the fleshy part) and a small, cherry-tomato-sized placenta—the gummy seed-bearing portion of the tomato.[67] These qualities are what make the San Marzano ideal for sauces, but they also indicate a closer connection to Mexican ancestral varieties. Today, the San Marzano is big business for Campania, the region where all *Denomin-azione d'Origine Protetta* (DOP)–protected San Marzanos are grown.

Receiving DOP protection requires San Marzano tomatoes bearing the label to be grown in a specific region in the volcanic soil around the Sarno River, harvested by hand, and packaged whole. The DOP is intended to protect traditional foods and create a luxury market for agricultural products. Plenty of eligible farmers don't bother acquiring the licensing because of the expensive, bureaucratic process. In a daisy chain of licensing, another bureaucratic agency, the *Associazione Verace Pizza Napoletana*, the "true Neapolitan pizza association," responsible for protecting authentic Neapolitan pizza, requires DOP San Marzano tomatoes. More often in the United States, San Marzano tomatoes include in the label "Italian style," referring to the cultivar rather than the protected, regional food.

Perhaps unsurprisingly, Italian immigrants were less concerned with authentic tomato varieties than we are today. Accustomed to living in rural areas where they grew their own vegetables, many immigrants set up garden patches to grow household vegetables, including tomatoes. The best tomatoes for making sauces tend to be elongated varieties, such as the plum tomato, Roma tomato, and San Marzano. They should be sweet, fleshier, with fewer seeds, which can be bitter. When making sauce from fresh tomatoes, some cooks remove the seeds to improve the flavor of the sauce.

Red sauce cuisine developed an association with Italian culture during the twentieth century. Although Sicily and Naples had strong, existing tomato-based foods, the wide availability of the fruit in the United States meant it was an easy way for Italian immigrants to connect with old-world recipes. Furthermore, because the tomato had largely been relegated to

consumption as a condiment in the United States, there were few reasons
to associate the tomato with other ethnic groups when the Italians arrived.
Today, of course, the tomato is strongly linked to Italian culture as well
as America's immigrant Italian culture, but that might have as much to
do with the immigrants arriving in the United States as with the culture
in Italy.

7

❖ ❖

The Opening Acts

Early red sauce recipes emerged from the celebratory foods of the Italian peasant class, including dishes typically prepared for festivals, holidays, or special events like weddings. Restaurants at the start of Italian immigration tended to focus on these foods because eating out initially remained a luxury, albeit a more affordable one than possible in Italy. Often, when these immigrants did splurge, they ate meals with extended families, and because men usually arrived in the United States first and only later brought families, many of these meals served as a celebration of family reunification. Many of the laborers spent years without seeing wives or children and, on the family's arrival, splurged with fancy restaurant meals. As a result, dishes served at restaurants evolved to have heavier, richer qualities than the foods cooked in Italy and were served with plentiful proportions, large quantities of meat, and elaborate presentations.

Menus embraced dishes imitating the extravagance and lifestyle of the rich, or at least the idea of how wealthy Italians might live. Few of the immigrants, even those working in the United States as restauranteurs, had ever actually experienced the foods available to the upper classes while in Italy or even eaten in a restaurant before arriving in New York. The abbondanza, particularly the wide availability of meat, symbolized the great promise of immigration. Many of the dishes either drew inspiration from the idea of upper-class Italian cuisine or reinterpreted vegetarian dishes to include meat, while others evolved out of what had once been a rare holiday meal and became a commonly served dish.

Restaurant menus initially were designed to attract the broadest segment of immigrant patrons. Even with southerners dominating these groups, elements from many regions ended up sprinkled onto menus. Some elements, like the breadsticks commonly served at the start of the meal, come from the north, although the largest influences came from a mix of southern provinces. These traditions were combined in new ways and drew on influences found in America.

The tomato, so much a part of Sicilian and Neapolitan cooking, and widely accessible in America, became the recognizable and predominant ingredient. One of the earliest dishes to illustrate this connection between celebration, tomatoes, spaghetti, and small-scale trattorias is the dish spaghetti fra diavolo, originally called lobster fra diavolo or, even more simply, lobster diavolo. The phrase *fra diavolo* translates as "with or among the devil" or "brother of the devil," a nickname earned because of the spice of hot peppers. An early American invention, lobster fra diavolo draws inspiration from many southern Italian seafood dishes mixing heat and tomatoes with shellfish, but it does not have a direct analog in Italian cuisine.

In 1908, the Italian American restaurant Enrico & Paglieri opened in the basement of a townhouse in what is now the West Village of New York City,[1] then an Italian ethnic neighborhood. Like many restaurants serving the community, the owners lived above their place of business. They catered to not just ethnic Italians but also the new American bourgeois and their desire for adventurous ethnic eating with an affordable menu. Enrico & Paglieri were well known for serving lobster fra diavolo, so much so that half a century later, it was still their calling card. The *New York Times* explained in 1946 that Enrico & Paglieri offered a menu with little variation featuring minestrone soup as well as lobster diavolo.[2] For just fifty-five cents,[3] the restaurant provided customers an affordable but luxurious dining experience with a prix fixe price including antipasti, soup, salad, and spaghetti at a better price than similar restaurants offering meals à la carte.[4] The perception that Italian food provided good value and affordable luxury helped popularize the cuisine with non-Italian restaurant goers.

The first iteration of lobster fra diavolo began as a preparation for the lobster rather than as a sauce for pasta. The prix fixe meal from Enrico & Paglieri included pasta as primi piatti, with the lobster served as the entrée. The preparation of spaghetti fra diavolo as a sauced pasta likely evolved with imitators copying the popular offering, combining tomato sauce and lobster before tossing with pasta. Today, spaghetti fra diavolo is a pasta dish of black and red pepper, garlic, tomatoes, and mixed shellfish served over pasta. The shellfish is most often lobster, but some recipes will add crab or scallops. Further adding to the confusion, the modern conception of a fra diavolo sauce is sometimes interchanged with arrabbiata sauce, another spicy tomato sauce originating in Rome. Rao's, the impossible-to-get-reservations red sauce joint, offers in its line of gourmet jarred sauces a spicy red sauce named arrabbiata fra diavolo sauce, although no seafood is listed among the ingredients.

All evidence points to lobster diavolo originating in New York City, but among both Italian American and Italian food writers, there remains a disagreement as to whether the dish is more American or more Italian. There is a link between Neapolitan tomato seafood dishes and the early twentieth-century version of lobster diavolo. American lobsters are another way the American abundance was expressed. Maine lobsters served in the United States are larger, have bigger claws, and continue to be available in ample supply. The Mediterranean lobster, bug-like, petite, clawless, and rare, was even then (and continues to be) an expensive luxury. Overfishing in the Mediterranean meant the tiny lobsters, even in the nineteenth century, were unlikely to be a staple. American lobsters, by contrast, were once so plentiful that laws limiting how often they could be served to servants became necessary. Lobster diavolo took this bountiful American product, sauced it in a traditional Italian method, and served it at an affordable price.

The inspiration for lobster diavolo may have come from a spicy chicken dish known as *pollo* alla diavolo, a spicy chicken entrée. In this case, the *alla diavolo* indicates the meat is prepared with coarsely ground black pepper.[5] Black pepper was at one time considered a strong spicy flavor. Pellegrino Artusi includes a recipe for pollo alla diavolo in the 1891 *La scienza in cucina e l'arte di mangiar bene*, and the 1912 American cookbook *Simple Italian Cook Book* also presents pollo alla diavolo. This latter recipe calls for cayenne pepper but adds a note: only for those who like it—suggesting not everyone was ready for the heat brought on by capsicum.

By the end of the nineteenth century, New York City's young and wealthy feasted on lobster at large-format venues known as lobster palaces. Restaurants such as Rector's and Murray's Roman Gardens provided entertainment with music, dance floors, and vaudeville shows. They were a stark rejection of formal hotel dining rooms or restaurants like Delmonico's and became known for their ostentatious extravagance, including chorus girls, champagne, and lobsters. Ethnic restaurants like Enrico & Paglieri competed with these popular destinations by offering good value for money, like the prix fixe menu. Lobster fra diavolo in this context would seem a natural progression and prime example of the adaptability of Italian cuisine in America, where lobster replaces chicken in a familiar preparation, creating a new dish to satisfy the demands of a young, moneyed customer.

Early versions of lobster fra diavolo prepared the critters whole, with the sauce dressing the meat. This preparation is most likely how Enrico & Paglieri served their dish as part of their prix fixe menu. Commonly, the whole lobsters, sauced with hot pepper and tomatoes, are served in their shells over a pile of spaghetti or bucatini. The heaviness of the dish convinced Marcella Hazan that it must have been invented by Americans rather than Italians, while the Italian American food writer John Mariani claims the recipe originated somewhere in southern Italy.[6]

With the whole lobster resting on top of the pasta, the lobster's sauce essentially became a condiment to the spaghetti underneath. Innovation prevailed. Shelling the lobster and tossing the meat in the sauce not only made the dish easier to eat but also had the benefit of allowing the chef to reduce the amount of lobster meat or add cheaper shellfish to the sauce. Today, a common variation replaces the lobster with shrimp. Another version removes the lobster from its shell, leaving chunks of meat mixed with sauce and served over the pasta. By the 1940s, lobster fra diavolo had become a well-known dish in Italian American restaurants and a mainstay of places like Patsy's and Angelo's.[7] Capri on West 52nd Street in Manhattan was serving a version of lobster fra diavolo with the whole lobster fried and then cooked with tomatoes.[8] Spaghetti was not included. The dish made its way into the English translation of Ada Boni's *The Talisman of Italian Cooking* but is absent from earlier Italian editions of the book.

James Beard has claimed the dish originated in France, as lobster *à l'Americaine*, with lobster fra diavolo merely an Italianized variation of the French dish. Beard's fra diavolo begins by preparing the lobsters according to his l'Americaine recipe. In this method, lobsters are broiled, cooked with oil, butter, onions, shallots, and garlic and then flambéed in cognac. Once the lobster l'Americaine is prepared, they then can be diavolo'd with oregano, parsley, cloves, mace, pepper, tomatoes, and more onions and cognac. His version lacks the spice of the hot pepper,[9] even if l'Americaine contains a pinch of cayenne. Furthermore, Beard's fra diavolo dish is served alongside rice rather than pasta. Certainly, it is possible Italian peasants might have been influenced by sophisticated French cooking techniques as Beard, a Francophile, contends, but, more likely, Italian immigrants simply combined a readily available American ingredient—the lobster—with an existing method they were familiar with.

In many ways, Enrico & Paglieri's fra diavolo epitomizes the creation of red sauce cuisine more generally. The restaurant combined an abundant luxury item, the lobster, with common and familiar foods, the spaghetti and the tomato, and served the dish at an accessible price, attracting not only ethnic Italians but also middle-class Americans of northern European ancestry, with the dish evolving as it disseminated throughout the ethnic community.

The broader and enduring success of Italian American restaurants relied on attracting more than just ethnic immigrant communities. In the nineteenth century, trendy and sophisticated restaurants were almost exclusively French in style and food and provided upscale, white-tablecloth dinner service. Delmonico's, the preeminent American restaurant for much of the nineteenth century, despite the Italian-sounding name, was operated by a Swiss family as a French-style restaurant. French cuisine was not considered an ethnic food as much as simply the standard available in restaurants generally. French cuisine was restaurant cuisine. The French restaurants of the period introduced Americans to spaghetti, but it was French spaghetti, rather than Italian spaghetti, meaning they served spaghetti l'Italienne, spaghetti in the Italian style. It was not at all Italian.

The competition between French and Italian cuisine can be seen too in chicken cacciatore, an Italian hunter's stew. Pollo alla *cacciatore* appears in Artusi's nineteenth-century cookbook, indicating origins in Italy, but with similar ingredients to French chicken *chasseur*. Cacciatore is sometimes considered the Italian version of this French dish, *poulet* chasseur. Both are chicken dishes stewed with vegetables, wine, and onions, and with variations including tomatoes, mushrooms, or other vegetables. Chicken cacciatore often appears on the menus of Italian American restaurants in some form, earning it a reputation as an Italian American dish, but having a long-shared history. Numerous stewed-chicken recipes share a common name, including the French dish rechristened as Italian. Given the popularity of French dining, including a hunter's chicken stew provided accessibility to diners unfamiliar and intimidated by Italian menus.

As Italian American cuisine grew into an acceptable ethnic food, and arguably as Italian food grew more popular than French cuisine, French cooking conceded to Italian influence. *Spaghetti l'Italienne* came to mean spaghetti with tomato sauce.[10] It was not, in context of French restaurants, spaghetti and meatballs, but a plain, thin tomato sauce served over spaghetti.

At first, Italian restaurants attracted other immigrant ethnic groups because they often lived in close proximity. In Manhattan, Chinatown and Little Italy overlapped. Chinese immigrants would eat in Italian restaurants, and Italians would eat in Chinese restaurants.[11] Indeed, *The Macaroni Journal* offers chop suey recipes using spaghetti alongside recipes for Italian and Mexican pasta dishes. Jewish ethnic enclaves also intermingled, especially when it came to food.[12] But the real success of Italian restaurants came when the bourgeois Anglo-Americans discovered the quaint ethnic trattorias.

The concept and image of an iconic red sauce Italian restaurant that persists today evolved in the late nineteenth century from the fantasy of old-world Italy. The immigrant owners of these trattorias recreated a concept of what they believed a restaurant should be, intending to remind themselves of a place they had left.[13] Even then, the red-checkered tablecloth, straw-wrapped Chianti bottles, and imitation villa atmosphere existed as a fictitious memory, a pastiche of a nonexistent history. The symbols chosen included a hodgepodge of styles and regional identities. The Chianti bottles came from Tuscany, a region outside of the south[14] and a location not sending large numbers of immigrants to the United States. The red-checkered pattern known as gingham was often used in a variety of ethnic restaurants in different colors and was produced for a global market in places like England. Restaurateurs invented a vernacular, merely suggesting a nostalgic idea of Italy without actually reproducing it. It was basic marketing, and it worked. Many of the early upwardly mobile, bourgeois diners sought out and wanted the quaint, rustic aesthetic even if was merely an artificial veneer. It was chic, romantic, and appealing. The style proved so desirable that a restaurant in Providence, Rhode Island, went so far as to thematically decorate in the Italian trattoria style despite exclusively serving dairy products inspired by the British island of Guernsey.[15]

Part of the success of the red sauce restaurant is owed to a growing middle-class desire to seek ethnic food. These original foodies wanted the experience of new and different flavors from what had become a stodgy French restaurant experience, and they found those new flavors in ethnic enclaves. In East Coast cities, ethnic immigrant communities mingled with middle-class Americans who now had disposable income and a thirst for adventure. As the United States matured on the global stage, the upwardly mobile sought new ways of comparing themselves to the old world. Consuming the food of continent gave them claim to status of European peers, even if only in their mind.[16] More important, Italian food was inexpensive,[17] allowing easier access for the young bourgeois to experiment with a low risk. The hipsters of their day, the urban bourgeois were tempted by exotic flavors like garlic,[18] and so the immigrant-owned restaurants in places like Manhattan's West Village began attracting these adventurous bohemians.

Artists and writers found low-cost meals. They also found inspiration in the restaurants they frequented, with the restaurants themselves serving an important role: "scarcely a memoir or novel of the period 1880 to 1910 fail to include a nostalgic scene set in an Italian cellar restaurant in Greenwich Village."[19] Although popular with bohemians, the era's East Coast elites, the broad appeal of Italian American restaurants to nonimmigrants would not penetrate the hinterland until after the First World War.

Perhaps, then, the most important factor in the development of red sauce cuisine was the arrival of Enrico Caruso, the famed tenor who sang at the Metropolitan Opera. Caruso was born the son of a shoe peddler in 1873 in Naples, Italy. He began singing in his local church at the age of eleven.[20] He debuted in the opera *L'Amico Frencesco* in Naples in 1894 before touring around Italy and Europe; by the time Caruso arrived in New York City in 1903, he was a well-known star. He lived in the city almost two decades, where he met his wife, Dorothy Parker Benjamin. They married in 1918. His fame and celebrity at the time could well be compared today to Beyoncé, both trendsetters and talented vocalists. As a foreigner, Caruso was seen as an ethnic other, but he profoundly influenced Italian American cuisine in the United States and advanced the cause for accepting Italian Americans, all while changing the course of Italian American cuisine.

Enrico Caruso debuted at New York's Metropolitan Opera in the 1903–1904 season, on opening night of *Rigoletto*.[21] Already very much in demand, he arrived in New York looking to earn a big payday. His arrival boosted the image of Italians in America, and he attracted crowds nationwide, such as with a performance in San Francisco the night before the great earthquake of 1906.[22] Luckily, his experience with earthquakes in Naples had prepared him to bolt from the bed to the window when he felt the shocks just after five in the morning. Caruso inspired future generations of Italian Americans, like Tony Bennett, who grew up listening to Caruso's recordings.[23]

Caruso's time in America was not without hiccups. The Black Hand, an extortion ring, sent him threatening letters looking for payments. The organization often targeted immigrants, who had little recourse but to pay. Since Caruso had access to money and influence, he refused. He also refused to pay his personal chef, Carlo Ragozzino, who sued for back wages. Caruso insisted the chef cooked poor-quality food, and Caruso's wife even testified that Ragozzino prepared rancid calf brains and left her kitchen messy and cluttered.[24] The judge eventually ruled against Caruso, finding it impossible that the food was as bad as the family claimed. In another incident highlighting the tension between Italian immigrants and other ethnic groups, an

Irish policeman—New York's police force was dominated by Irish at the time—sought to discredit Caruso by arresting him for solicitation. James J. Kane, a patrolman, arrested Caruso on charges of disorderly conduct at the Central Park Zoo's monkey house for making untoward advances directed at a woman. The victim, Mrs. Graham, never appeared in court, and Caruso paid a modest fine. Later that year, Kane was accused of making false statements and eventually revealed the invention of eight other similar claims with the assistance of a woman for hire.[25]

Caruso earned significant performance fees, as much as $1,500–$2,000 per night, a considerable sum at the time. A rigorous schedule and poor lifestyle choices lead to declining health. He left New York in 1921 to return to Naples for rest and recovery. He departed at the end of May, and on board the ship there was enough spaghetti to measure it in miles for his personal use.[26] He died three months later in Naples after an unsuccessful operation.

Beyond his larger-than-life celebrity, the important legacy of Caruso's time in New York is that his mere presence helped popularize Italian American restaurants. The middle-class diner followed him first to the select restaurants he patronized, but then more generally to other bohemian haunts he didn't. Caruso, an influencer of his day, helped make Italian cuisine cool, and crowds of diners followed. He was known to push his way into restaurant kitchens and supervise or instruct the preparation of pasta dishes.[27] Frequently he was spotted eating out at many Manhattan Italian American restaurants around the city, but he had favorites. He often lunched at Pane's on Forty-Seventh and ate dinner at Del Pezzo on Forty-Sixth.[28] He kept a standing, nightly reservation for himself and small party at Del Pezzo.

His impact on Italian American cuisine didn't end there. Caruso convinced Luisa Leone to open her restaurant, Leone's,[29] later Mama Leone's, a legendary red sauce restaurant serving hundreds of diners a night. For a half a century, Leone's operated as an independent restaurant serving up red sauce classics until it was acquired by the conglomerate Restaurant Associates. Restaurant Associates expanded it into a chain, spreading red sauce Italian across the country, and continued serving food from the Manhattan location until 1994.

Luisa Leone's path to success was exceptional, but not an uncommon story among Italian immigrants. Luisa Leone departed Italy shortly after the birth of her son, Gene, around 1898, with her husband, Girolamo, a wine merchant. She and her husband lived in New York City and cooked for Caruso out of her kitchen.[30] Caruso encouraged her to open a formal restaurant,[31] although her husband disliked the idea of his wife working.

When the restaurant first opened in 1906, Leone served food out of the family living room,[32] not an uncommon arrangement for many Italian restaurants in the early decades of the twentieth century. Leone's had just twenty seats when it opened, with Caruso filling them with a party on opening night.[33] Then it catered to an ethnic immigrant crowd, like Caruso. In 1914, Leone's husband died, and her sons started working at the restaurant. They pushed their mother to expand,[34] but Prohibition slowed their plans until 1934.[35]

Twenty years later, Leone's had moved to Times Square, where the then-35,000-square-foot restaurant catered to more than just an immigrant population. The location attracted crowds of middle-class Americans on their way to Broadway shows and eager for what eventually became a red sauce favorite well known outside of immigrant circles. Mama Leone's grew from a twenty-chair restaurant into one with 1,250 seats, serving 700,000 meals a year,[36] in eleven dining rooms at its peak. Luisa Leone died in the early 1940s, and her son Gene took over. The restaurant took on the name "Mama Leone's" as a sign of respect and then made it official when Gene sold it to Restaurant Associates. While Leone's may represent the ultimate success story, similar parlor restaurants operated in the ethnic Italian neighborhoods, with many growing beyond their owner's living rooms as Italian cuisine grew more popular over the early years of the twentieth century.

Meanwhile, Leone's was not the only restaurant for which Caruso is at least partly responsible. Caruso's, a "spaghetti house" chain, opened in Manhattan serving a variety of low-cost pasta dishes. Spaghetti houses sold large plates of spaghetti and other pasta, a kind of fast food of their day, and Caruso's was not alone in the concept. Other brands and independent restaurants spread spaghetti and Italian American–style pasta dishes across the country, competing with other casual restaurants. These spaghetti houses positioned themselves as lower-cost options than fine-dining establishments, competing in the same space as casual chains like Howard Johnson's and luncheon counters like Schrafft's rather than upscale dinning. The Caruso's chain had six New York restaurants and an outpost in Newark, New Jersey, serving a wide array of Italian-influenced foods at affordable prices.

In addition to the naming the restaurant chain, the Caruso brand landed on a wide array of products from sewing needles to olive oil, cheese, and soup mix, for most of which he earned endorsement royalties. The most lasting of these legacies is the red sauce pasta dish spaghetti alla Caruso, sometimes known as bucatini alla Caruso. The dish featured a tomato-based sauce containing mushrooms and chicken livers. Some recipes indicate mushrooms are the defining ingredient rather than the chicken livers, but at the Caruso's chain, mushroom sauce is listed as a separate item. The popularity of Caruso sauce continued well into the 1950s, appearing on menus of cruise ships and casual restaurants. Considering the volume of chicken liver included in the recipe, the decline in popularity is perhaps unsurprising, as Americans generally have shifted away from organ meats. An Italian version of this recipe is known as spaghetti *con fegatini*,[37] but it became popular in the United States because of the Neapolitan tenor.

The American version of spaghetti alla Caruso most likely originated at Del Pezzo on Forty-Sixth.[38] Enrico Caruso's regular presence popularized the restaurant, and he frequently ordered spaghetti topped with a red sauce containing mushrooms and chicken livers. The owners of Del Pezzo saw such a large upswing in business—customers wanted their chance to bump into Caruso—they renamed the dish in his honor.[39] Caruso was not a one-restaurant diner, though; he also frequented the restaurant in the Knickerbocker Hotel.[40] He lived at the hotel for thirteen years, beginning in 1908.[41] The iconic Times Square hotel attracted tourists to the neighborhood and became a hot spot for celebrity sightings. Caruso's regular patronage at the hotel dining room is perhaps the source of confusion of the origins of spaghetti alla Caruso. The chef of the Knickerbocker Hotel, Louis DeGouy, published a recipe he named "spaghetti Caruso" in his 1947 *Gold Cook Book*. That recipe is missing the heaping piles of chicken livers,[42] focusing instead on the mushrooms. Most other spaghetti alla Caruso recipes include chicken livers, setting DeGouy apart in this regard.

Another early spaghetti Caruso recipe comes from Diana Ashley's *Where to Dine in Thirty-Nine*, a recipe collection featuring restaurant recipe selections from popular chefs. The book contains a recipe from chef Antonia Riconda, an employee of the Caruso spaghetti house chain. Caruso died almost twenty years before the publication of Ashley's book, but the chain bearing his name was still serving up spaghetti.

Enrico Caruso was not the only Italian opera singer to lend an Italian name to an Italian American spaghetti dish. His contemporary, soprano Luisa Tetrazzini, is perhaps now best remembered for the spaghetti and poultry dish named in her honor. Many variations of chicken or turkey Tetrazzini have evolved over the course of its existence. The main base of the recipe consists of cream, mushrooms, parmigiana cheese, topped with breadcrumbs and tossed with spaghetti and turkey or chicken. Knickerbocker Hotel chef Louis DeGouy claims the original version contained turkey,[43] but variations include chicken and even seafood as the protein.[44] Later American variations adulterate the recipe with canned cream of mushroom soup, part of the convenience-food craze and marketing gimmicks of the canned food industry. Regionality also influences the recipe, and there is no particular standard preparation, as some versions convert the sauced pasta into a baked casserole.

Tetrazzini first sang opera in New York in 1908, just a few years before the recipe began to appear in print.[45] She also spent much of her career in San Francisco, where the recipe is said to have originated as chicken Tetrazzini.[46] Once more Louis DeGouy's *The Gold Cook Book* is at odds with history. Since the dish is absent from *The Sunday American Cook Book* (a pamphlet including the singer's favorite recipes),[47] there is no definitive protein either way. The popularity of the dish grew through the 1930s, when it began appearing in America's hotel dining rooms and places like Sardis.[48] From then onward, the dish continued evolving, eventually becoming a casserole disassociated with Italian American cuisine but, like so many other red sauce dishes, becoming simply American.

These first Italian American dishes epitomized the way red sauce recipes began to enter into the zeitgeist. Chefs and home cooks adapted the recipes they were familiar with, using ingredients more readily available and often in greater quantity. The following decades would bring more memorable and more everlasting recipes onto American menus, but these early dishes remain proto–red sauce dishes that set the stage for the Italian American invasion.

8

❖ ❖

Meat and Tomatoes

Higher wages had a huge impact on immigrants' lives once they arrived in America. Despite sending money home, higher incomes allowed many people to regularly add meat to their diets for the first time. Southern Italians ate half as much meat as those in the north,[1] with many immigrants rarely eating meat before coming to America. After immigration, even the poorest families found they could eat quality meat as frequently as once or twice a week.

One method for increasing meat consumption was simply enriching tomato sagu with meat. The hearty meat sauces known as ragù have since become a mainstay of Italian American culture. Ragù, like sagu, is similarly cooked for a long period of time but includes meat. The word itself comes from the French *ragoût*, meaning a stew, with that phrase originating with *ragoûter*, "to arouse or enhance the taste."[2] The combination of time and meat creates a heartier, thicker sauce, and it typically is darker in color. American ragù often includes several meats in a single sauce, including sausages; ground beef, pork, or veal; and whole cuts. Braising the meat in ragù over a long period of time softens the tough muscles of cheaper cuts.

Provincial variations of ragù in Italy have traditions of specific meat stews, with either the animal or cuts distinguishing them. In Verona, for instance, a ragù is made with horse meat and game like duck, but hare and boar are common in Tuscany and Umbria, cured meats in Rome, and lamb in Abruzzo and Molise.[3] Americans cook variations on Neapolitan ragù (with the Americanized spaghetti and meatballs a derivative) and, despite Bologna's decidedly northern orientation, variations on Bolognese ragù. American ragù combines multiple types of meat. Meat ragù became famous in part because of depictions in popular films, like *The Godfather*, in which protagonist Mikey learns how to make a ragù thick with sausage and meatballs. The memorable scene depicts the epitome of the idea of Italian American culture, of old men sitting around cooking a tomato and meatball sauce for their dinner. A similar scene occurs in prison in *Goodfellas*, depicting the Italian American protagonists cooking a ragù with veal, beef, and pork. The depiction of Italian Americans as gangsters in popular culture also increased the popularity of red sauce cuisine as early as the era of Prohibition, and film and television (such as *The Godfather*, *Goodfellas*, and *The Sopranos*) continued to highlight red sauce dishes throughout the last century.

In southern Italy, the price of meat kept ragù off the tables of working-class peasants. If the poor ate meat at all, it was reserved for holidays a few times a year. Meat dishes represented celebrations and parties rather than the ordinary daily meal. Even then, for the poorest, the meat they had access to was often only sausages,[4] leftover pieces, and scraps ground up with fat. The general availability of food, especially meat, in the United States—and at a price even average laborers could afford—was one of the appeals of emigrating. Immigrants wrote to relatives who remained behind in Italy describing the bounty,[5] sometimes with embellishment, and these descriptions encouraged more immigrants to follow.[6]

At first, meat remained a luxury, albeit an attainable one. Meat once a week was still better than once a year. When it was scarce, meat was reserved for Sunday dinner. In many Italian neighborhoods, this meat-filled Sunday sauce became known as "gravy," a mistranslation of ragù. The richer the family became, the more meat would end up in their ragù.[7] An early recipe published in America suggests making a gravy by boiling chunks of whole meat, usually beef, in water, and adding tomato paste and butter. The meat, boiled for up to eight hours, produces a gravy for a meat ragù "à la Napoletaine"[8] and appeared in an early issue of *Good Housekeeping* in the 1880s. The author refers to the gravy sauce as a dressing and suggests combining it with spaghetti.

The image of an old Italian American grandmother standing beside a stove cooking a sauce is really the image of a woman who grew up a poor peasant sustained on a vegetable-rich diet now accustomed to regularly cooking a meat-rich ragù. The gathering of family around hearty, meaty pasta sauces became an important ritual for ethnic Italians, and as the immigrants grew wealthier, they increased their meat consumption throughout the week. Still, Sunday gravy remained a special part of their tradition because of the required cooking time of several hours, and the social aspect of gathering family. Following the conventions of formal Italian dining, Italian Americans would often reserve the meat from the sauce as the secondi piatti, serving the surplus sauce over the pasta as a primi piatti. As spaghetti and meatballs evolved into a mainstay of American restaurants and weeknight meals, this practice of separating the meat grew less common, but many Italian American families retained the tradition on Sunday meals.

Sunday gravy, the all-day ragù, is most commonly a variation of Neapolitan ragù, a slow-cooked sauce filled with meat. Neapolitan ragù begins with a *soffritto* heavy with onion. Early Neapolitan cooking would employ only onion or garlic, not both, although contemporary interpretations usually call for a combination. Since garlic and onion are both alliums, Italian cooks believed adding both was redundant. This Neapolitan soffritto rarely includes celery and carrots, although both are considered essential in Bolognese. The Neapolitan cooking that arrived with Italian immigrants was based on poverty and shortage, and the efficiency of ingredients reflects that. The meat in a Neapolitan ragù is kept in larger pieces rather than using ground meat. The meats within the sauce varied by the chef or the family budget but included pork, salt pork, veal, beef, sausages, or a combination.

Sunday gravy often featured *braciola*,[9] meat cutlets that are pounded thin, rolled, and stuffed with a variety of fillings. Braciola goes by many names in Italian recipes, including *vraciola*,[10] *braciole*, *involtini*, *messicani*, *braciolone*, and *braciolette*,[11] and it has long been part of Italian cuisine. Pork and veal rolls are some of the most common in Americanized versions of the dish, and fillings can include ham, herbs, breadcrumbs, and cheese. In 1912, *Simple Italian Cooking* included a recipe for involtini of beef alla *Siciliana*. These beef cutlets are stuffed with butter, ham, bread, and onion, rolled up "like sausages,"[12] and cooked off on a grill. Braciola, like meatballs and sausages, was added to the Sunday gravy for cooking, but it was usually not served during the week as the other meats sometimes were. Breaded eggplant provides a cheaper substitute for the meat in the Italian dish involtini di *melanzane*, and immigrants may have been more familiar with preparing involtini of eggplant than of involtini of meat. The eggplant dish took on the name *rollatini*, a word unknown in Italian. Eggplant rollatini today is most often stuffed with ricotta, like a manicotti, baked in tomato sauce, and topped with mozzarella cheese to provide a vegetarian alternative for the meat averse.

Neapolitan ragù, sometimes known as sugo della *guardaporta*[13] ("the sauce of the gatekeeper"), earns its name because the *portinai*, translated as "doorman" or "gatekeeper," sat at the entrance to villa courtyards of tenement buildings watching both the property and the slowly simmering pot of stew. Ragù must cook long and slow to correctly braise the meat, but it also requires the occasional stirring to prevent burning and, in the era before electric or gas stoves, someone to tend the fire over a long period of time.[14] To achieve this thickness, the sauce must cook for several hours, concentrating flavors and softening the meat, another challenging task when cooked on an open fire.

Ragù Neapolitan in many forms became one of the most common dishes served by Italian Americans for Sunday meals. These dinners served as the gathering point for immigrant families, who often lived within the same building or on the same block, and in myth and in popular culture, the ragù Neapolitan is the dish families gathered to eat. The tradition took on significant meaning for families separated by long periods of time. The pasta, sauced with the ragù, would be served as a primi piatti, with the reserved meat served as the secondi piatti. As Italian Americans grew wealthier, and meat more plentiful, it was eaten during the week as well. The formality of meals grew unnecessary, and serving meat and pasta together became more common outside of celebrations, holidays, and Sundays.

Spaghetti and meatballs evolved from the tradition of cooking ragù. The sauce at its base is a Neapolitan-style ragù using hand-formed balls of ground meat in place of a whole cut of veal, pork, or beef. Spaghetti and meatballs was entirely the creation immigrants and the restaurants in America, a combination of several regional culinary traditions into a single dish. Italy does not have a tradition of serving spaghetti with meatballs, nor do Italians serve the entrée meat alongside the pasta. Although each component of the dish is rooted in Italian culinary traditions, the invention of the dish required the convergence of immigrant nostalgia and American abundance.

Italian cuisine is filled with examples of meatball recipes, known as *polpette* or polpettone (meatloaf), but these dishes are never served over spaghetti in sauce.[15] Polpette are traditionally served as the secondi piatti, the entrée following the pasta. They come in various sizes but are generally smaller than American meatballs, with some as small as marbles. Italians also serve a larger meatball portioned as a single ball, provided as the second course. For both the very small and the very large meatballs, sauces act as condiments to the meat. Recipe variations adjust the ratios, but meatballs begin with ground meat, often a combination of pork, beef, and veal, and then are combined with breadcrumbs, parmesan cheese, herbs, eggs for binding, and sometimes onion or garlic. The balls are fried in oil and then baked in the oven or braised in a tomato sauce. The American meatball, often the size of an egg and drowning in a tomato ragù, has no recognizable counterpart in Italy.

Meatballs are not just a symbol of Italian American cuisine but also a product of how Italians in America adapted. Southern Italians were long accustomed to finding ways of extending luxury foods like meat with lower-cost foods and food waste. In the case of meatballs, ground meat substitutes for expensive whole meat. Adulterating the meatballs with breadcrumbs not only helped bind the balls together but also reduced the cost of each ball by expanding the total volume. Breadcrumbs were commonly used in southern cooking to increase the calorie counts of an individual portion at a low cost. Nothing is more economical than finding a use for stale bread. Breadcrumbs found their way into all sorts of dishes and serve as a substitute for more expensive foods peasant farmers had little access to. For instance, some southern tomato ragù recipes call for adding breadcrumbs directly to the sauce. The starch thickens the sauce and adds volume to what might otherwise have been a lean meal. Vegetables are mixed with breadcrumbs browned in oil, and even pasta is topped with breadcrumbs instead of cheese. Meatballs are no different in this regard, with the bread adding volume to otherwise-expensive meat. Red sauce, pasta, and meatballs were a means of feeding a large family with limited resources.

The exact origins of spaghetti and meatballs as a combined, American dish are difficult to pinpoint. For holidays and celebrations, meatballs were braised alongside sausages and veal shanks. Similarly, the Neapolitan lasagna di *carnevale*, a single-plate dish served on Fat Tuesday leading into the Lenten fast,[16] contains small meatballs alongside sausages and other foods prohibited during Lent. These meatballs are smaller in size than those served with spaghetti and meatballs but show a tradition of mixing meatballs with sausages. Artusi offers a meatball recipe using boiled meat and gruel of milk and bread, flavored with raisins and pine nuts. These meatballs should be the size of eggs—not all that different than the typical American meatball—but are fried off and served alone rather than with spaghetti or tomato sauce.

An early recipe in *The South Bend Tribune*[17] describes a casserole featuring meatballs of Hamburg steak. The steak is chopped up and combined with breadcrumbs, egg, onion, salt, and paprika, formed into balls, and fried before adding tomatoes, green pepper, onion, and butter and baked in a casserole dish. After forty-five minutes of baking, boiled spaghetti is added into the sauce along with some cheese, and the casserole is baked again. Although this recipe has some commonalities with red sauce spaghetti and meatballs, the second baking of the casserole distinguishes it as more of a distant cousin. Variations of spaghetti and meatball recipes had been circulating in newspapers as far west as Chicago in the early 1900s, when American canning companies like Heinz and Campbell's wanted markets for their tomato products.

By the 1920s, spaghetti and meatballs had a fateful meeting. The *New Macaroni Journal*, the trade publication for macaroni manufacturers, published an article revealing Rudy Valentino's favorite recipes. An Italian actor based in the United States, Valentino was a silent film star and a sex symbol of the 1920s before dying prematurely at the age of thirty-one. The *New Macaroni Journal* is not necessarily reliable as a factual account—it is the same publication responsible for spreading the myth that Marco Polo brought spaghetti back from China. But the publication did claim to publish two of Valentino's favorite recipes, one for spaghetti with tomato sauce and another for meatballs. The spaghetti à la Valentino recipe includes a not-very-memorable tomato sauce, a basic recipe common for the time, but immediately following this recipe was one for Valentino's favorite meatballs. Valentino's "Savory Meat Balls"[18] recipe includes a serving suggestion of plating alongside fried potatoes. The inclusion of a starch other than pasta suggests these meatballs are intended as a side dish, or perhaps a separate meal entirely. The recipe never mentions combining the meat with tomato sauce and pasta. The invention of spaghetti and meatballs could be attributed entirely to a misreading of the magazine's article and the American public's adoration of celebrities.

Around the same time, spaghetti and meatballs appears in an advertisement for American Beauty macaroni.[19] The recipe calls for combining ground beef and pork, onion, bread, egg, parsley, and grated onions, formed into balls, and fried. Unlike the earlier meatball casserole, the American Beauty recipe suggests serving with pasta and tomato sauce together on a plate without baking the dish together. There is also a helpful image of a plate of spaghetti with two meatballs and portion of sauce on top—just as might be expected today. American Beauty wanted to sell macaroni, and there are few better ways to sell it than as the base to an affordable meat dish.

The popularity of meatballs continued to grow over the next decade, and during the period following, spaghetti and meatballs migrated from domestic kitchens to restaurant menus. Since meatballs could be adulterated with less expensive ingredients, restaurants could squeeze higher profits without leaving customers feeling cheated. As restaurants became less formal, the rigidity between first and second plates also began to blur, and combining meat and pasta in one dish provided good value. Lastly, meatballs found even greater appeal with the arrival of the Depression. Italian-inspired menu items generally, but meatballs in particular, offered low-cost, high-calorie meals. The Depression brought about the invention of porcupine meatballs, a variation in which the inclusion of rice in the balled mixture further extends the expensive ingredients with a cheap additive and typifies how red sauce recipes were adapted by need.

Spaghetti and meatballs with tomato sauce was entrenched in red sauce cuisine by the Depression era. Recipes began appearing in American cook-books designed to appeal to mainstream American readers. It was during this period that Ettore Boiardi's Chef Boyardee, known for spaghetti and meatballs, began offering cost-effective, prepackaged canned pasta meals on grocery store shelves. Boiardi provided a line of canned ethnic food products, including everything diners needed like Italian cheese.[20] Chef Boyardee had taken staples of red sauce cuisine and condensed them (both literally and metaphorically) into cans for mass-market production. Product lines from Chef Boyardee helped develop spaghetti and meatballs into an American food, and by the onset of World War II, Boyardee was positioned to sell canned spaghetti products to the military.

More indicative of the special position spaghetti and meatballs achieved, the U.S. Army included a recipe for spaghetti and meatballs with tomato sauce in their army manuals for the Second World War. The military cook-books provided large-scale recipes for feeding a hundred people at a time all while drawing from a standard commissary. The army's spaghetti and meatball recipe was not a single recipe. The meatballs could be combined with other sauces such as brown gravy, with one serving option combining the meatballs with tomato sauce and spaghetti. The army's recipes also adapted to available ingredients, with instructions for both ground meat and whole animal carcasses. The tomato sauce called for a single clove of garlic for six quarts of tomatoes, and that one clove was meant for a serving portion of one hundred. The tomato sauce included cinnamon, cloves, and cayenne; the pasta was to be cooked until soft and then braised in the tomato sauce, along with the meatballs, for thirty minutes,[21] further soften-ing the already-limp macaroni.

The mere inclusion of spaghetti and meatballs shows just how far Ital-ian American ethnic cuisine had traveled by World War II. The only other ethnic foods in the manual are two Chinese American–style noodle dishes. The army's version of spaghetti and meatballs, designed to appeal to sol-diers from a wide spectrum of backgrounds, and limiting strong flavors like garlic, helped shape a generation's palate but also drove the American demand for red sauce cuisine in the years after the war, even if it was as processed, Americanized food. Spaghetti and meatballs became so in-grained in the American conscious by the postwar period that the famous spaghetti eating scene in the 1955 *Lady and the Tramp* includes meatballs amid the spaghetti strings, a departure from depictions of spaghetti in films just a few decades earlier.

The evolution of Italian tomato ragù in the United States followed the immigrants' pursuit of a more luxurious life. They replicated where they could and improvised when they couldn't, but ultimately the resulting dishes are the product of a once-poor people growing richer and imitating wealth as they perceived it.

9

Red Sauce Enters a Golden Age

Italian immigration slowed in the years between the first and second world wars. The First World War disrupted immigration and transatlantic trade, and later in the 1920s, new immigration laws in the United States deterred incoming immigrants, and the Italian fascist government simultaneously attempted to restrict emigration. Italians still arrived, particularly those with family already in the United States, but in smaller numbers. The reduction of new arrivals impacted the Italian American restaurants in two ways. Fewer immigrants meant fewer new tenants for boarding houses. Renting spare rooms depended on the continuous flow of immigrants replacing previous tenants as they established themselves and moved on. Once the tsunami of immigrants slowed, these landlords required new revenue streams, and many turned their boarding houses into parlor-level restaurants, not unlike Luisa Leone had done when she opened the original Leone's.

Second, the reduction in new immigrants required immigrant-owned restaurants to appeal to customers from outside their ethnic community to survive. By the 1920s, with fewer immigrants and more competition, menu innovation became essential. The need for a larger customer base also pushed ethnic restaurants to reinvent or adapt dishes to accommodate nonethnics.

Italian restaurants attracted non-Italian patrons by offering good bargains. These patrons expected to eat a plentiful amount of food at a low price in Italian restaurants, and value became a hallmark of Italian American cuisine. Multicourse prix fixe meals anchored with a pasta course, like those offered at Enrico & Paglieri's, and large portions of low-cost ingredients like pasta at the spaghetti houses helped Italian American restaurants compete on value. As the spaghetti houses spread outside of ethnic-centric cities, they acted as ambassadors of Italian American cuisine by tempting diners with affordable price points while introducing them to the frightening world of garlic-laced tomato sauces. Spaghetti houses opened in cities, pulling back the curtain on ethnic Italian food,[1] and spaghetti and tomato sauce eventually even appeared on the menus of wholesome American chains like Howard Johnson's and Schrafft's, a casual restaurant appealing to young women. Italian cuisine would come to displace French cuisine as the premiere dining experience in American restaurants, but these changes were built on a foundation of low-cost Italian American food.

The most critical event bolstering Italian American restaurants may have been the introduction of Prohibition. By that time, red sauce restaurants had established the general look and feel patrons had come to expect, from checkered tablecloths and murals depicting Venice or the Aventine Hill. But red sauce restaurants took on a new dimension as a destination where patrons could acquire illicit alcohol. Prohibition had a compounded benefit for Italian restaurants. The older French restaurants found it impossible to survive without alcohol sales to bolster their bottom line.

Delmonico's, the famous and influential New York City restaurant, shuttered shortly after the start of Prohibition. The restaurant had operated since the nineteenth century with a French-inspired menu and set a new standard for restaurants, primarily decoupling the hotel from the dining room. The founding family sold the establishment at the start of Prohibition, but without the sale of alcohol, the large restaurant could not generate enough revenue to continue operations. Delmonico's was not the only French-influenced restaurant impacted by the new law, and the end of alcohol sales marked a temporary end to formal, fine French-style dining in America. Many French chefs threw in the towel rather than serve a meal without French wine.

However, Prohibition didn't prevent Italian restaurants from continuing to serve. Italian immigrants were uniquely positioned to survive the era. The production of wine alone wasn't technically illegal, and immigrants had long embraced their ability and right to cultivate a small patch of urban garden. They were well suited to produce their own wine, from grapes either grown in their yards or purchased from markets. In the restaurants, the Italians often were more than willing to continue serving wine furtively in mugs or coffee cups that might stand out in more formal restaurants.

Like the French, the Italians considered wine essential to a good meal and were willing to simply ignore the new laws. What had become a bourgeois adventure to wander into a West Village Italian trattoria suddenly became more of thrill with the promise of an illicit drink.

The illegality of alcohol sales also bolstered another enterprise among Italians. Organized crime flourished, with vices like alcohol creating a need for suppliers and protection from the law. Mobsters became myths and legends in their own right, and eventually both historical figures like Al Capone and fictitious characters like Tony Soprano and Vito Corleone integrated into American mythology. The romantic qualities of checkered tablecloths and straw-wrapped Chianti bottles pale in comparison to the romantic notion of these lovable outlaws. The imminent threat of death enticed diners to Italian restaurants with the hope of glimpsing gangsters firsthand.

Although both restaurant kitchens and domestic cooks replicated some tomato-based pasta dishes directly from the recipes they left behind in Italy, they also expanded their offerings with new inventions. Competitors inevitably copied the successful variations and expanded their menus adapting to changing consumer expectations. New York City led the way. The city's restaurants benefited from established wealth, a large immigrant population, and a restaurant culture dating back to the nineteenth century, and in New York, diners were willing to experiment with ethnic foods. The confluence and diversity of other ethnic groups in close proximity further facilitated the evolution of Italian American recipes, as we will examine later with veal parmigiana.

During the 1920s, Italian Americans reinvented the traditional Bolognese ragù as a sauce served over spaghetti. The dish combined the popular spaghetti pasta with a high-value meat sauce. The Americanized dish is a hearty meat ragù derived from a traditional recipe from Italy, and yet spaghetti alla Bolognese is about as authentic as the vegetarian Bolognese suggested by the investment group looking to overhaul Olive Garden. The people of Bologna do cook Bolognese ragù, but the addition of spaghetti is strictly an American combination. Instead, the Italians serve Bolognese ragù exclusively with tagliatelle, a type of flat pasta. The dish is so ubiquitous that the pairing of tagliatelle and Bolognese requires no explanation in Italy. Tagliatelle pasta are long and flattened noodles, essentially a thinner variation of a lasagna noodle, and the same pasta known in Rome as fettuccine.[2] Spaghetti, by contrast, are cylindrical tubes. This distinction might seem minor to American diners, but not so in Italy. American recipes also tend to include more tomatoes with the spaghetti alla Bolognese, giving it more of a southern Italian influence.

Henry Russell, a British opera critic, references spaghetti Bolognese as early as 1926.[3] Bolognese sauce served with spaghetti, a meat sauce, was well established in New York by the 1930s. Rian James, in his 1930 book *Dining in New York*, explains that spaghetti Bolognese is one of the famous sauces of Moneta's.[4] Ralph's, a midtown Manhattan restaurant, served a spaghetti *Bologneze*, according Diane Ashley's *Where to Dine in Thirty-Nine*. Del Pozzo in New York served a *taglierini* alla Bolognese, a pasta from the Molise region paired with the Bolognese sauce, in 1936.[5] Documentation of taglietelle alla Bolognese in the United States begins in the postwar period, largely in travel books and guides, and then later as Italian restaurants began to rebrand themselves with the terms *authentic* and *northern Italian*. Americans had only just grown accustomed to spaghetti—and, even then, remained skeptical—and likely the use of the familiar pasta was merely to placate the delicate American consumer.

The standard Bolognese sauce begins with the "holy trinity" of *soffritto*—onions, celery, and carrots. Butter provides the fat rather than olive oil. Bologna is a northern region, and it sits above the veal line,[6] an imaginary line across the peninsula. In the north, where milk is a major part of the culinary tradition, male calves are slaughtered as veal, creating a greater availability of meat, while in the south animals were used to pull plows and carts. Work animals with tough muscle meat are undesirable as food, and Neapolitan ragù, where meat is braised for a long period of time, will soften the tough, well-worn meat. The veal line also corresponds to cultural access to fresh dairy products like butter, milk, and cream. These products were generally unavailable in the south and absent from southern cuisine (or made from heartier animals like goats and sheep). Although not every Bolognese ragù will contain all three ingredients, usually at least one makes an appearance.

To the chagrin of tagliatelle purists, Italian Americans have also applied Bolognese sauce as a lasagna filling, combining it with mozzarella cheese for a meaty baked-pasta dish, although this concoction should not be confused with Bolognese lasagna, a specific preparation of the baked pasta dish originating in Bologna. Bolognese lasagna al *forno* layers a meaty ragù with béchamel sauce, not mozzarella or ricotta cheese. Although Bolognese lasagna has grown in popularity throughout Italy in recent years, now that the dish is a widespread phenomenon, the ubiquity has meant a decline in overall quality.[7] American colloquial usages confuse Bolognese ragù and Bolognese lasagna, but the original dishes were distinct, with the name referencing the geographic region. Spaghetti Bolognese evolved in the United States at a time when consumers had grown to expect the spaghetti-shaped pasta but may have been unfamiliar with other pasta types. Restaurateurs coopted the term *Bolognese* to designate hearty meat sauces and distinguish them from marinara or other tomato-based sauces, even if the meat sauce did not imitate ragù based on Bolognese traditions.

Another prominent dish to evolve in the decades prior to World War II was veal parmigiana. Veal alla parmigiana, veal parmigiana, veal *parmigiano*, or veal parm, along with other variations of the name, is a breaded cutlet of veal topped with tomato sauce and mozzarella cheese and baked so the cheese melts around the cutlet. The breaded cutlet is usually pan or deep fried before adding sauce. The dish became pervasive on restaurant menus during the prewar decade, with the popularity of the dish coinciding with the decline of a similar preparation, steak pizzaiola. Steak pizzaiola is a slice of beef braised in a simple tomato sauce, but it became much less common later in the twentieth century.

Early iterations of veal parmigiana likely evolved from a southern dish featuring eggplant. *Melanzana* alla parmigiana, or eggplant alla parmigiana, originated in or around Naples. Europeans accepted the eggplant before even the tomato, and it is a significant ingredient in the south of Italy. As with eggplant involtini, breaded eggplant was a mainstay in poorer kitchens but was substituted by meat once it was financially possible in the United States. The abbondanza served as a catalyst for reinvention. Melanzana alla parmigiana morphed from a simple vegetable recipe into a whole style of preparation applied to various meats, vegetables, and seafood; in addition, it appeared on menus as an entrée and was adapted into sandwiches and, later, a pizza topping. By the middle of the twentieth century, veal parmigiana had become the standard-bearer of the "alla parmigiana" genre and earned a reputation beyond the ethnic Italian community.

Tomatoes and eggplants had a lot in common, as both were part of the nightshade family. Initial recipes for tomatoes describe treating them in a similar manner as eggplants, essentially fried in oil with salt and pepper.[8] The eggplant became a popular crop in southern Italy in places like Campania[9] and Calabria,[10] despite negative associations, and remains an important ingredient in southern cooking.

Those early recipes for frying eggplant in oil matured into the more sophisticated melanzana alla parmigiana. Sicilians fried sliced eggplants in olive oil but then layered them in a pan before baking. This method of cooking eggplant grew popular even before the addition of the tomato sauce, and sometimes it is still served as *en bianco*.[11] A Neapolitan version begins by flouring the eggplant prior to frying, providing a faint crust.

Although the name *alla parmigiana* suggests the dish's origins are in the city of Parma, it is unlikely the case. Parma has little to do with even the prototype version other than supplying Parmigiano-Reggiano cheese,[12] and even this cheese remains a disputed ingredient. Sicilians typically cook with *caciocavallo* cheese.[13] A more likely explanation is that the name stems from a similarity in appearance to the Sicilian window shutters used to keep out the hot sun. The lengthwise slices of eggplant, layered in baking dishes, are said to resemble the wooden slats of the shutters, known as *palmigiana*. The phrase evolved phonetically because in Sicilian dialect, the word sounds like parmigiana.[14]

These early versions of eggplant alla parmigiana met with tomato sauce near the beginning of the nineteenth century when Neapolitans were adding the newly discovered condiment to spaghetti. Corrado's 1773 *Il Cuoco Galante* provides a recipe for *a zucche lunghe alla parmegiana*,[15] a zucchini dish in which medallions are fried, topped with cheese, and baked. A modern-style eggplant parmigiana, *molignane a la parmisciana*, is included in the Neapolitan cookbook by Ippolito Cavalcanti.[16] This first edition of the cookbook was destroyed, and only subsequent printings from 1839 on remain.[17] The American cookbook *Simple Italian Cookery* mistranslates a zucchini parmigiana recipe as one for pumpkin.

Italian American eggplant parmigiana—the *alla* is often dropped today, although early menus included it—begins by slicing eggplant, battering it with flour and egg, covering in breadcrumbs, and frying it, before layering it with tomato sauce and mozzarella cheese, and baking in the oven. The cheese should melt and slightly brown. Variations include substituting the eggplant for zucchini, medallions of chicken or veal, meatballs, whole shrimp, portabella mushrooms, and even spaghetti, making alla parmigiana one of the most versatile dishes from Italian American cuisine. Veal parmigiana stands out as the most common red sauce menu variation, appearing widely and becoming synonymous with the cuisine itself. At the time Italians were establishing themselves in places like New York City, veal parmigiana represents the epitome of celebratory foods Italian immigrants consumed and served on a regular basis.[18]

Several factors contributed to the importance of veal parmigiana as a mainstay of the red sauce menu. Foremost, New York produced excess amounts of veal from the dairy industry in upstate agricultural regions. Even in New York City itself, a limited dairy culture existed. Breweries fed their waste product to dairy cows, producing swill milk, a low-quality and near-poisonous product. All of these cows produced calves, and many of those calves ended up as surplus animals sold as veal. The southern regions of Italy where immigrants had arrived from had few cows and little in the way of cow-milk dairy culture, so veal itself would seem extra special to a population accustomed to domestic animals like sheep, goats, chickens, and pigs. Cattle, if they were kept in the south, remained working animals and, even when they were slaughtered at the end of their lives, produced tough, stringy meat. Additionally, New York already had an established culture of eating beef. Steakhouses played an important role in New York's restaurant culture and, as beef production moved westward, in Chicago as well. By the 1940s, Americans ate ten pounds of veal per capita.[19] Beef was everywhere in America, and Italians mirrored consumption of it in their own kitchens.

Availability and existing consumption patterns in American cities such as New York likely contributed to the of rise veal parmigiana among Italian Americans. The more common meat in southern cooking was pork, and Neapolitans did already have a pork dish with a similar combination of meat and tomato sauce known as *carne* alla pizzaiola, pork stewed or braised in a light tomato sauce. In the United States, carne alla pizzaiola became steak pizzaiola, likely for the same reasons veal parmigiana grew popular. Beef, a luxury product, was far more available in American cities than southern Italy.

Steak pizzaiola had been popular in Italian Americans restaurants in the twentieth century. The term *pizzaiola* translates roughly to "pizza maker" or "pizza seller," and the translation of *carne alla pizzaiola* or *spaghetti alla pizzaiola* is "a meat or spaghetti in the style of the pizza makers." The style of the pizza makers originates in Naples, where pizza was a popular dish, but became widely available.[20] A steak pizzaiola is a cut of meat braised in a loose tomato sauce similar to marinara or stewed with other vegetables. Preparing a carne alla pizzaiola is simply a method of braising meat and tenderizing it. *Spaghetti alla pizzaiola* usually refers to a spaghetti tossed with the braising sauce along with the meat served alongside, not unlike a Neapolitan ragù. By cooking the meat in the tomatoes, cheap cuts are transformed from tough, stringy meat into something soft and tender.

In Italian American cooking, alla pizzaiola never achieved the kind of widespread acclaim as alla parmigiana. More common in the first decades of the century, meat pizzaiola dishes did exist concurrently alongside veal parmigiana in the same way Neanderthals and humans once coexisted. Steak pizzaiola faded into the background as veal and chicken parmigiana grew in popularity, and the similarity of the preparations—especially the

Americanized version with a more tomato-forward flavor—likely cut into the popularity of the dish. Today, a chicken or veal parmigiana dish is far more often available at a local red sauce joint than a steak alla pizzaiola.

Veal parmigiana's origination draws on a number of other influences, and one of these sources was likely veal scaloppini, sometimes *scaloppine*. The phrase derives from the French term *escalope* and indicates boneless pieces of veal[21] or other meats, better known to Americans as a cutlet. The lesser-used term *paillard* is more or less interchangeable in the American culinary tradition, but in French restaurants of the nineteenth century, *escalope* and *paillard* referred to different parts of the animal.[22] Paillards were thin, flat, and juicy, but escalope came from tougher muscles and required a good pounding to flatten and tenderize. Scaloppini tended to look like paillards but beaten flat. Like braising, scaloppini was a way to turn cheap cuts into tender meat. Neapolitan domestic cooks likely cooked up veal or pork scaloppini alla pizzaiolo at the same time immigrant groups began arriving in America, but these were still a few steps away from becoming the Italian American veal parmigiana. The essential distinction between veal parmigiana and earlier dishes from Italy like veal scaloppini alla pizzaiolo is the addition of breading created by a three-step flour-egg-breadcrumb batter and a topping of cheese.

Germans made up a large portion of the immigrants arriving in the United States prior to the Italian immigration. They established significant ethnic enclaves, as did other immigrant groups. Germans played a particularly significant role in New York City, arriving before the Italians and entrenching themselves as part of the dominant cultural force. By the 1880s, Germans had established restaurants and offered their ethnic cuisine to the growing middle class, the same group of patrons who would eventually discover ethnic Italian red sauce restaurants. These restaurants served German specialties including wiener schnitzel.[23]

The traditional German schnitzel is a veal, pork, or chicken cutlet pounded flat, breaded, and fried. The accompanying sauces vary by region within the German-Austrian culinary sphere. Schnitzel's popularity in German enclaves in New York City influenced the evolution of veal parmigiana. Although the cut of meat is similar to the French paillard or the Italian scaloppini, the schnitzel is always coated in batter and fried, an essential distinction between the meat used for veal parmigiana and the preparation of carne alla pizzaiola, which is never breaded. German-style restaurants, bolstered by large immigrant populations, also had seen a surge of popularity during the early twentieth century. Italian American restaurants, needing to appeal to a broader customer base, may simply have been mimicking the popular schnitzel as a way of luring in non-Italian customers.

Further hinting at this connection between the schnitzel and veal parmigiana is another Italian American dish, veal *Francese*. "Veal Francese" simply means veal in the French style, but the French style varies depending on who is interpreting it. In Italian American cuisine, veal Francese is a veal cutlet battered and fried and topped with a sauce of lemon, garlic, white wine, and parsley. This combination is not a common recipe in Italy,[24] but the sauce is similar to one commonly served alongside German schnitzel, suggesting another crossover between German and Italian immigrant foods once both groups arrived in the United States.

Before surrendering the origins of veal parmigiana to the Germans, we must also acknowledge a famous dish from Milan, *cotoletta alla Milanese*. Translated as "veal in the style of Milan" and frequently referred to as veal Milanese, this dish is a thinly pounded slice of veal breaded and fried. Although few of the immigrants arriving in places like New York came from the north, the Milanese had been eating their breaded cutlets for at least a century. And by some accounts, Austrian wiener schnitzel (schnitzel of Vienna) owes its existence to Milan's cotoletta. This legend begins during the reign of the Hapsburg monarchy, when the Austrian empire ruled over parts of northern Italy and eastern Europe. In 1848, the emperor had sent Austrian field marshal Earl Joseph Wenzel von Radetzky to Milan in an effort to thwart revolts against the empire. While in Milan, Radetzky dined on cotoletta alla Milanese and loved the dish so much he fawned over it in letters to the emperor. His letters home, it has been claimed, helped birth Vienna's most famous culinary creation.

There are a number of problems with this legend. First, schnitzel appears in the cookbook of Maria Anna Neudecker published as early as 1831,[25] almost two decades before Radetzky arrived in Milan. Second, the Milanese and the Viennese employ different cuts of meat, with the Italians using meat from the rib and Austrians using meat from the leg.[26] Despite these somewhat-obvious inconsistencies, the Radetzky myth was popularized, and the reason dates back to the 1960s when diplomatic relations between Italy and Austria were strained. An Italian journalist, looking to stir up trouble, concocted a scheme to take away the pride and joy of Austria, the schnitzel. Felice Cùnsolo invented and began to spread the funny anecdote about Milan inventing schnitzel in order to seize Austrian cultural history and erase any Austrian claim to it. Like all good lies, there are hints of truth to it. The story appeared in the 1969 publication *Touring Club Italiano* and eventually led to a German translation publishing the tale.[27] In reality,

Austrian- and German-style breaded schnitzel existed at least as early as the eighteenth century.[28]

Although wiener schnitzel and cotoletta alla Milanese developed independently, these foods were far from the south of Italy. The invention of veal parmigiana is likely a fusion of all these influences made possible because of the melting pot of New York City, where the confluence of Italian and German immigrants at a specific moment in time came together to create the delicious dish.

By the middle of the twentieth century, as Italian American restaurants ascended into the popular cultural zeitgeist and consumers began to view Italian-influenced food as a sophisticated cuisine, veal parmigiana became an essential menu item for red sauce restaurants. It epitomizes a second-wave red sauce restaurant appealing to wider range of consumers looking for more complicated dishes than spaghetti and meatballs. Since then, parmigiana has become a staple. Placed between bread or an Italian-style hoagie roll, parmigiana entrees become sandwiches available in places like pizzerias. Even chains like Subway offer a chicken parm sub, and competitor Blimpie sells a meatball parmigiana sandwich. Parm, a mini-chain in New York City, sells chicken, eggplant, and meatball sandwiches alongside entrée portions. Meat and vegetables alla parmigiana have grown into a widely available dish beyond even the confines of Italian American restaurants.

Domestic cooks and restaurants expanded the very idea of alla parmigiana with multiple iterations—the combinations are endless. Shrimp parmigiana was invented to serve as a meat alternative for Catholics observing Lent or to eat on Friday nights. Shrimp breaks a common rule of Italian cuisine—mixing cheese and seafood is often verboten. There is, of course, no shortage of vegetarian versions beyond the traditional eggplant parmigiana, such as using cauliflower. In Buffalo, New York, a restaurant called Chef's claims credit for creating a spaghetti parmigiana in 1988.[29] Eggplant or veal or chicken—or whatever else the mind can dream up—alla parmigiana is an ideal representation of the Italian American cultural experience, adapting a traditional food and then expanding it into a caloric celebration of tomatoes and plentitude.

Red sauce cuisine experienced its golden age in the years surrounding the Second World War. Spaghetti and meatballs and veal parmigiana were fast becoming cultural norms. Italian American restaurants, at least in larger cities, had begun to offer a common selection of dishes consumers could expect to find on the menu of "Italian" restaurants more generally, regardless of the local ethnic community creating a national cuisine. American consumerism too helped push red sauce cuisine into the kitchens of non-Italians. Marketing campaigns for the growing pasta industry, as well as the canning industry, all delivered macaroni and spaghetti to the American dinner plate. The Depression years also bolstered red sauce. An economical cuisine, pasta proved a low-cost, calorie-rich diet. Because Italian immigrants had started from a place of poverty, the dishes they produced had always been economical. Ground meat for meatballs and sausages could be cut with cheaper meat or additives like breadcrumbs without impacting flavor. This economy was also reflected by the very government agencies that had once attempted to convert Italian immigrants with "American" food, turning the tables and suggesting spaghetti to other ethnic groups.

Still, before the start of the war, Italian food remained an ethnic experience. A 1939 *Life* magazine cover story featuring Joe DiMaggio explains how the legendary Italian American baseball player had adapted well to American life since he never smelled of garlic.[30] The prevailing view of many Americans with northern European ancestry at the time was that garlic was a fundamentally foreign flavor; they even went as far as referring to garlic as "Italian perfume"[31] and Italian immigrants and their descendants as "garlic eaters." Even American-born Italian American heroes like Joe DiMaggio faced discrimination. However, the Second World War would change everything.

10

❖ ❖

The Other Red Sauce

The 1920s Hollywood icons Douglas Fairbanks Jr. and Mary Pickford helped introduce Americans to a Roman pasta dish that contradicted contemporary expectations of Italian food. Their celebrity influence, along with the endorsement of food writers at the time, helped make fettuccine alfredo part of the recognized Italian American pasta repertoire, despite the omission of the signature red fruit. Fettuccine alfredo's popularity grew through the 1920s until eventually becoming emblematic of twentieth-century Italian American dining. Fettuccine alfredo emerged in Rome just as Italian American restaurants gained a foothold among middle-class American diners. A few years after its creation, the dish immigrated from Italy into American culture. Thick, creamy in texture, and prepared with freshly made fettuccine pasta, the original version of the dish includes a simple list of ingredients: butter and cheese. Since then, the recipe has morphed from the simple sauce into an extravagant celebration of fat and calories, with modern incarnations adding many more sumptuous ingredients, the fresh fettuccine replaced by other shapes, proteins like chicken or vegetables mixed in, and "alfredo" sauces have even been substituted for marinara on pizza.

In many ways, alfredo sauce is the exception to many of the generalities that can describe red sauce cuisine. Unlike many other Italian sauces, fettuccine alfredo has a clear origin at a specific restaurant in Rome. While the original concoction is based on one of the oldest preparations for pasta in Italy, the creation of the dish occurs after the start of immigration to the

United States, and yet still ends up ingrained as part of Italian American culture and served regularly at red sauce restaurants. By the postwar period, alfredo sauce had earned a devout following in American restaurants, and now acts as a signifier of Italian cuisine in chain restaurants and nationally sold canned goods.

Fettuccine alfredo is also sometimes referred to as pasta *al triplo burro*, meaning pasta of triple butter. Although Americanized versions of the recipe contain cream, the original dish did not. The basic recipe begins as pasta al burro, a dish consisting of butter and cheese. Pasta al burro combines the two ingredients with a splash of starch-filled water from the boiled pasta. The process is similar to the preparation for cacio e pepe, where the starchy water emulsifies with the butter and cheese to create a thicker sauce. Pasta al burro is one of the oldest pasta preparations. Pasta or "maccheroni" al burro recipes appear in the earliest English-language Italian cookbooks. A richer version known as pasta al *doppio* burro—double butter pasta—starts in the same way, but with extra butter added over the pasta after the emulsion is made. Fettuccine alfredo earned the nickname "al triplo burro" because it includes even more butter than either of these preparations, combining the dish with the center core of the Parmigiano-Reggiano wheel.

Alfredo Di Lelio invented the pasta dish bearing his name while caring for his ailing wife, Ines.[1] In 1908, she had given birth to their son Armando, but she remained in a weakened condition. Di Lelio wanted to build her strength by adding calories to her diet, though without upsetting her stomach. The first step in enriching her diet had been to add extra eggs to the fettuccine noodles, the flat ribbons of pasta native to Rome. Pasta prepared with extra egg yolks can end up having a yellow or golden color and have a richer flavor. Looking to further boost the calories of her meals, he added extra butter to the simple dish, using one with a high butterfat content. Butterfat can vary depending on the process used and typically ranges from 75 to 85 percent fat, with industrial processes able to reduce the water content to a greater degree.[2] Today, imported butter often has a higher fat content than American butter, along with a higher expense associated with squeezing out extra water. To finish the dish, Di Lelio mixed in the dense center of the cheese, creating a creamy sauce for his wife's noodles. Di Lelio's remedy worked, and Ines survived. The world may never have known fettuccine alfredo had Ines not suggested adding the dish to the menu of Alfredo's restaurant.[3]

Sometime between 1910[4] and 1914, Alfredo finally gave in to his wife and placed fettuccine alfredo on offer at the restaurant Alfredo's on the Via della Scrofa in Rome. Di Lelio turned the dish into a signature spectacle of the restaurant. He served it tableside, emulsifying the butter and cheese together in front of diners as a performance, and included a musical accompaniment of a tenor and violinist. The act earned him the nickname "Il Maestro."[5] Alfredo's showmanship was well known in Rome as a result, and the restaurant attracted a number of Italian politicians and celebrities. Despite this popularity, the dish would remain unknown in the United States until about 1927, when the confluence of several events helped make fettuccine alfredo an international star.

In 1927, Prohibition was in full swing. Italian American restaurants found ways around the laws, but other more famous establishments shuttered as a result of the lost revenue. Among the casualties was Rector's. The restaurant had once been known for lobsters and champagne, and the closure led third-generation hotel and restaurant operator George Rector to pivot to a writing career. George Rector had grown up cooking in his father's Chicago restaurant, but after he married a chorus girl, George and his father had a falling out.[6] George operated several restaurants in New York, including the family namesake, a destination for high society, such as entertainers from Broadway and the banking class[7] of the era. Rector's attracted attention, whether it was sailors brawling in the dining room[8] or the marvelous revolving door, then a new-age technology.[9]

George Rector grew into a celebrity in his own right, so he was well positioned to pivot to writing about food when Prohibition killed the restaurant industry. He wrote cookbooks and columns and consulted on restaurant services. A trip to Rome in 1927 led George Rector to Alfredo's, by then known for the chef's tableside service. Alfredo's, like Rector's, attracted the rich and powerful. Upon his return, Rector praised fettuccine alfredo in his *Saturday Evening Post* column and described the tableside preparation. He claimed it included as many as five eggs to two pounds of flour.[10] He later published a recipe collection, *The Rector Cook Book*, in which the instructions include adding three lumps of butter the size of a small egg.[11] His fascination with fettuccine alfredo certainly helped popularize the dish, although many Italian American restaurants likely already served a lesser-known version of pasta al burro.

During the same year Rector was praising fettuccine alfredo, Hollywood power couple Douglas Fairbanks Jr. and Mary Pickford married and then honeymooned in Rome. Like Rector, they ate dinner at Alfredo's. The couple were enamored with the restaurant and especially with Di Lelio's performance, eating there regularly during their time in Rome. Before leaving, Fairbanks and Pickford presented him with a golden fork and spoon engraved with the words "To Alfredo the King of the Noodles."[12] Di Lelio served the dish tableside using his golden utensils, continuing to attract celebrities and politicians, until he sold the restaurant.[13] After returning to California, Fairbanks and Pickford began serving fettuccine alfredo to guests at dinner parties held in their Hollywood mansion. The richness of dish and the endorsement by America's sweethearts no doubt bolstered the dish's appeal to American diners at the same time that George Rector was singing its praises in his food column.

Di Lelio sold his restaurant, celebrity photos and all, to a waiter during World War II. The new owners kept the restaurant intact, and Di Lelio declared himself retired from the business in 1943. Like most celebrities, Di Lelio's retirement did not last long. After the war, in 1950, Di Lelio saw an opportunity when the Roman Catholic Church announced a jubilee celebration. The event promised to entice large crowds of pilgrims to Rome. He opened a new restaurant at 30 Piazza Augusto Imperatore.[14] The location sat across from the mausoleum of Augustus, a Roman monument destroyed by time, but that had recently been reconstructed by the Mussolini regime's attempt to link the fascist regime with the power and prestige of ancient Rome. The location is not far from the Spanish Steps and Via Del Corso. Put another way, Di Lelio opened his new restaurant in the heart of tourist Rome, and he was rewarded with a flood of customers.

Continuing to use his gold-plated fork and spoon to serve tableside, his reputation once more brought in American celebrities visiting and living in Rome. He rebuilt his collection of celebrity photographs, and they adorned the walls of his restaurant with the images of the famous people he served. On his death in 1959, Armando, known as Alfredo II and the son whose birth inspired the dish, took over. The restaurant, Il Vero Alfredo, continues to operate today under the leadership of Alfredo III.

Fettuccine alfredo truly became Americanized when it was coopted by a noodle company marketing fettuccine egg noodles publicizing a recipe for the famed fettuccine alfredo. The Pennsylvania Dutch brand introduced the product in 1966, allowing an easy way to make American version of the recipe. This new version included adding a cup of cream and a quarter cup of Swiss cheese to the butter and parmigiana.[15] The cream and extra cheese helped inexperienced chefs replicate the consistency of the original alfredo without requiring an emulsion.

Cream's intrusion into the recipe continued through the 1970s. Marcella Hazan, maven of authentic Italian cuisine, included an alfredo recipe in her 1973 *The Classic Italian Book*. Her version has less butter than the original and a cup of cream, plus a dash of nutmeg. Hazan perhaps can be forgiven for adding cream.[16] Born in Emilia-Romagna, her culinary focus remained in the northern half of the country, where dairy cows were more common, and the addition of cream in her recipe may simply reflect a regional difference in the preparation of the Roman dish.

Americans continued to make variations of the sauce richer and thicker, often adding heavy cream and extra cheese. The Olive Garden has a recipe with milk, cream, and both parmesan and Romano cheese.[17] These modern Italian-themed restaurants rely on adulterated alfredo sauce as a base for other dishes, using it in place of a béchamel. Alfredo sauce appears as the base for a chicken carbonara at Buca di Beppo, a rigatoni pasta with sausage and mushroom dish at Macaroni Grill, and an eponymous chicken dish at Carraba's. At the high end, Thomas Keller introduced a version of the dish at his Surf Club in Miami and short-lived TAK Room in New York. The menus are intended as a twentieth-century throwback and featured fettuccine alfredo topped with truffles. Highbrow or lowbrow, Alfredo Di Lelio's creation remains one of the most iconic sauces of the Italian American tradition despite the lack of tomatoes.

11

As American as Pizza Pie

The first half of the twentieth century introduced Americans to the flavors and tastes of Italian American cuisine. From this foundation, even nonethnic Americans in larger cities like New York and Chicago had started regularly eating this once-foreign-seeming food. Spaghetti and other macaroni shapes had become pantry staples during the Great Depression, and the war cemented red sauce in American culinary traditions in part because American troops had been to Italy, eaten Italian food, and fought alongside Italian Americans. The foreignness and exoticism had waned, but Italian American food had not yet come to dominate American mainstream culture. That was about to change.

Pizza represents one of the most visible and lasting effects of Italian immigration to the United States. It transformed from a working-class Italian street food into a symbol of twentieth-century American imperialism, demonstrating not only the influence of Italian American cuisine on America but also the transformation of foreign ethnics into fully integrated members of American society.

Early American pizzerias provided prepared food to immigrant ethnic groups within urban enclaves. The first pizzerias began as bakeries exploiting bread ovens. These neighborhood eateries transitioned into hybrid restaurants serving not just pizza but also an array of red sauce menu items like pasta dishes or veal parmigiana sandwiches. Pizzerias offered casual versions of the more formal Italian American red sauce restaurants, and, not coincidentally, as pizza grew in popularity among Americans, it also ended up on menus at those formal restaurants. Neapolitan pizzerias, where American pizza has its origins, traditionally remained segregated from formal (and respectable) restaurants, focused on serving poor and working-class diners.

The history of pizza begins with the history of bread. Dough made from grain flour and mixed with water and combined with heat yields unleavened flat bread. Baking it a second time further dries it out, facilitating long-term storage and preservation.[1] Although flatbreads existed throughout the Mediterranean basin, Jewish maza, similar to modern matzo, was one of the most common. Roman soldiers likely developed a taste for the Jewish bread and added cheese and oil from their rations, inventing an early form of pizza.[2] Other early flatbreads, such as Greek pita, where the term *pizza* may have origins,[3] likely also served as a primitive form. In Italy, variations on flatbreads exist across the different regions, including *spinata* in Sardinia[4] and *piadini* in Emilia-Romagna. The first "proto-pizza," baked from a dough of flour, milk, oil, and pepper, was called *strepticius*. All of these initial attempts are varieties of pizza *bianche*, a sauce-less pizza still served today. The Middle Ages brought about a dark period as bread baking generally shifted to an exclusively domestic activity. The public bakeries of the Roman empire closed, disrupted by invasion, food shortages, and political turmoil.

Stability eventually returned to the Italian peninsula, and regional flatbreads like focaccia, piadini, *farinata*, *panelle*, *sfincione*, and *schiacciata* with it. At this point though, the term *pizza* still referred only to cakes and breads generically, often with a descriptive word following like *fritta*, for fried, or *al forno*, for oven pizza.[5] Between 1500 and the early 1800s, *pizza Napoletana* referred to a sweet tart, usually with almonds.[6] As early as the seventeenth century, Neapolitans began baking flatbreads with the qualities of the pizza Italian Americans would eventually make famous, although it's absent from *Il Cuoco Galante*, Corrado's collection of recipes. Several common varieties existed then, with the most basic of these topped with nothing more than garlic, lard, and salt.[7] The *mastunicola* was topped with cheese and basil, and pizza alla marinara included clams and mozzarella cheese.[8] The term *pizza*, though, would not become synonymous with Naples until the end of the nineteenth century, primarily because before then, outside of Naples, nobody talked about pizza.[9] Calzones (better known in Italy as *calzoni*) also developed during this time. In a calzone, standard pizza fillings are sandwiched between dough that is fried or baked. Early versions of calzoni consisted of two sheets of dough with the filling in between[10] or a sheet of dough rolled up into a tube, suggesting the shape of a leg of a pair of trousers also known as calzoni.[11]

The tomato and the pizza met around the end of the eighteenth century, at about the same time the tomato was canoodling with vermicelli. By the nineteenth century, fresh tomatoes had become an essential ingredient in the region, leading to the more recognizable pizza alla marinara—a topping of tomatoes, garlic, anchovies, and oil—and the pizza alla mozzarella—consisting of tomatoes, garlic, mozzarella, basil, and oil.[12] The latter would be christened the pizza Margherita by the end of the century. In Naples, pizza fed the working men of the city, as well as the lazzarone (the street urchins known for eating boiled macaroni by the fistful). Pizza was not a well-regarded food. Indeed, the lazzarone ate pizza during the week to save money for vermicelli on Sundays.[13] By 1850, pizza outsold the pasta.[14] Pizza offered two advantages: First, the versatility of pizza as a vessel for various toppings created a variety in diet. Second, soft flours are used in pizza, and the durum wheat used for pasta cost significantly more. With a lower price point and greater adaptability, pizza's appeal grew among the poor as an unavoidable street food.

The Neapolitan pizzaioli, or pizzamakers, were licensed merchants. Pizzerias caused something of a problem in the city since the large ovens presented a fire hazard, and either fear of fire or simply opposition from cantankerous neighbors often meant the pizziaolo's biggest challenge was obtaining a license. The police inspected the wood-fueled ovens for safety, and the pizzaiolo was the license holder. The license holder was expected to be on the premise when the shop was open, so they often napped in the back of their shops. The lucky ones lived in apartments above the shop, allowing them to remain on premise even when they were home. These permanent pizzerias were known as *pizzaioli fissi*,[15] but they competed with or sometimes augmented their incomes by hiring *pizzaiolo ambulante*. These roving pizza salesmen would traverse the city selling pizzas from a cart or carrying case, meaning even early pizza was a fast food for delivery. Fried pizza (*pizze* fritte) proved a popular dish, but it fell out of favor with the pizziaoli because of the high cost of keeping hot fry oil ready throughout the day.

The pizzerias in Naples usually had a slab of marble for making pizza in the shops and displayed the ingredients for customers to see. They used fresh tomatoes, garlic, basil, caciovallo cheese, small fish, and copper canisters for pouring olive oil. The wood-fired ovens also left behind a thin layer of ash, and this ash flavored the pizzas. Ash mixed with salt had long been a way the poorer classes salted foods when salt was too expensive.[16]

Pizza grew in popularity among working families and the poor while remaining mostly unappreciated by the upper classes until 1889. King Umberto I and his royal consort, Margherita of Savoy, visited the city of Naples in May of that year. Wanting to sample the famous (if low-class) pizza, the king summoned the pizzaiolo Raffaele Esposito and his wife Giovanna Brandi to the Palace of Capodimonte to cook the dish. Esposito prepared three pizzas: pizza alla marinara, pizza bianche, and pizza alla mozzarella.[17] Esposito allegedly renamed the pizza alla mozzarella in Queen Margherita's honor after she declared it her favorite of the three. Whether or not this is true, Epsosito did smartly obtain a letter signaling his participation in feeding the queen and establishing himself as the "father" of pizza.

The licensing of Neapolitan pizzaioli helped protect dynasties, and some of those families survive as pizzaioli today. They often intermarried with each other as well, further complicating the lineages of historic pizza makers. One of these pizza dynasties that still survives today is the Lombardi clan. At the turn of the century, Errico Lombardi served as head of the family and, falling on hard times, took a voyage to New York. Whether he made it to New York remains unclear, but he did return to Italy after traveling and eventually opened a pizzeria that operates still.[18] Gennaro Lombardi, founder of Lombardi's in New York, likely belonged to part of this extended Lombardi family.[19] He lays claim to serving the first pizza in America.

Given the importance of pizza to both American and Italian cuisine, unsurprisingly, there is some dissent about the accuracy of Lombardi's claim. Lombardi, like many Italian immigrants at the time, first operated a grocery store. The shop opened in 1897, but it didn't start selling pizzas until 1905. The shift in business might be owed to another famous New York pizzaiolo, Anthony "Totonno" Pero.[20] Totonno, a Neapolitan immigrant, worked in the grocery store and suggested selling the pizzas to immigrants who could not easily bake the food at home. He eventually left Lombardi's to open Totonno's in 1924, another famed pizzeria, in Coney Island, Brooklyn.

Pizza likely had already been sold in New York before Totonno suggested making it, and even before Lombardi's opened as a grocery. As early as 1885, just a few years into the heavy Italian immigration, pizza probably had been sold as a low-cost food.[21] Another Neapolitan immigrant, Filippo Milone, is thought to have built and then sold several pizzerias around New York City, and Lombardi may have benefited by buying one of these locations.[22] But Lombardi has two important claims, even if he wasn't the first actual purveyor. He was the first to receive a mercantile license to sell pizza,[23] making his pizza official. Licensing was of course always an important part of true Neapolitan pizza, and it remains today an essential hallmark of "authentic" Neapolitan pizza. The second (and perhaps more important) contribution was baking pizza in a coal-fired stove to replicate the wood-burning ovens used in Naples.[24] Coal was far more cost efficient in New York than wood, and it burns much hotter. The higher heat produces crispier pizza crust. Today new coal ovens are nearly impossible to install in New York because of pollution regulations, but a century ago, many of the early New York pizzerias relied on them. Existing coal ovens continue to operate, although even these face increasingly difficult and expensive pollution regulations.

Pizza caught on among the ethnic Italian enclaves. The pizzeria often credited as the second in the United States opened in Trenton, New Jersey, around 1910[25] or 1912.[26] Joe Papa opened Papa's, serving Trenton tomato pie, a variation of the New York style with the sauce on top of the cheese. Papa's grandson Nick Azzaro claims that Lombardi's lost the title of oldest pizzeria because it actually closed up shop between 1984 and 1994,[27] but Lombardi's holds an outsized influence on New York's pizza scene by seeding pizzaiolos around the city. Former Lombardi's employees kept leaving in order to open their own shops, like John Sasso, who opened John's in 1929, and Patsy Lancieri, who opened Patsy's in 1933,[28] and of course Totonno. Other notable pizzerias opened during this time include Mario's in the Bronx and Pepe's in New Haven in 1925.[29] New Haven's pizzas are known for their particularly thin crusts,[30] achieved with a higher-moisture dough, and have a long-standing rivalry with New York–style pizza.

Frank Pepe was born in Italy in 1893[31] before emigrating to the United States. Like so many immigrants before him, Pepe began with a pushcart before opening a brick-and-mortar shop. He distinguished his New Haven pizzeria by selling white pizza made with olive oil, oregano, and anchovies, and developing the now-famous white pie topped with clams.[32] Joining Frank Pepe Pizzeria Napoletana in New Haven in the 1930s was Modern Apizza in 1934 and Sally's Apizza in 1938,[33] with the latter founded by Sal Consiglio, a nephew of Frank Pepe.[34] The term *apizza* is specific to New Haven's pies and draws on the accents of the local Italian immigrants.[35] The burgeoning rivalry of pizzerias like that in New Haven in the prewar years was a common occurrence in Little Italy neighborhoods and Italian enclaves across America, but especially along the East Coast.[36] However, despite the growing availability in regions with a high number of Italians, before the Second World War, pizza remained an ethnic food.

The pizzas sold in Italian American pizzerias in the first half of the twentieth century directly drew inspiration from Neapolitan pizza. The Italian American pizziaoli made only modest changes. Oregano was substituted for basil owing to availability, and the use of garlic was limited, largely because the flavor proved too strong for descendants of northern Europeans.[37] Another difference was access to tomatoes. Although fresh tomatoes had become available in the United States throughout the year, canned tomatoes were cheaper. With a warmer climate in Naples, the availability of fresh tomatoes for much of the year resulted in Neapolitan pizzas using crushed, fresh tomatoes. Canning industries in America and the high cost of transporting winter tomatoes to cold cities like New York and Chicago meant American pizzas are more likely to have a prepared sauce, often a quickly cooked marinara. And because early American pizzerias made use of bread bakery ovens, larger in size than the dedicated Neapolitan pizza oven, the pies themselves grew larger. The regional variations in the United States, like Trenton's tomato pies and New Haven's flatter pies, derive from a New York pizza tradition with origins in Naples. But eventually new pizza styles would emerge, drawing on influences from other regions.

Pizzerias populated ethnic enclaves up and down the mid-Atlantic states in what would eventually become the Pizza Belt, a term first coined by Ed Levine[38] describing a region of the country with easily accessible, high-quality pizza. Generally, it extends from southern New Jersey through southern Rhode Island. Before the Second World War, the largest obstacle to widespread consumption was the ovens. Although wood and coal bakery ovens worked adequately, obtaining and maintaining the right amount of heat proved difficult and labor intensive. Bread ovens were costly to install and maintain since much of their heat came from the heavy stone construction. Pizza makers could close up shop at night having extinguished the fire, or with nothing but hot coals remaining, and return in the morning to find the oven still hot enough to bake bread. But if a pizza oven remained unused for a day or more, it would require added time and fuel to dry out and bring back up to temperature. All this work maintaining the ovens prevented the pizzeria from spreading beyond communities with built-in Italian consumers.

Yet, in the postwar period, pizza entered into the American zeitgeist, and consumption skyrocketed. In a 1947 issue of *Good Housekeeping*, pizza is described as a pancake, the toppings are a mixture of tomato and cheese, and the article offers an explanation on the pronunciation of the new food.[39] A *Ladies Home Journal* article from 1948 attempts to explain how to eat a pizza, comparing it to eating an apple pie,[40] an all-American food. Indeed, in the years directly after the war, Americans were literally learning how to eat it. Pizza arrived at just the right moment. Americans wanted convenience foods—whole meals that were fast and easy to make. It was the dawn of frozen TV dinners and restaurants designed for takeout meals. Pizza offered convenience, flavor, and an attractive price point, fitting all of these requirements. Pizza had always been a food eaten away from the point of production, even in Naples. Take-away food found a natural place in the American suburban culture created after the war where a family car quickly carried food from a restaurant to domestic table.

What allowed for pizza's success was the invention of a new kind of oven. The gas-fired pizza oven overcame the primary obstacle preventing pizza from becoming an accessible and widely available food. Ira Nevin, an oven repairman who had learned to love pizza while stationed in Naples during the war, invented a ceramic-lined gas-powered oven specifically for pizzas and founded a company called Baker's Pride,[41] launched in the Bronx, New York. Nevin was a third-generation oven builder who constructed brick ovens as a child, and in engineering school, he wrote a thesis on oven construction.[42] In his professional career, he worked in aviation engineering before the war.

Nevin neglected to patent the first gas-fired design, and a copycat competitor began selling knockoffs. His wife encouraged him to further develop the oven technology leading to a newer model. He would go onto patent numerous oven-related inventions, including a variation on the gas oven to mimic the intense heat of wood-burning pizza ovens.[43] But his 1945 oven would pave the way for corner pizzerias across America by providing a far simpler and lower-cost system of baking pizza than had previously been available.

The 1950s saw the Americanization of this strange ethnic food that just a few years earlier nobody even knew how to pronounce. In 1955, Hunt's, known for its canned tomato products, picked up on the pizza craze by advertising a ten-minute pizza prepared with Hunt's tomato sauce, English muffins, and mozzarella cheese. Mozzarella was called the "pizza cheese," but Swiss or any other good melting cheese can be substituted, the ad suggests.[44] Inspired by the ad, a Florida man invented the first bagel pizza.[45] As would happen with lasagna, the frozen food aisle offered another avenue for pizza to enter into domestic kitchens. The Celentano brothers introduced frozen pizza in 1957, and Chef Boyardee sold box pizzas with canned sauces and cheese.[46] Neither of these proved especially tasty; nevertheless, pizza's popularity grew. The combination of convenience, pizza's acceptability as a meal across generational and gender lines, the willingness to eat in more casual settings (like in front of the television[47]), and new leisure patterns among the middle and upper classes all contributed to the success of pizza in America.[48]

Concurrent with the plentitude of domestic options for eating pizza, the expansion of pizzerias with Nevin's gas-fired oven ultimately allowed pizza to become commercialized on a large scale in the form of fast-food chains. While East Coast cities with large Italian American enclaves were dominated by New York–style, neighborhood pizzerias, the Midwest adapted the pizza into an American icon. Here, in the nation's bread basket, the big names in chain pizza were founded within a few years of each other. Pizza Hut was founded in Wichita, Kansas, in 1958; Little Caesars in Garden City, Michigan, in 1959[49]; and Domino's in Ypsilanti, Michigan, in 1960.[50] Papa John's Pizza, an Indiana pizzeria, joined them in 1984.[51] Unlike the pizza sold in local shops and micro-chains in the mid-Atlantic Pizza Belt, the Midwestern pizzas shifted further from Neapolitan-style pizzas. The crusts grew thicker and puffier, more like bread than pizza. Sauces became sweeter, a combination of preserving mass-marketed sauce and appealing to Midwestern palates. These chain pizzerias expanded rapidly and soon became a symbol of American culinary imperialism. By 1990, Pizza Hut cut a deal to open two Moscow locations, the same year it opened a location in Beijing.[52] Pizza Hut had access to the Russian market because its parent company, PepsiCo, had a working relationship with the Soviets. Pepsi exported its cola to Russia but refused to accept rubles as payment. At first Pepsi swapped cola for vodka, but when Americans boycotted Russian products, even the vodka lost value. The company offered soda in exchange for a number of old ships, with the Soviet ships eventually sold for scrap. For a brief period of time, though, Pepsi's ships represented one of the largest navies in the world. Pepsi owned Pizza Hut since 1977 as part of a food and restaurant division. The existing relationship selling Pepsi products helped pave the way for Pizza Hut to expand into the Soviet Union.

Other variations of pizza also evolved into regional styles. Chicago, the de facto capital of the Midwest, would invent a wholly American food: the deep-dish pizza. Many in Chicago today advocate the superiority of Chicago's local pizza over the thinner pies from the Pizza Belt region on the East Coast. If New York's pizzaiolo constructed a pizza tradition honoring the Neapolitan legacy, Chicago's cooks invented one to honor the sensibilities of middle America. The story of Chicago-style pizza begins with Ike Sewell, a Texan, who came to Chicago looking to open a Mexican restaurant. He partnered with Italian-born Ric Riccardo, and in preparing to open the restaurant, they sampled a meal of the Mexican-inspired menu. The food left Riccardo ill, and he convinced Sewell to start a pizzeria instead. Their concept, opened in 1943, temporarily was named Pizzeria Riccardo; they finally settled on the name Pizzeria Uno in 1955.[53]

Success was slow. Pizzeria Uno's tiny dining room was dark and cramped, and it went largely unnoticed by the local population.[54] The signature dish was a "pizza" built to satisfy the palate of middle America: a thick crust set in a deep, metal pan filled with cheese and meats, covered in sauce. They invented a thicker, heavier meal, requiring a knife and fork, unlike the flimsier New York–style slices. And unlike thinner pizza, the heavy deep-dish pies took upward of forty minutes to cook. By comparison, Neapolitan pies in a wood-fired oven could cook in less than a minute, and even New York–style pizza only required a few minutes' cooking time in a gas oven for a whole pie. Slices of premade pies reheated within in a minute or two. The long cooking times and the dark, out-of-the-way location almost led Pizzeria Uno to fail, until a write-up by a local reporter caused a spike in business. Soon afterward, the pair of restaurateurs opened Pizzeria Due. Smartly, as the chain expanded, they did not continue to count upward in Italian but expanded as Pizzeria Uno and then Uno Pizzeria Grill.

Neither Sewell nor Riccardo had much experience cooking, so while they backed the restaurant, the invention of the Chicago-style pizza likely fell to someone else. The two contenders are either Adolph "Rudy" Malnati Sr. or Alice Mae Redmond. Malnati managed Pizzeria Riccardo in 1951 and had a handshake partnership with Riccardo and Sewell. As with most handshake deals, it never worked out quite as intended. Lou Malnati, Rudy's son, opened Malnati's, another standard-bearer of deep-dish-style pizza, but his father never saw a piece of the Pizzeria Uno empire. Alice Mae Redmond worked as the cook at Pizzeria Riccardo and is also a likely candidate for having invented the deep-dish recipe. She disliked the original deep-dish crust, thinking it too hard.[55] Redmond continued improving the recipe, working toward softening the crust, and took the new recipe with her when she left to work in the kitchen of competitor Gino's East. Since then, Chicago's deep-dish has caused an ongoing debate between the superiority of New York– or Chicago-style pizza.

Another regional pizza worth mentioning is Detroit-style pizza. Gus Guerra introduced the Detroit pizza at his bar in 1946. The rectangular pies are baked in metal boxes common in the auto industry for storing parts. Toppings like pepperoni and cheese go on before the pie is baked and then are topped with hot marinara.[56] He based the recipe on a Sicilian pizza from his mother-in-law.[57] In the East Coast Pizza Belt dominated by New York–style pizza, a tradition of rectangular "Sicilian" pies also exists, and they tend to be fluffier and softer. These rectangular pizzas are made from thick dough and originally were served with sauce and parmigiana cheese, not mozzarella. New York–style Sicilian has come to simply mean a fatter, square-shaped slice of pizza topped with tomatoes, mozzarella, and whatever other toppings are available. A thinner variation known as the Grandma pie began appearing in the 1980s. Introduced by Umberto's Pizzeria in New Hyde Park, New York, Grandma slices were Americanized with the addition of mozzarella cheese compared to a traditional Sicilian base of tomatoes and anchovies.[58] The Grandma slice started off as a homestyle pie served to friends and family before being introduced to the then-modest restaurant menu sometime between 1986 and 1989.[59] Over the next decade, the style spread rapidly through the tri-state region. Detroit, Sicilian, and Grandma pies are all variations on the sfincione bread, a pizza from Sicily. Sfincione is traditionally sold in bakeries or street stalls and is topped with a thin tomato sauce, onions, anchovies, and breadcrumbs.[60]

Today, pizza has a worldwide following. Pizza Napolitano is recognized throughout Italy as a food of value rather than cheap meal for street urchins. Neapolitan-style pizzerias have become a major export from Italy, like the Irish pub from Ireland. The Eurozone helped facilitate Italians relocating across the continent, and with them they brought Neapolitan pizzerias serving their flat-crusted pies. The toppings can vary and often reflect local tastes, like smoked fish in Scandinavia.

To protect the brand and the legacy of pizza, two organizations were founded. In 2010, the *Associazione Verace Pizza Napolentana* (AVPN), "Association for the True Pizza Napoletana," and the *Associazione Pizzaiuoli Napoletani*, "Association of Neapolitan Pizza Makers,"[61] received the legal protection status known as "Traditional Specialty Guaranteed," allowing them to protect and define authentic Neapolitan pizza's preparation and ingredients. The AVPN began with just seventeen members and regulates the ingredients and preparation of true Neapolitan pizza. There are two recognized and licensed pizzas: the marinara and the Margherita. Marinara pizzas may be topped only with peeled tomatoes, oil, garlic, and oregano, while the Margherita contains cheese. The guidelines outline specific tomatoes (San Marzano), specific cheese (mozzarella di *bufala* or *fior di latte*), specific oil (cold pressed), and oregano and basil. The tomatoes and cheese must also be certified under the DOP (Denominazione d'Origine Protetta—protected designation of origin) laws. Members must make pizzas to the standard and pay a fee to become certified.

The traditional Italian American pizzeria is in decline. The assault comes from both the low and the high ends of the financial spectrum. On the low end, dollar-slice joints that began in the 2010s undermine the neighborhood pizzeria's bread-and-butter business of a low-cost meal or a late-night snack. The low-margin, high-volume slices invaded New York City and sliced into the business of neighborhood pizzerias by undercutting their individual-slice sales. Neighborhood pizzerias serving an expansive menu with red sauce pasta dishes, sandwiches like chicken parm, and entrée portions of red sauce recipes have larger kitchens and higher overhead than the tiny, takeout-only dollar-slice joints. By grabbing the single-slice market, dollar pizza cut into a high-margin item on the pizzeria's menu. The threat to local pizzerias even inspired residents of the Lower East Side to launch a petition to ban the discount pizza stands.[62] Further disrupting the pizza ecosystem, at one point, the dollar-slice joints in Manhattan entered into a price war with each other, with competitors undercutting even the dollar price point with combo deals. Pizza slices in New York City have long paralleled the cost of a single ride on the city's subway. Most neighborhood pizzerias hold to this—and an increase in the average slice of pizza has often served as a portent to a coming subway fare hike. When the dollar-slice joints entered the market, subway fares were $2.75 a ride. Most slices in the city sold for between $2.50 and $3, and the dollar slice hurt the traditional pizzeria.

More recently, Neapolitan-style pizza came into fashion in New York City, offering an upscale dining experience that competes with the local pizzerias serving the distinct New York–style pies. These pizzas—baked in wood-fired ovens, smaller in size, and with a thinner crust—have become popular at sit-down restaurants, which also cut into the take-away and delivery market share of the neighborhood pizzeria. Opening in trendy neighborhoods, these new pizzerias are competing with high-end restaurants. Roberta's—founded in 2007 in the East Williamsburg, Brooklyn, industrial zone—has grown into an international chain with a global footprint selling Neapolitan-style pizza rather than larger-format Brooklyn-style pies. Similar imitators included Motorino, Houdini Pizza Laboratory, Franny's, Paulie Gee's, Ops, and others. There are even three AVPN-certified producers of Neapolitan pizza in New York, including La Pizza Fresca Ristorante, Ribalta, and Song 'e Napule. These developments have threatened the traditional Italian American neighborhood pizzeria in the same way fine-dining Italian restaurants and low-cost chain restaurants have threatened the Italian American red sauce restaurant.

Pizza selling in New York has grown increasingly competitive. When Patsy Grimaldi, the nephew of Patsy Lancieri, opened his coal-fired pizzeria, he was immediately sued by Patsy's for using the same name. He renamed the pizzeria Grimaldi's, after himself, and in 1998 sold off the Brooklyn location to Frank Ciolli.[63] The popular pizzeria attracted crowds of tourists, particularly as the Brooklyn waterfront in the DUMBO neighborhood gentrified. Ciolli's sons expanded Grimaldi's into an Arizona-based chain with forty-two restaurants. The Brooklyn outpost remained a separate business entity, and eventually rising rents pushed Ciolli to relocate the original Grimaldi's several storefronts down the street. The first problem Ciolli faced was his coal-fired oven. The laws had changed since the oven in the first location had been installed, and New York City's environmental regulations required special allowances to install a new one. After some delays, Ciolli eventually received the required permission.[64] The second problem Ciolli faced was that Patsy Grimaldi decided to un-retire and open a new pizzeria—in the former Grimaldi's location Ciolli was leaving behind. Patsy Grimaldi, unable to use the name Patsy's or Grimaldi's, opened Juliana's Pizza, serving pies from the same oven he had previously sold to Ciolli, along with his name. The Arizona-based Grimaldi's has since purchased the lone Brooklyn outpost, adding to the eleven-state chain. Grimaldi's is currently in the process of launching franchises to further expand the Brooklyn-style pizzeria nationwide.

As is happening with red sauce cuisine, nostalgia is driving a desire to return to old traditions. Paulie Gee's has opened a "slice shop" imitating the classic pizzeria atmosphere, themed around the 1980s, serving upscale New York slices. Even the dollar-slice guys want in on the luxury pizza market. Eli Halali, who founded the 2 Bros dollar-slice chain with his brother Oren, opened a new venture, Upside Pizza, with Noam Grossman serving high-end slices.[65]

Pizza has become an all-American food. It represents the reach of American capitalism with chain restaurants penetrating a global market. Pizza sales across all styles and genres now account for more than $46 billion in annual sales in the United States alone, making it one of the most successful fusions of Italian and American culinary traditions.

12

Curds and Whey

The mainstreaming of pizza probably did more to make Americans comfortable with eating Italian-style cheese than any other event in the twentieth century. Americans now eat more than eleven pounds of mozzarella per person each year.[1] The bulk of that consumption is driven by pizza sales, with rapid growth beginning in the 1970s.[2] As of 2001, mozzarella surpassed cheddar cheese production[3] in the United States. Still, there are than four hundred varieties of cheese documented in Italy, with many more small-scale, hyperlocal varieties of cheeses produced in domestic kitchens and small farms yet undocumented. Only a handful of these cheeses entered the American food system with the arrival of Italian immigrants, and red sauce cuisine leans heavily on a few specific varieties. Although today imported Italian cheeses are widely available, for most of the twentieth century, Italian and Italian-style cheeses had been limited to specialty stores within immigrant enclaves, often in large cities. Grocers like Di Palo's in New York were instrumental in bringing these products to American consumers before they appeared in national grocery chains, and they continue to offer a superior selection of imported products. American cheese production grew out of varied immigrant influences, drawing on the most common or most popular selections from different groups as they arrived and settled in the country. During the expansion of Italian American cuisine, especially the rapid expansion of the pizzeria in the postwar period, commercial production of Italian-style cheese grew alongside it.

Cheese plays an important role in providing a steady supply of food throughout the year, especially hardened aged cheeses. Milk spoils easily, and cheese creates a method of preservation, extending the shelf life of those calories. The process of turning milk into cheese can also control naturally occurring pathogens contained in raw milk, an important step before the era of pasteurization. Bacteria and yeasts known as SCOBY exist in a symbiotic balance, and the cheese-making process will usually successfully push out harmful microbes and bacteria.[4] Cheese also helps to make milk digestible by breaking down the proteins humans have difficulty consuming. Lactose intolerance persists in people of Mediterranean descent, but they likely find aged cheeses easier on their stomachs.

Today Americans most often think of cow's milk cheeses, but early cheese production began with other domesticated animals. Southern Italy rarely kept cows for milk, instead relying on sheep, goats, and buffalo, with cow's milk cheeses more common in northern Italian traditions.

Mozzarella cheese serves as the workhorse of red sauce cuisine, topping pizza, veal parmigiana, lasagna, and other baked pasta dishes. It is, after tomatoes, the quintessential ingredient of Americanized Italian cuisine, and the richness of a cheese-laden dish epitomizes the evolution of Italian food in America. American mozzarella greatly differs from the original Italian creation, where traditionally it was made fresh and consumed immediately. Italian mozzarella is always made from the milk of the water buffalo, while mozzarella-style cheese made from the milk of cows is called fior di latte, meaning "the top of the milk." The same is not true in America. Water buffalo were and continue to be rare domestic animals in the United States, and the majority of American mozzarella is manufactured from cow's milk, with the most common variety containing a low moisture content.

The term *mozzarella* is derived from the Italian *mozzare*, meaning "to pinch off,"[5] referring to the process of pinching off portions of the cheese from a larger mass. These pinched-off portions are then formed into the familiar mozzarella balls in a standard size of 250 grams. Different-size mozzarella balls have unique names and specific sizes, measured in grams: *bocconcini*, "mouthfuls," 125 grams; *ovilini*, "eggs," 100 grams; *ciligegini*, "cherries," 15 grams; *perline*, "beads," 10 grams.[6] Cow's milk and buffalo milk produce different end products because of the variation in water and fat content. Buffalo produce richer and creamier milk than dairy cows, and it has twice the butterfat and less water.[7] The milk, and resulting cheese, is bright white in comparison to cow's milk and remains a highly prized product. Yet water buffalo are fickle milk producers. Convincing them to produce milk at all is a challenge, and even in the best of times they produce only a fraction of the milk dairy cows produce.

A relative of the cow, but also of yaks and aurochs, the water buffalo is not native to Italy. They arrived as working animals, but historians disagree on precisely when. The earliest estimates point to the arrival of the buffalo along with Hannibal, of ancient Carthage, carrying his war treasure on the backs of the animals upon returning from Asia.[8] Another possibility is that they arrived from eastern Europe following the fall of Rome, around the sixth century.[9] The Greeks may have introduced buffalo to Sicily, with the animals eventually migrating to the mainland peninsula by the twelfth century following the Norman conquest.[10] Today there are more than 400,000 in the country.

By the twelfth century, production of mozzarella had begun. The bishop of Capua describes a cheese known as *mozza* or *povature* that fits the description.[11] By the fourteenth century, buffalo milk mozzarella had become a commercialized product in Italy, and by the fifteenth century, buffalo provided butter, ricotta, mozzarella, and the aged cheeses known as *provole* and caciocavallo.[12] Cheese created demand, and capacity expanded, but buffalo milk was not produced on a large scale until the seventeenth century. By then, farmers had established *bufalare* (buffalo pastures)[13] designed specifically for the animals, which paved the way for broader consumption. Only in the eighteenth century did mozzarella become a widely consumed product, and at that point it became a mainstay of pizza Napoletana, made famous on the pizza Margherita.

Italian immigrants recreating dishes from home had limited access to buffalo mozzarella. Although today there are experiments with farming water buffalo in the United States, at the time Italian immigrants arrived, the primary source of dairy came from cows. During this period, dairy farms were common in upstate New York, sending milk and cheese to the cities. Substituting cow milk for buffalo milk provided immigrants an easy solution for producing cheeses domestically, particularly those like ricotta that spoiled easily. Cow's milk mozzarella quickly became the default norm, as did another mozzarella relative, *scamorza*, meaning "idiot" or "dunce."[14] Scamorza has a pear-like shape but is dryer than mozzarella[15] and has a stronger taste. It is smooth and slightly aged, and it peels apart in the same manner that industrial cheese products like string cheese do.

As American agriculture industrialized, large-scale cheese production replaced farmhouse cheese as a staple. As early as 1851, in Rome, New York, factory-style cheese production had started taking place.[16] Although industrializing cheese production brought down the cost of food, consumers experienced a decline in quality. Cheddar cheese, a staple of English settlers, suffered from the process first. Reducing the aging time and increasing the moisture-to-fat ratio lowered the cost of cheese production, but consumers paid the price in lost flavor. Americans didn't seem to notice.[17] Production and consumption of cheddar increased rapidly. The same crisis befell ethnic cheeses like mozzarella in the middle of the twentieth century, as the cheese evolved from an ethnic delicacy into an essential topping for the rapidly growing industry of fast-food pizza. Highly processed mozzarella has the consistency of scamorza and provides a longer shelf life than fresh mozzarella. The dry, processed mozzarella became an essential component for pizzerias without access to fresh-made cheese.

Making scamorza isn't the only way to extend the life of mozzarella cheese. Smoking mozzarella, known as mozzarella *affumicata*,[18] preserves the cheese behind a brown skin and adds a strong smoked flavor. Other variations of mozzarella include provolone, made using the layering process known as pasta *filata*.[19] The layering process creates a smooth texture similar to mozzarella or scamorza, but provolone is aged, albeit for a relatively short period of time. Provolone *dolce*, meaning "sweet," is aged for a mere two months. American industrial cheese production favors softer, sweet provolone. Provolone of the *piccante* variety ages for twelve months and has a spicier, peppery flavor.

Originally a southern Italian cheese, industrial production of provolone has moved to the north. In the south of Italy, provolone production continues on a smaller scale, and usually focuses on producing piccante cheeses. Another aged cheese in the mozzarella family is caciocavallo. Produced since the medieval era throughout the territory that had belonged to the kingdom of Naples,[20] it is now one of the most widely consumed cheeses. It is a semi-dry cheese with an edible rind and is good for grating. *Caciocavallo* means "horse cheese," a name it earned from the way the cheese had traditionally been aged. Two pear-shaped lumps of cheese were tied together on a rope. The rope then was draped across the neck of horses, where it aged and remained available for the rider to snack on. The cheese is no longer aged with this method.

One final member of the mozzarella family worth mentioning is *burrata*. This cheese is one of the newest invented, created at the beginning of the twentieth century. Burrata is formed by pulling mozzarella into a pouch shape and filling it with curd and cream.[21] It spoils within two or three days and should be eaten immediately. Developed in Puglia, the cheese is enriched with cream, making it a luxury product. Only in recent years has burrata grown in popularity, earning something of a cult following in the

United States, although, again, more often produced there with cow's milk than milk of the buffalo.

Perhaps the best-known cheese the world over is Parmigiano-Reggiano. Although technically a northern cheese, it was well renowned enough in the nineteenth century that even poorer immigrants from the south knew of it. Today Parmigiano-Reggiano is produced in a legally defined area within the region of Emilia-Romagna. Like other cheeses from the region, Parmigiano-Reggiano is a grana cheese, meaning granular. *Grana* is a generic term for cheese made in the style of Parmigiano-Reggiano but made outside of the DOC (Denominazione di Origine Controllata—controlled designation of origin) and DOP zones. Other similar cheeses exist, like grana padano. The commonalities of the cheeses are crystals formed by bacteria during the aging process, causing the final cheese to easily flake away. Variations on the recipe have been produced since the Roman era, with modern parmigiano produced for some seven hundred years. DOC status was granted in 1995.

Legally defined Parmigiano-Reggiano is cheese produced from dairy cows consuming grass and hay from within the protected zone. Initially, the cheese had to be made from raw milk collected from cows between the late fall and early spring, but as modern agriculture extended the milking season, the rules were relaxed. The seasons do impact the flavor of the cheese. While connoisseurs and the official industry group make these distinctions, the average consumer will never notice.[22] Parmigiano-Reggiano must age for at least a year, and as many as four, with *giovane* (young), *vecchio* (old), *stravecchio* (extra old), and *stravecchione* (super old) describing each age variety.[23] Today there are between seven hundred and eight hundred active producers[24] drawing from close to nine thousand dairies.[25]

Early immigrants imported plenty of Parmigiano-Reggiano. The aged cheese traveled well, and the immigrants had been accustomed to high food prices in Italy. American industrial farms, especially in Wisconsin, produce imitation parmesan. The name Parmigiano-Reggiano is protected under European law and trademarked, but the Italians today would prefer banning even the generic term. American parmesan is perceived in Italy as inferior cheese, and the Italians may not be wrong. As with American-produced mozzarella, American parmesan lacks many of the essential qualities of the real thing. American parmesan is often aged for less time, meaning the cheese has less time to form those delicious flavor crystals. A *Cooks Illustrated* taste test found domestic cheeses to have a wax-like consistency, and chemical sampling found American parmesan often contained too much water.[26] Short aging and excessive water are not the only scams to worry about when buying parmesan in the United States. Imported parmesan doesn't necessarily indicate a high-quality product from Italy; Argentina, with a large number of Italian immigrants, also produces imitation parmesan cheese products. Argentinian cheese, regardless of quality, is technically imported.[27]

Another cheese originating early on in the history of the Italian peninsula was a ricotta-type cheese. From the Latin term *recoctus*,[28] meaning "re-cooked," ricotta is derived from leftover whey produced in cheese making. Producing a hard cheese like a grana would leave behind whey, and this liquid is cooked a second time to produce ricotta. At 85 degrees Celsius, the proteins separate and form lumps that are skimmed off the surface and then left to drain. Using a byproduct from making other cheeses meant ricotta provided additional calories from waste products. In pre-Roman times, as early as 2000 BC, ricotta provided a substantial component of agriculture on the Italian peninsula.[29] It can be made from the milk of many animals, including cows, buffalo, goats, and sheep.

Salted ricotta, known as ricotta *salata* or *canestrata*,[30] is a salted cheese common in Sicily. The salt preserves the ricotta. Without salt, fresh ricotta spoils relatively quickly, meaning it was a cheese Italian American immigrants had to produce locally. Unlike with hard, aged cheese, even paying substantial amounts of money would not allow the importation of ricotta before the age of jet travel. Ricotta has grown into a staple in Italian American cuisine in both savory and sweet dishes. It is the filling for manicotti and rolled lasagna noodles, and often it is a substitute for béchamel sauce in American Bolognese-style lasagna. It also serves as the filling, along with sugar, for cannoli or is baked into ricotta cheesecake.

One final essential cheese to consider when discussing red sauce cuisine is pecorino Romano. A hard, aged sheep's milk cheese produced originally in Lazio,[31] the region outside of Rome, the cheese has long been an essential ingredient in the Italian American household. For one thing, sheep's milk cheese was significantly less expensive than Parmigiano-Reggiano, but it can serve as substitute in many instances. The term *pecorino* is derived from the word for sheep (*pecora*) and indicates sheep's milk cheese. There are pecorino cheeses other than pecorino Romano, derived from sheep in other locations. It is one of the oldest cheeses in Italy and was a food that fed the Roman legions.

Although these cheeses were mainstays in Italian-immigrant enclaves, they had remained relatively unknown outside of those communities for decades. In the postwar period, as red sauce cuisine started going mainstream, Italian cheeses needed to be introduced to Americans. A 1949 *Woman's Day* article[32] presents ricotta, provolone, parmesan, Romano, mozzarella, gorgonzola, and *bel paese* as the Italian cheeses produced and available in the United States.[33] Bel Paese, less common today, was a twentieth-century invention, created by the cheesemaker Egidio Galbani in 1906 in Lombardy.[34] Consumption of Italian cheeses grew rapidly, with Americans consuming twenty-four million pounds in 1956, up from less than a million in 1930.[35] The varieties and availability of imported cheeses and domestic variations have grown exponentially since the start of the postwar period, but this finite list represents the cheeses widely available through most of the mid-twentieth century. Italian American importers like Di Palo's in New York City have made a huge business of importing many other cheeses as consumers sought more authentic Italian foods. Tariffs on European goods threatened as much as 95 percent[36] of the store's stock during the Trump-era trade disputes.

Italian cheese mirrored the Italian American experience as a once-exotic dairy product soon became a mainstay in gourmet grocery stores nationwide, and in the case of mozzarella, it eventually evolved into a commodity distributed in vending machines and convenience stores.

13

❖ ❖

One Lasagna, Many Lasagne

Pizza was not the only red sauce dish to achieve wide-reaching popularity in the postwar period. Baked lasagna appeared often on Italian American menus before the war, but, like pizza, it became an American household staple in the 1960s as a convenience food. Lasagna noodles are one of the oldest pasta shapes in Italy, and various forms of lasagna arrived with the earliest Italian immigrants. *Lasagna* can refer simply to the noodles, but more commonly in the United States it is a specific dish consisting of several layers of wide, flat noodles, tomato sauce, cheese, and meat, baked in an oven, with variations on this basic form evolving over time in the United States. The simplest preparations appeared on the earliest restaurant menus of ethnic restaurants and remain a common offering even today. Lasagna transitioned from exotic ethnic food into an American mainstay in the postwar period with the introduction of frozen foods in grocery stores nationwide.

Fresh-made lasagna noodles predate dried macaroni. Even today, a true lasagna should be made with fresh egg noodles rather than a dried macaroni, although the prebaked noodles promise to balance convenience and flavor. Lasagna noodles are directly related to the Roman lagana, also sheets of flattened dough. Because of the simplicity, lasagna noodles are pervasive and widespread throughout all the regions of Italy, with each area producing unique dishes, widths, and combinations of fillings based on locally available ingredients. In addition, many common pasta shapes descend directly from the lasagna noodle, including tagliatelle and fettuccine, and stuffed pastas often start life as sheets of lasagna. The lasagna family of shapes contrast in preparation from pierced pastas like bucatini or shapes extruded through a die in that they can be produced with elemental equipment.

Roman lagana were often baked in an oven with liquids, but, unlike modern lasagna, they were not boiled prior. The liquid in the pan cooked the lagana as it baked. During the medieval era, cooking techniques evolved the Roman-era lagana into a dish recognizable as today's lasagna. Instead of baking or braising the dough in liquid, the pasta sheets were cut to size so as to fit the baking vessel and boiled in water, broth, or milk.[1] For a period in the twelfth to fourteenth centuries, Roman lagana and lasagna coexisted as the culinary traditions transitioned.[2] Lasagna in this era was a leavened dough rolled flat, boiled, and served with cheese, and it could be served as single-level constructions or have alternating layers of noodles and cheese stacked together with the addition of spices.[3] The variations are documented in the Neapolitan cookbook *Liber de Coquina*, from the fourteenth century, and the book contains step-by-step instructions.[4] These were primarily dishes of wealthy households. Lasagna became the preferred fresh pasta dish in the medieval era.

Lasagna continued to grow in importance over the next few centuries. While dried pastas required hard durum wheat, lasagna noodles often were made with cheaper, softer flour. Lasagna made from soft wheat flour sold for less than the dried macaroni, and the city of Palermo even went as far as establishing set prices to enshrine the price disparity into law.[5] Although using fresh pasta meant lasagna offered no long-term preservation benefit for the wheat, it did help make the dish available to a broader segment of the population. Lasagna makers, known as lasagnari, grew in importance during the Renaissance era. The guilds also served to protect quality and reduce competition. In Florence, the lasagnari had first served as members of the cook's guild but eventually abandoned the cooks for the wafer-makers' guild.[6]

Since *lasagna* refers to the style of noodle rather than a specific dish, as with other pastas, lasagna noodles can be served either en brodo (as in soup) or with a sauce. Another quirk of the Italian language is that in the north, the plural, *lasagne*, is generally employed, while the south always uses the singular *lasagna.*[7] Since the majority of immigrants came from the south, Americans use the term *lasagna* for a singular dish. Lasagna in the Italian American kitchen almost exclusively implies a specific style of baked casserole with noodles layered with cheese, sauce, sometimes meat, and then baked in the oven. In Italian cuisine, these dishes are usually referred to by the more specific term *lasagna al forno*, or "oven-baked lasagna." As with variations of lasagna noodles, in Italy, lasagna al forno recipes vary by region.

What Americans think of as lasagna is also broadly a stuffed pasta dish, sometimes known as a lasagna *imbottite*. These oven-baked dishes consist of layers of lasagna noodles with red tomato sauce, mozzarella and ricotta cheese, and often (but not always) a variety of meats ranging from ground beef, sausage meat, or meatballs. Lasagne vary across the regions of Italy, and American recipes draw inspiration from on all these. Neapolitan-style lasagna includes a mix of meats, usually pork and cured pork, or veal, beef, or sausages. Another variation, also from Naples, is the *lasagna di carnevale*, originally reserved for Fat Tuesday feasts celebrating all the many foods prohibited during the Lent period.[8] Layers of ricotta, tiny meatballs, sausage, and sometimes eggs are piled into layers along with Neapolitan ragù. Neapolitan lasagna is most often constructed with boiled, fresh-made pasta. In Italy, this dish is served at religious celebrations and was for many people one of the few times a year they would eat meat. Because of the abundance available in America, dishes like festival lasagna were consumed with greater frequency.

Another regional lasagna to influence Italian American cooking in the United States was the lasagne Bolognese. Layers of lasagna noodles are alternated with Bolognese ragù and *besciamella* sauce—Italian for béchamel—and topped with parmigiana cheese. American versions of the dish often substitute ricotta cheese for the béchamel, to simplify cooking, or do away with the béchamel entirely. American versions of lasagna Bolognese also tend to have a lot more sauce than the Italian original.[9] As with lasagna di carnevale, lasagne Bolognese originally was served as celebratory food—throughout the Emilia-Romagna region, lasagne was served to celebrate the birth of a daughter—but has since become a regional specialty. Today, lasagne Bolognese has grown popular throughout Italy, and nearly every restaurant in Bologna serves their own variation, leading to a decrease in quality.[10] Northern recipes rarely require the noodles to be boiled before baking, instead absorbing moisture from the cheese and sauces while in the oven, and allowing the noodles to crisp under the heat.[11]

Lasagnas are absent from the early Italian American cookbooks, but by the 1930s, the recipes begin to appear.[12] The first general cookbook to include a lasagna recipe is likely the *Ladies Home Journal Cook Book* published in 1960.[13] But restaurants served the dish, and a recipe appears in *Where to Dine in Thirty-Nine*, the survey of New York's restaurants featuring recipes from the chefs. Ashley highlights Colucci's restaurant on West 51st Street and includes a variation of a Neapolitan lasagna with ricotta, chopped meat and pork, tomato sauce, Romano, and mozzarella, although it's perhaps worth noting the book misspells *mozzarella* as the phonetic *mazzarella*.[14] Maria Lo Pinto's *New York Cookbook* includes lasagne but refers to it as a baked macaroni, while Maria Luisa Taglenti refers to Neapolitan lasagna as old fashioned. Mama Leone's recipe collection included a variation of a lasagna di carnevale. The restaurant was famous for preparing huge trays of lasagna for their massive dining rooms.

There is no consistent, authoritative American lasagna, but Neapolitan, Neapolitan carnevale, and Bolognese all exert a strong influence on the lasagnas served in places like Colucci's, Enrico & Paglieri's, and Leone's. Lasagnas and stuffed pastas often served as a means of using leftover food, leading to limitless combinations.[15] The typical red sauce lasagna combines layers of tomato sauce, ricotta, mozzarella, and ground meat, with a final layer of parmigiana on top, but may eliminate any of those ingredients or substitute in others.

Another common lasagna variation to eventually make it to the United States was lasagne *verde*, green lasagna. In the original recipe from the Emilia-Romagna region (Bologna and Modena), spinach colors the lasagna noodles green.[16] American adaptions of this dish included wilted spinach, rather than a green pasta, and the white noodles are layered with béchamel or ricotta.

Lasagna was fast becoming a popular, well-known food by the 1960s, but not because of ethnic Italian restaurants. It had become national grocery store item available as a frozen food. By the 1960s, with American women entering the workforce, food marketing shifted toward time savings and ease of preparation. American housewives found many complicated foods simplified by canning, freezing, and microwavable packaging. Since lasagna is essentially a casserole, a one-pot meal, combining meat and pasta, it became a natural fit for the trend. Even in Italy, lasagna is sometimes treated this way, acting as a combination of the primi and secondi piatti. Neapolitans, for instance, serve the "shit" lasagna on New Year's Eve to celebrate the new year, avoiding a complicated cooking preparation while producing a large quantity of food for family and friends. Another element of this tradition includes buying factory-made lasagna noodles. According to myth, Neapolitans believe they will have financial success in the coming year if they spend money buying the noodles.

Lasagna was also a food conducive to freezing, and as America warmed to frozen meals in the 1960s, frozen lasagna took center stage. One of the great innovators in this regard was Stouffer's, a Cleveland-based restaurant chain. Stouffer's initially launched a mediocre line of frozen casseroles, with all but the lasagna resulting in lackluster sales. Frozen Stouffer's lasagnas became ubiquitous in Cleveland grocery stores[17] and were eventually sold to the food conglomerate Nestlé. The Stouffer's lasagna is a combination of tomato-meat sauce and cheese, layered with noodles, and through national marketing campaigns, it created a standard for lasagna.

Lasagna noodles also serve as the base for several other pasta dishes, with the flat sheets proving a versatile vehicle for cheese and sauce. Ravioli developed in the fourteenth century from lasagna sheets. The flat pasta was folded over and filled with meat, fish, or cheese before being fried in a pan. Ravioli originated in predominantly northern kingdoms and percolated through the general population over time, with the fillings distinguishing a regional variety more than shape and construction technique.[18] Ravioli traditionally have a ricotta filling, while the term *agnolotti* refers to other fillings,[19] but the term is rarely used in the United States. *Ravioli* became a more universal term between the First and Second World Wars.[20] Ravioli also benefited from artificial refrigeration since the fillings and fresh pasta wrapped around it spoil easily. As grocery stores installed more and more freezer space, the pasta became widely available.

Another common use of lasagna noodles is for cannelloni, more often called manicotti by Italian Americans. Cannelloni are fresh pasta cut into squares, boiled, rolled, and filled with meat, fish, or cheese—anything that a cook can stuff into a ravioli—and then baked usually with butter and cheese. The filling of cannelloni should be thicker and firmer than stuffing on a sealed pasta to avoid leakage, since cannelloni have open ends.[21] Manicotti are similar, though usually exclusively filled with ricotta cheese. Manicotti are then covered in tomato sauce and parmigiana cheese before baked. The term *manicotti* is strictly an American invention. The term means literally "cooked hands," and the noodles resemble the fur muffs women wore in winter to keep their hands warm.[22] Hand muffs had been popular for men and women since the sixteenth century. Despite falling out of fashion for men, women continued using them through 1950s, and the fur muff would have been a widely known reference. In a 1951 issue of *Ladies Home Journal*, manicotti is mentioned as better than lasagna and included as a thrifty meal suggestion.[23] American versions of these dishes, like with other pasta dishes, have more sauce and cheese than the Italian counterparts.

Another common baked Italian American pasta dish is baked ziti, a combination of ziti noodles, tomato sauce, and mozzarella, baked in the oven and topped with more cheese. Ziti al forno was a common wedding dish in

Naples, and in Italian American communities long after immigration, rarely was there a wedding without ziti to celebrate. The dish persists today as a common celebration dish for other qualities—the ease of producing a large number of portions and a meatless menu option.

Baked pasta dishes in America have undergone the same evolutions of other red sauce dishes. Chain restaurants have reinvented the traditional combinations, adding more cheese and sauce than even early Italian American cooks. But the evolution of lasagna didn't end there. The popularity of the dish, and the possibilities for adaptation, proved too tempting. Julia Child presented a "lasagne a la Francaise" on her famed PBS show, and Tex-Mex variations substitute tortillas for lasagna noodles.[24] Purists decry these as abominations. But the adaptability of lasagna is also one of its greatest attributes. All the variations of Italian lasagna surely offended the sensibilities of purists in their day, but that doesn't make them any less delicious.

14

❖ ❖

A Taste of Rome

In the postwar period, Italian American cuisine had transitioned from something exotic into something American. Spaghetti and meatballs could now be found on the restaurant menus alongside blue-blooded Yankee pot roasts and New England clam chowder; in casual, family-friendly places; and on grocery store shelves and in home pantries. Pizza made inroads across the country, removing the air of foreignness from flavors like oregano and garlic. By 1959, the red sauce behemoth Leone's was acquired by Restaurant Associates,[1] a conglomerate that monetized the restaurant into a commercial powerhouse, demonstrating the staying power of Italian American food, and in the 1960s, even Howard Johnson's was offering spaghetti and ravioli on its menus.[2] Red sauce penetrated the culinary consciousness of mainstream America with a chicken parm in every pot.

Once American consumers had grown familiar with the general concept of Italian cuisine, the groundwork was laid for expanding on those flavors. The postwar years saw pasta preparations with origins in Rome and the surrounding province of Lazio enter into the Italian American lexicon. These traditional Roman sauces consist of cacio e pepe, *gricia*, carbonara, amatriciana, and arrabbiatta. This region sent many immigrants to the United States during the early twentieth century, and therefore it is likely these sauces were part of their food traditions before the 1950s. However, these only begin to appear in publications, recipe collections, and menus in the postwar period. The confluence of American soldiers occupying Italy during and after the war and a growing interest in Italian American food in this period helped propelled Roman recipes to the forefront of red sauce menus.

Today, variations of these sauces are generally available in some form or another at red sauce joints, chain restaurants, and even as prepared, jarred sauces, although they are not all, strictly speaking, an actual sauce. Like spaghetti and meatballs, the Americanization of traditional recipes has resulted in adulterations that would scandalize native-born Italians. The Italian American variations primarily consist of larger portions and thicker sauces with the sauce dominating the dish rather than complementing the pasta. But a dish like cacio e pepe is a product of mixing ingredients directly in the pasta and cannot be made ahead of time. In some cases, the Americanized recipes substituted local ingredients, or added ingredients for convenience or to simplify the labor of cooking. American domestic cooks in the postwar period were especially enthralled with easily prepared foods, and as many recipes were adopted by mainstream society, the dishes were inevitably altered to accommodate their palates and tolerances.

Amatriciana had an inauspicious introduction to the American public a few days after Christmas in 1952. That year, Remo, a young elephant held captive in the Rome Zoo, died from an intestinal infection, and his obituary circulated on newswires across the country. The nationally distributed story reported Remo had enjoyed eating spaghetti al amatriciana, a dish regionally associated with Rome.[3] Remo's love of spaghetti and the hefty amount fed to him likely contributed to his demise. The intestinal infection was assumed to have been caused by eating too much pasta, a food not ordinarily in the diet of an elephant. Within a few years of Remo's death, spaghetti al amatriciana began appearing on restaurant menus throughout the United States, and recipes for the dish began circulating in periodical publications.

Pasta alla amatriciana and pasta alla gricia are two similar pasta preparations consisting of salted pork (usually *guanciale*), pepper, and pecorino cheese, with tomatoes or tomato sauce added to amatriciana. Gricia, or *grici* in Rome, has origins in the countryside outside the city. It is inseparable from amatriciana, and sometimes even called amatriciana bianca.[4] Gricia is the older preparation, having origins as far back as the fifteenth century. The inclusion of tomatoes in amatriciana sauce indicates it is a more recent creation, as tomatoes would have arrived only with the Columbian Exchange. Gricia began life as a food for shepherds. The salted pork and aged sheep's cheese traveled well when the shepherds herded their flocks to grazing land away from their homes. The shepherds often would remain with their flocks on remote hillsides for long periods of time, camping out in the fields to ward off predators and to prevent the sheep from wandering away. Simply prepared over a campfire, salt pork, pasta, and cheese provided a substantial meal.

The debate over the origins of these dishes begins in the hillsides overlooking Rome. Two rural towns have a centuries-long feud over the rightful inventor. The small city of Amatrice has long claimed to have originated pasta all'amatriciana, first as a recipe now known as amatriciana bianca, and then later adding tomatoes. The city remains the guardian of an authentic recipe. But Amatrice lies only a short distance from the city of Grisciano, which lays claim to having invented pasta all'gricia,[5] for which the tomato-less version of the dish is seemingly named. But the dispute does not end there.

Pasta gricia is known by the alias grici, especially on menus in Rome. The discrepancy exists because of bread makers; a fifteenth-century Roman word for bread-maker was *gricio*, derived from *i grici*. The term referred to immigrants from Switzerland, a region that at the time was divided into small independent cantons. The members of one of these cantons, the Grey League, or *Lega Grigia*, wore gray clothing, not unlike the gray coats of the Roman baker's guild. The term *griscium* eventually came to be synonymous with bakers and immigrants from Switzerland. Over time, the term *grici* slowly became increasingly generic, referring to other vendors of household goods like olive oil but seen as crude and backward. By the nineteenth century, grici had become money lenders, offering small loans and posting credit notes to their doors. In the interest of collecting their money, they stayed open late. Charcoal stoves allowed them to cook without taking breaks from collecting money for their meals. The pasta they ate thus became the pasta alla gricia.[6]

Another Roman variation on the alla gricia is sometimes known as spaghetti alla *carrettiera*, translated as "the coachman's spaghetti." The name is derived from the simplicity of the preparation, which allowed cart drivers to prepare it while traveling.[7] In Rome, alla carrettiera is essentially an alla gricia finished with mushrooms and canned tuna.[8] A Sicilian version of this dish is simpler: garlic, cheese, salt, pepper, and breadcrumbs.[9] Unlike gricia and amatriciana, carrettiera—in either form—is not a common dish in Italian American cuisine.

It is not just pasta alla gricia the Romans have claimed from the Lazio shepherds. Roman chefs insist amatriciana also originated in Rome. Here, bucatini all'matriciana has a slight variation to the recipe served in Amatrice. Although both versions include tomatoes, guanciale, and cheese, only in Rome does bucatini all'matriciana also contain onions.[10] This more recent variation of the dish is attributed by the Italian Academy of Kitchens to a man residing in Rome but born in Amatrice. The original recipe used *casalino* tomatoes, a fruit with thick ridgelines and local to Rome. A clue is provided in the recipe—alla amatriciana versus alla matriciana. The former is cooked in the style of Amatrice, while the other is in the style of the cook from Amatrice.[11] Another clue is in the choice of pasta. In Rome, amatriciana is almost exclusively served with bucatini, a long thread of pasta with a hole through the center of it. Pasta alla gricia and amatriciana from Amatrice usually use spaghetti or even shorter pasta, suggesting the Roman and Amatrice versions are different recipes, if only slightly. If this explanation would seem to satisfy the questions of origin, rest assured, it does not. Adding to the confusion, the province of Abruzzo may hold a claim to pasta all'amatriciana as well. The borders of Lazio and Abruzzo have shifted over time, and the amatriciana style is common in Abruzzo, as are the sheep and shepherds considered responsible for inventing gricia.[12]

Despite all the uncertainty, nothing has stopped the town of Amatrice from fostering a cottage industry around the recipe by declaring themselves arbiters of authentic amatriciana. There was a collective outrage a few years ago when Italian celebrity chef Carlo Cracco went on national television to cook his version of pasta all'amatriciana and revealed his secret ingredient: garlic. According to locals in Amatrice, the addition of garlic threatens the soft and sweet flavors of guanciale.[13] The mayor of Amatrice was so outraged by Cracco's garlic foible that he issued an official city recipe.

Italian American versions of amatriciana often ignore these stringent rules. Guanciale, pork jowl meat, is a hard-to-find specialty food, even today. Guanciale is sweeter and more tender than other preserved pork products. Pancetta is often substituted in American recipes, although Maria Luisa Taglienti's early recipe calls for chopped salt meat.[14] Taglienti also describes the dish as originating in Abruzzo, which might explain the difference in protein. The strong flavor and smokiness of American bacon is considered undesirable. Most American recipes, like with Cracco's version, include garlic or onion (or both). Although variations of amatriciana had become a mainstay of Italian American menus from the late 1950s, it achieved new notoriety in 1998 when Mario Batali opened Babbo Ristorante e Enoteca, with the restaurant lauded for the inclusion of an Americanized version of bucatini alla amatriciana on the menu.[15] Batali added garlic and red onions, two violations of the strict traditional recipe.

Another related dish introduced to American menus in this period was spaghetti carbonara, arriving in the early 1950s. A Chicago area guidebook from 1952 attributes a carbonara recipe to Armando's, a restaurant from the north side.[16] Carbonara also appears in the 1955 publication of *The Italian Cookbook* by Maria Luisa Taglienti, with this latter volume more widely known than the Chicago guidebook. Taglienti, born in Rome, married an American military officer in Florence before emigrating from Italy.[17] The couple lived in Paris for two years and then returned to the United States to settle in New Jersey. In addition to growing up in Rome, Taglienti spent three months traveling in Italy researching the recipes for *The Italian Cookbook*. Her book continued to circulate long after publication. Variations on carbonara continued to grow in popularity. Carbonara also earned a celebrity endorsement in 1966 from Italian actor Ugo Tognazzi at the 1966 New York premiere of the film *Marcia Nuziale*.[18]

Traditionally made spaghetti carbonara combines pancetta, pecorino cheese, black pepper, and pasta, over which a raw egg is cracked and cooked by the warmth of the other ingredients rather than on direct heat. Modern, Americanized versions of the dish will add cream, helping to smooth the sauce, or garlic to spice up the flavor, and prior to pancetta becoming available in the United States, bacon would be substituted. Taglienti's version calls for bacon, adds white wine, and mixes parmigiana cheese with the pecorino as well, although these ingredients are not considered traditional.

The bacon and egg ingredients earned carbonara a reputation as an American dish allegedly invented by or for American soldiers during World War II.[19] Several competing mythologies attempt to explain these origins. In one narrative, the Americans' well-documented love of bacon and eggs inspired Italians to offer the soldiers a taste of home, or Italians created the sauce when mistranslating an American breakfast. However, products like cured pork and eggs were both rare and expensive in liberated Italy. They would fetch a high price on the black market, suggesting no Italian in their right mind would offer them up to occupying American soldiers. Although American officers might have had the finances to pay for such rare ingredients, enlisted men were unlikely to.

Another possibility suggests carbonara came straight from soldiers' ration packs, and that the pasta dish was named for those packs, which were a dark black charcoal color. The average American soldier in Italy was equipped with K rations, packs provided to enlisted men with meals, toilet paper, cigarettes, and chocolate. The packs contained bacon, cheese, and eggs, the essential ingredients for carbonara. The soldiers may have tired of eating the provided rations and instead combined those ingredients with local pasta. Alternatively, these same ingredients were distributed by Americans to the local population, who were on the brink of starvation.

Soldiers distributed food including powdered eggs and tinned meat, and inventive Italians used these poor-quality ingredients with their native pasta for a delicious, high-calorie dish.

One of the most compelling arguments supporting the connection between American soldiers and the dish is the lack of published carbonara recipes. In essence, carbonara doesn't exist as a dish in printed form before the Second World War. Carbonara is absent from Artusi, and it doesn't appear in Ada Boni's prewar collection either,[20] nor in a prewar book about Roman cuisine.[21] And yet even amatriciana finds its way into eighteenth-century recipe books shortly after tomatoes enter into the Italian culinary tradition.

Further complicating the origin issue, pasta alla carbonara translates to "pasta in the style of *carbonari*"—men who worked with charcoal and coal.[22] Charcoal is produced by slowly burning timber since the charred remains are concentrated carbon ready for hot fires, but the process was time consuming and occurred in the forest away from villages. In Rome, that timber was available in the mountainous Lazio region surrounding the city where alla carbonara is also said to have origins. The most common explanation is that the dish was consumed by the men cutting the wood responsible for watching the fires burn. Salt pork, cheese, and pepper were readily available pantry items, and even isolated in the woods, finding a bird's egg was possible—in essence, these carbonari were eating a version of alla gricia topped with an egg. From there, legends vary. In some versions, the men introduced the dish to Romans when they delivered charcoal. In others, a worker of the carbonari occupation opened a restaurant specializing in the dish. The latter version is linked with the mythology of the restaurant La Carbonara on Campo de' Fiori, operating since 1912.[23]

One even less likely theory is the recipe was somehow linked with a secret society, also known as the Carbonari, a nineteenth-century organization that worked to topple conservative Italian governments.[24] They are also credited with preparing the various disassociated kingdoms of Italy for unification.[25] Similar to the Free Masons, the Carbonari hosted extensive rituals and built lodges around the country. Is it possible spaghetti alla carbonara played a role in their rituals? Have they hidden the dish's origins to protect their organization? Perhaps it would be easier to document if they were not a secret organization. However, while some truths may exist in these stories, they are primarily fictions.

A Bolognese chef by the name of Renato Gualandi claims to have invented the most common iteration of carbonara in 1944 for a celebratory banquet between British and American commanders. Gualandi, who became a celebrated Italian chef in the twentieth century, had enlisted in the Italian army at the start of the war and was subsequently stationed near the Yugoslavian border. After the surrender of Italy and the collapse of the Italian army, he attempted to return to his native Bologna but made it only as far as Riccione, a seaside town around the resort communities near Rimini. He began working for a local mayor waiting out the war. When allied forces liberated Riccione, they planned a banquet for the commander of allied forces in Italy. Gualandi volunteered to cook the celebratory meal, as he had some experience working in hotel kitchens. The Americans first accused him of being a communist because of his military service spent in the north of Italy. Yet, lacking any experienced cooks, they eventually allowed Gualandi to prepare the grand luncheon. Only belatedly did he realize the war rationing had limited the availability of ingredients, and instead of cooking a feast from the bounty of a hotel kitchen pantry, he had to make do with limited ingredients. Wanting to at least serve meat, Gualandi drew on the soldiers' rations containing salt pork, processed cheese, and powdered eggs, and he prepared the resulting carbonara sauce.[26]

Crediting Renato Gualandi with inventing spaghetti alla carbonara may be too easy an explanation, even if he did serve one iteration of the dish. The name *alla carbonara* may have been invented around the middle of the twentieth century, but the recipe is likely much older. Ippolito Cavalcanti's nineteenth-century Neapolitan cookbooks included a recipe for pasta cacio e *uova*, a dish of cheese and eggs.[27] Numerous recipes had their names changed around the Second World War, and carbonara's sudden appearance may simply be the result of a fresh new name. Ada Boni's recipe for alla gricia before the war is titled *spaghetti alla marchiciana*, meaning in the style of Le Marche, an Italian region.[28] Another Roman sauce, arrabbiata, materialized from nowhere in this era, but it is most likely just a new name for alla piccante, a spicy sauce.

Many recipes acquired new names during or after the fascist period, a time of cultural upheaval when the government actively worked toward a greater sense of national identity. Fascists advocated for Italian rather than regional identity, and recipes reflected those desires. To this end, Ada Boni argued in favor of dishes with Italian names and specific naming conventions.[29] Renaming regional dishes to make them more universally Italian was an intentional scheme to unify the old local identities.

Whatever its true origins, today carbonara is considered the pasta dish most likely to be adulterated or falsified, according to *l'Accademia Italiana della Cucina*.[30] Americanized versions of carbonara often include heavy cream and American bacon rather than pancetta. As with the other Roman pastas, the smoky flavor of American bacon is said to overwhelm the dish, while chopped ham rather than pancetta or prosciutto underwhelms it. Using cream provides a shortcut to re-creating the silkiness of the eggs but makes a much heavier dish. *Carbonara* in American restaurant parlance has come to refer to cream and bacon sauces often poured on chicken, shellfish, or even pizza. The Olive Garden serves a particularly famous carbonara dish with both chicken and shrimp. So much for an authentic Italian menu. In Rome, the dish remains true to its origins, relying on the emulsion of starchy water and cheese for creaminess rather than substituting cream or milk.

Carbonara, gricia, and amatriciana all have a common origin, a now-popular pasta dish known as cacio e pepe, translated as "cheese and pepper." Cacio e pepe is prepared directly in hot pasta by mixing finely grated cheese, black pepper, and a bit of starchy pasta water, a method similar to that employed by Alfredo Di Lelio in creating his namesake recipe. The starch and fat emulsify with the melting cheese to form a creamy sauce without actually adding cream. Gricia expands on this dish by adding salted pork; carbonara builds further by adding an egg, and amatriciana by adding tomato.

Cacio e pepe is one of the earliest preparations of pasta, at least as old as the medieval era, and perhaps even as far back as ancient Rome. Aged cheese stored well even without refrigeration. In ancient Rome, soldiers were provided cheese as a standard provision, one of the earliest condiments for pasta. Pecorino Romano, a sheep's milk cheese, is the authentic original ingredient, ground down into small grains that melt in the heat of the pasta.

The luxury ingredient of this dish was the pepper, particularly in the medieval period. Spices like pepper often only made it to the plates of aristocrats and often disguised the rancid flavors of rotten foods. Pepper disseminated through Italy from Venetian and Genoese merchants who controlled trade routes with the East, where black pepper originated from. Black pepper flavored foods on the Italian peninsula as far back as the ancient Roman empire.[31] Romans used the spice not just for flavoring food but also as medicine. They imported the spice from Asia by way of Middle Eastern trade routes, but otherwise the source of their pepper remained nebulous in the West for centuries. The price also remained high because of the scarcity and the number of intermediate merchants involved in the trade.

During the Middle Ages, Venice controlled much of the black pepper trade across the Mediterranean. The city-state bolstered its near-monopoly by forcing crusading knights to sack its competitor, Constantinople, during the Fourth Crusade. Intermediaries continued to control pepper east of the Mediterranean, and they took a sizable piece of the profits. Marco Polo's expedition east centered on finding sources of black pepper to create trading networks to usurp the various merchants between Italy and India, where the spice grew. Huge profits could be made if Italian merchants, or European merchants more generally, were able to circumvent the Arab middlemen, and the desire for black pepper catalyzed the investment in exploration.

The early sea routes navigated around the southernmost point of Africa and crossed the Indian ocean to connect Europe with pepper sources in Sumatra. The journey was perilous. The most dangerous segment was crossing the Indian Ocean. Ships departed India ideally in the autumn to avoid spring storms around the Cape of Good Hope.[32] Many failed to leave on time and ended up at the bottom of the sea. The pepper trade proved deadly, but also highly profitable. The Portuguese, English, and Dutch all sought fortunes along this route and set up colonial empires in southern Asia to supply their pepper trade.

To compete with these networks, Spain set sail to the west. Christopher Columbus had struggled for years to fund an expedition, and Spain took the bait, hoping to find competing pepper sources. Columbus came across two sources of pepper, neither of which actually were the highly valuable black pepper. Black pepper is a berry that grows in bunches on vines. Columbus had brought samples with him to help identify sources of it. Presenting these berries to the native people of Jamaica, they offered up a similar-looking aromatic berry, larger than pepper but otherwise similar in appearance.[33] What the Jamaicans offered was allspice, as yet unknown to the Spanish. Despite the size difference, the Spanish returned to Europe selling the spicy counterfeit.

Nevertheless, black pepper remained in high demand. The British, Portuguese, and Dutch desire to import pepper from Sumatra continually put the empires into conflict with each other. They also created abusive systems of labor to exploit the pepper-growing regions. Farmers had contractual obligations to fill their pepper quotas, often forgoing the planting of rice to feed their families and creating food shortages.[34] Queen Elizabeth I chartered the East India Company, and after she died, James I granted the company a monopoly on pepper to push out the Dutch. The East India Company continued to hold the monopoly and then became a bureaucratic administration standing in for the British government in many of its Asian holdings. The corporation also held monopolies on trade of certain items within the American colonies.

Americans had found another way of lowering food costs, this time by wresting control away from the British East India Company.[35] After the American Revolution, with the American colonies liberated from the British crown, the new nation continued to purchase pepper from the East

India Company out of necessity. In 1803, shipping merchants from New England set out to break the European monopolies. They sailed to Sumatra and cut their own pepper contracts directly with producers. Huge profit margins helped build Salem, and later Boston, into major shipping centers. But Americans were not yet heavy pepper users.

Pepper also set the tone of nineteenth-century American foreign policy, especially in the Pacific Ocean. Pirates attacked the American pepper ship *Friendship*, and so, in 1831, the newly launched frigate *Potomac* was sent the Pacific to rectify the situation. Loaded with marines and sailors, the ship destroyed the Sumatran town of Kuala Batee in retaliation. The attack marked the beginning of American gunboat diplomacy, an international public policy program where American businesses exploited the power and reach of the American military.

The American merchants forced down the price of pepper through oversupply. The one-time delicacy of the rich soon became a kitchen cabinet staple in the United States.[36] By the era of Italian immigration, black pepper had become another common ingredient readily available to them. Meanwhile, American palates were not particular warmed up to spicy food even generally, with even garlic too spicy for their delicate palates. Black pepper was more or less as spicy as Americans were willing to go well into the twentieth century.

Even though pepper had been a relatively expensive ingredient until the nineteenth century, cacio e pepe was a relatively austere preparation relying on the trick of emulsification to create a thick creaminess. A well-made cacio e pepe will taste as though rich with cream but should not contain any. The thick consistency comes only from the small portion of the starchy water the pasta was cooked in and the melting cheese. From a historic perspective, the lack of cream is simply a practical matter. Cream is difficult to store and keep fresh. The starch from the pasta water, when heated, will thicken with the fat in the cheese. Preparing this dish correctly can prove challenging for the inexperienced cook.

Cacio e pepe experienced a resurgence in popularity beginning in the mid-2000s, both in Italy and in the United States, with chefs like Nancy Silverton, an associate of Joe Bastianich and Mario Batali, adding the simple dish to the menu of Osteria Mozza in Los Angeles, but also drawing criticism for adding butter to the recipe. Not long after, cacio e pepe became a calling card for restaurants and even had chefs working out fusion variations, such as one not-so-popular[37] variant by Dave Chang and Josh Pinsky, who substituted fermented chickpea paste for cheese on the menu of Momofuku Nishi.[38]

Black pepper dishes like cacio e pepper may not seem especially spicy today, but the bite of pepper had long been considered strong. But in the postwar era, a spicier dish began appearing in American Italian restaurants known as arrabbiata. The name means literally "an angry sauce," earned from the spiciness of the recipe. English speakers will sometimes use the name *arrabbiata* in conjunction with or in place of *fra diavolo*, but this is incorrect. Al diavolo in the original Italian recipe is spicy because of black pepper, while arrabbiata is spicy because of chili pepper, also known as crushed red pepper. Spicy red peppers became a popular dish in southern Italian cuisine as a cheaper way to add spice after peppers were introduced to Europe from the Americas.

Roman arrabbiata sauce consists of hot peppers, usually pickled pepperoncino, garlic, tomatoes, and salted pork, either pancetta or prosciutto. Unlike with amatriciana sauce, the sweeter guanciale is unnecessary, as the spice from the chili pepper overwhelms any delicate flavors. The Italian version of arrabbiata recipes suggests a link to the other Roman preparations as a spicier variant, part of the larger family of pasta preparations, but American versions frequently omit the pork. In modern American restaurant usage, *arrabbiata* has become synonymous with *spicy*, with *pasta all'arrabbiata* in red sauce restaurants often referring to a spicy tomato sauce, instead of alla piccante. In the prewar period, tomato sauce laced with chili peppers were common, usually listed as *sugo al piccante*, meaning literally spicy sauce. Arrabbiata appeared in Italy after the war, and, as with most variations of American arrabbiata sauces, many of these recipes omit salted pork.

The one component all variations agree on is pasta all'arrabbiata contains hot peppers. Peppers, like tomatoes, originated in Central America and did not arrive in Italy until after the Columbian Exchange. Columbus came across *Capsicum annuum*, better known generically as chili peppers. Peppers were cultivated by the Aztecs, who by the arrival of the Spanish had cultivated dozens of varieties.[39] Peppers were readily available alongside tomatoes in the markets of Tenochtitlan when the conquistadors marched through Mexico. Though quite evidently not the black pepper berries, some of the chili pepper varieties had spicy heat, and the Spanish referred to these new fruits as *pimiento*, like *pimienta* (black pepper).[40] The linguistic link to black pepper stuck in Spanish, but it was eventually lost in many other European languages. Although not the expensive black pepper so desired by the Europeans, *C. annuum* proved fairly useful and spread quickly through Europe along with the other foods of the Columbian Exchange.

Chili peppers arrived in Sicily by way of North Africa in the early part of the sixteenth century.[41] Italians developed several cultivars, including the

Italia. The term *pepperoncini* refers to chili peppers generically, although Italian Americans often specifically refer to preserved green peppers pickled in vinegar when they say pepperoncini. These spicy chili peppers were common in the south of Italy. In the last few decades, the use of spicy chili peppers in the rest of Italy had grown more popular. Even though chili-pepper-spiced foods were common in the south, few recipes document their use since cooks used chili pepper spice to taste, in the same way one might salt and pepper a dish for seasoning.[42]

Not all the members of the *C. annuum* family are spicy, and the sweet peppers also found a use in Italian cuisine in sauces like chicken cacciatora or *scarpariello*. Chicken scarpariello consists of chicken and sausages sautéed or braised in a sauce of peppers, onions, vinegar, and white wine, but disagreement on this list of ingredients exists. Some recipes add roasted potatoes, pickled peppers, or even tomatoes, and sometimes it is served over pasta, but not always.

The name *scarpariello* implies a relationship with shoemakers, but the reason for this attachment remains a mystery. Most people take it to mean "chicken of the shoemaker," but there are a lot of other possibilities. These meanings vary and include a dish invented in the cobbler district of Naples; a dish cobbled together by various ingredients; the chicken bones in the mouth of a diner resembling a cobbler's shoe tacks protruding from a mouth[43]; or a dish so basic even a poor cobbler's family could afford to assemble it. The ending *-iello* implies a meager dish.[44]

The restauranteur Lidia Bastianich described scarpariello as particularly well known in America,[45] but there are few references to it before the 1980s. In 1981, Craig Claiborne, food critic of the *New York Times*, wrote in the paper that it was a dish with dubious Italian origins, although he also cited it as sometimes attributed to a Sicily or Calabria.[46] In the 1980s, scarpariello became something of a fad dish, appearing throughout *New York Magazine* in advertisements and restaurant listings,[47] but, unlike veal parmigiana or spaghetti and meatballs, midcentury magazines make no mention of it. The peppers play an essential role in scarpariello, especially given the absence of tomatoes.

The immigrants in America replaced the pepperoncino with cultivars more commonly found in America at the time. Sweet peppers are a mainstay with Italian sausages, commonly served at festivals celebrating Italian heritage, like the San Gennaro festival held on Mulberry Street in Manhattan's Little Italy. The festival celebrates St. Gennaro, who is said to have saved Naples from an eruption of Mt. Vesuvius.[48] First celebrated in 1926,[49] the event started as a single block-long party with a group of Neapolitan immigrants led by Alexander Tisi grilling chickens in the street.[50] Since then, the party has grown, expanding to an eleven-day event, and attracting more than a million attendees, with over three hundred street vendors.[51] The festival in 1959 featured a tunnel constructed of provolone cheese promoting a half-ton wheel.[52] Since the 1980s, the food offerings have expanded to included Chinese foods from nearby Chinatown and foods influenced by other ethnic groups in the city, such as South American *arepas*. Sausage and peppers are a constant, though, often served as hero sandwiches. San Gennaro festivals have expanded beyond Mulberry Street to the Bronx, Staten Island, and elsewhere, and festivals celebrating other saints are also held. Sausage and peppers are served nearly universally.

Although green peppers are common and often cheapest, it is because they are immature fruits and are harvested fastest. Almost all peppers are green until they ripen into varying shades of amber, yellow, red, purple, or mottled variations in between. Immature peppers are green because of chlorophyll in their skin.[53] As they ripen, other vitamins come to dominate, and those colors come through. The skin also imparts a bitter flavor[54] and usually is removed in cooking by scorching the skin and then enclosing the peppers in a bag, allowing the steam to separate the skin from the flesh.

In the south of Italy, mature chili peppers are hung to dry. These can be crushed, forming red pepper flakes, a common pizza topping and occasional substitute for fresh chilis. Crushed red pepper consists of a mix of no particular varieties of dried chili peppers crushed with seeds and all. These are not related to the red or pink pepper berries sometimes mixed in with gourmet black pepper. Those red peppercorns are not a pepper of any kind. Black pepper comes in just two colors: black and white. Like green and brown olives, black and white pepper actually come from the same plant, but black pepper is picked when the berries are green, and the white pepper is picked later, when the berries have turned from green to red.[55] Both have an outer shell that must be removed, usually by soaking in water.

Arrabbiata recipes sometimes call for dried pepper flakes, but pepperoncini pickled with vinegar are more commonly used. The vinegar adds a layer of flavor to the sauce. Pepperoncini often are yellow, but they are not banana peppers. Dried peppers are hung out in autumn after the harvest and can provide spice all year long as well, with the dried fruit crushed along with the seeds, where most of the heat resides. The Accademia Italiana della Cucina provides two variations for penne all'arrabbiata, both listing Lazio as the region of origin. One recipe contains prosciutto; the other does not.

There is a good bit of disagreement on the origins of the name *all'arrabbiata*. Food historian Diane Seed claims the sauce developed in the 1940s as a result of Italy's relationship with Libya. According to Seed, Italian soldiers interacting with Arabs were introduced to hot and peppery Arab cooking and developed a palate for spicy foods. The Libyan dish *mbekbka* is perhaps the nearest relation, a spicy tomato soup of pasta boiled in sauce with chili powder and turmeric. There are several problems with this hypothesis. First, Roman-style arrabbiata sauce contains pork, a food forbidden by Islam. Second, southern Italians and Arab populations had long-standing food pathways before the 1940s. Surely southerners would have been introduced to hot and spicy "Arab" food alongside the introduction of dried pasta. Those relationships between Sicily and Arabs existed even before peppers were imported from the new world.

The Italian pasta company La Rustichella presents an alternative. They claim the penne all'arrabbiata was created in the 1930s at the restaurant Alfredo alla Chiesa Nuova in Rome,[56] an establishment frequented by writers and poets. Arrabbiata sauce was a favorite of the Italian poet Carlo Alberto Salustri, who wrote under the pseudonym Trilussa,[57] and who reportedly frequented the restaurant.

More likely though, arrabbiata suffered the same indignity of carbonara and so many other sauces during the postwar period and was rechristened. The dishes lost their regional associations and gained occupational ones. Although this shift in usage is documented, the explanation as to why remains a mystery. The emergence of pasta alla arrabbiata corresponds with the disappearance of sugo al piccante, and so even though arrabbiata is only documented in the postwar period, it likely existed before that time.

Recipes for arrabbiata began appearing in the United States in the 1960s alongside the other Roman sauces in Italian restaurant menus. Despite the general availability, arrabbiata truly came into vogue around the turn of the millennium. In 2000, *SF Gate* taste-tested all the jarred arrabbiata sauces available—just five it could find at the time. When it followed up eight years later, the newspaper found more than fifteen. Today there are more than thirty brands offering an arrabbiata, representing a full spectrum of price points from jars imported from Italy to Walmart's house brand; the sauce has found its way to mainstream menus.

The Roman sauces represented a new era for red sauce America. Southern Italian cooking continued to dominate the conception of Italian American food in the United States for a few remaining years, but the more complicated sauces demonstrated red sauce was more than simply spaghetti and meatballs.

15

The Last Red Sauce

By the 1970s, the American public's conception of Italian food began to shift away from red sauce as other regional styles of cooking entered the American zeitgeist and fad diets encouraged lighter dinner meals. The pursuit of authenticity would further drive diners to seek alternatives to the Italian American food they were familiar with. Two final sauce preparations were added the red sauce repertoire during this period. Spaghetti alla puttanesca and penne alla vodka quickly became mainstays of Italian American cuisine, representing the final notes of an ethnic symphony of tomato-based, southern-influenced Italian food. Italian food would soon come to mean a very different kind of cooking in America.

Puttanesca sauce primarily refers to a spicy tomato sauce made from anchovies, black olives, capers, and garlic, with some recipes including hot peppers. Regional differences, however, mean *puttanesca* can refer to somewhat different sauces, and, in some instances, what is now generally considered puttanesca sauce has held other names. Italian American restaurants in particular likely served variations of the sauce under aliases. When the sauce first started appearing, restaurant reviews often raved about the puttanesca pasta dishes, and this may have led to a more universally recognized use of the term as competitors sought to benefit from the positive press.

Spaghetti is almost exclusively the pasta of choice for puttanesca sauce, although unlike many other Italian pasta dishes, there are no practical or methodical reasons for the decision.[1] The substitution of other shapes has no ill effect on the sauce. While the sauce contains tomatoes, the primary flavor here is savory umami from anchovies, black olives, and capers— three ingredients naturally filled with glutamate. Glutamate is the flavor identified as providing a sense described as savory. Tomatoes and parmigiana cheese also naturally have glutamate, but the addition of these other umami powerhouses make puttanesca sauce especially rich and fragrant.

A frequently repeated legend surrounding the origin of puttanesca is that the sauce served working girls in the Roman neighborhood of Trastevere. While tourism and gentrification have reinvented this neighborhood as a destination for nightlife, for many years the area had been considered a dangerous working-class ghetto. It also had a reputation for prostitutes, a legal industry in Italy during the midcentury. Puttanesca is rooted in the word *puttana*, an Italian word that can mean "tart" or "whore." The legend held that the sauce's quick preparation allowed sex workers a meal between customers without losing much time, because there is nothing a john wants more than the heavy stench of anchovies and garlic on the breath of his prostitute.

Another name for the sauce in certain periods is spaghetti alla *buona donna*, translated to mean "good women's spaghetti."[2] The brothels of Italy, state-owned institutions, were known as *case chiuse* (closed houses). The windows of the brothels were required to remain permanently shuttered as way of mitigating the intrusion of unsavory activity in the neighborhood.[3] The visitation and hiring of prostitutes was perfectly fine just as long as nobody could see it happening and the workers themselves remained ostracized from polite society. Along with the requirement to keep the house closed, the prostitutes faced restrictions on the hours they could leave the house.[4] These restrictions also limited when they could visit the market and, by extension, limited their access to fresh foods. These facts more accurately align with the legend that puttanesca sauce originated with these working women because the ingredients are shelf-stable products they could keep in their pantries. In this regard, puttanesca contradicts the main ethos of Italian cuisine to use the freshest locally available ingredients.

Nevertheless, puttanesca is a practical sauce. Some variations include tossing uncooked ingredients with the hot pasta and serving it at room temperature, potentially hours after preparing the dish. This variation might have lent credence to the myth that the sauce was a favorite of prostitutes, since a woman called to action midway through cooking her dinner could let it sit without ruining the dish. Despite the fanciful and delightful tale, prostitute's pasta seems highly unlikely. The closed houses shut down in the 1950s, some years before the sauce began to achieve any kind of notoriety.

The more credible origin story of puttanesca sauce begins on the island of Ischia. Ischia sits just off the coast of Naples, less famous perhaps than nearby Capri, but no less beautiful. Today, Ischia has gained fame as the summer destination of Elena Ferrante's heroines in her Neapolitan novels, and Americans might also recognize the island from scenes in the film version of *The Talented Mr. Ripley*, employed as the stunning location for many of the film's beach and yacht scenes. Otherwise, Ischia has remained a lesser-known destination except to local tourists. At the time of puttanesca's emergence, Ischia was even more remote than it is today, and the island attracted artists and free spirits. It's these artistic misfits who are responsible for inventing the puttanesca sauce during a long night of heavy drinking.

Early in the 1950s, painter Eduardo Maria Colucci summered in a small house on the island. Colucci was a native of Ischia, and, born in 1900, Colucci's primary influence was art styles of the 1920s. He was not especially prolific as an artist but was recognized as a skilled practitioner. Summers on Ischia in the 1950s passed with a bohemian vibe. Several varying accounts of the creation of puttanesca mention an assortment of creative guests attending a party Colucci had organized. On the night puttanesca supposedly came into existence, Colucci had been offering his friends wine and apertivo drinks—one can imagine history may have downplayed how many drinks they had—when his now-hungry guests demanded dinner. The problem, it seems, was Colucci had very little food in his house. He had only *puttanata*, or shit, to toss with pasta. Here might well be the origin of the whore's spaghetti: while *puttana* translates to "tart" or "prostitute," *puttanesco* translates to "whoreish," and *puttanata* translates to "fuck up."[5] The sauce might very well be the "shit" sauce or the "fuck up" sauce, rather than the prostitute sauce. To feed his friends, Colucci searched his pantry and concocted a spaghetti dish to feed the ravenous guests. The mixture of garlic, anchovies, capers, olives, and tomatoes proved pleasing. This ingredient combination sometimes goes by the name "marinara"; however, Colucci preferred the name puttanesca.[6] Colucci's nephew, Sandro Petti, in attendance that evening, cooked at the Ischia restaurant Rangio Fellone, where spaghetti alla puttanesca was introduced commercially.

In some variations of the story, Sandro Petti invented the dish rather than his more famous uncle. Petti, who eventually would become a respected architect, has claimed credit for the sauce.[7] Petti's story is similar to Colucci's, but it features Petti's drunk friends rather than Colucci's. According to this version, his inebriated friends showed up at the restaurant and demanded dinner. Since Petti had been in the process of closing the restaurant, he had nothing to offer his pals except leftovers—the puttanata.

His friends insisted Petti feed them, and so he eventually gave in, creating suga alla puttanesca. Proving a successful dish, Petti then introduced the sauce to the restaurant menu.[8] There remains the possibility that Petti, the professional cook, actually cooked the spaghetti for the drunken artists on the night puttanesca reportedly was invented at Colucci's house, and the effects of time and memory have changed the details. Either way, Petti is almost certainly the conduit to Rangio Fellone's menu. To bolster his claim, Petti cites a reprimand from the local bishop, Ernesto De Laurentiis, who chastised him for calling the pasta dish "shit spaghetti." De Laurentiis passed away in 1956,[9] suggesting the sauce had its origins before then.

The puttanesca story would be all too simple if that's where it ended. Spaghetti alla puttanesca makes an appearance in the 1961 novel *Ferito a morte*, by Raffaele La Capria. He describes the "spaghetti alla puttanesca" as a wonderful sauce made in Siracusa,[10] a city in the south of Sicily. The novel won the Premio Strega prize that year, an annual prize awarded to Italian novels. The narrative follows several young men partying on the island of Capri and Ischia—and the inclusion of puttanesca might very well have been a way of making the book feel contemporary or mocking the wealthy young men depicted in it. La Capria reportedly began writing the novel as early as 1953, shortly after publishing his debut. Born in Naples, La Capria also fits the profile of the kind of bohemian artist who summered on Ischia and traveled in the circles with artists like Colucci. The dates align, so that he could have borrowed the name spaghetti alla puttanesca after Colucci or Petti "invented" (or renamed) the sauce.

Whether or not La Capria ate puttanesca on Ischia, his reference might offer another clue to the true origins of the sauce. His description of puttanesca as a sauce from Siracusa, a city on the eastern shore of Sicily, offers a starting point. Ada Boni's *Talisman* cookbook also contains a recipe, spaghetti Syracuse style. Boni's recipe includes eggplant, absent from most puttanesca recipes, but otherwise offers a similar composition with olives, anchovies, and capers. The sudden emergence of this dish might owe less to a drunken night of a group of artists than it does the simple renaming a more traditional pasta sauce, as happened with carbonara, arrabbiata, and numerous other regional dishes in the postwar period. Perhaps, then, puttanesca's late arrival resulted from the fact that it was merely the renaming of an existing recipe. Pellegrino Artusi even provides a similarly composed sauce as far back as 1891 known as salsa del *papa*. The sauce, it is noted, is not named for the pope, as a direct translation suggests,[11] but the composition is similar to suga alla Siracusa. That so many similar recipes share ingredients but have different names highlights how a seemingly new sauce may appear from nowhere through a simple rebranding.

Suga alla Siracusa and spaghetti alla puttanesca share a flavor profile common in Sicilian pasta dishes. Another, very similar sauce, suga alla *norma*, first came about in the nineteenth century and consists of tomatoes, eggplant, onions, and salted ricotta, with some variation regarding whether the eggplant is fried. The preparation is popular in Catania, a city in eastern Sicily,[12] but only became popular in the United States very recently despite the large number of Sicilian immigrants. A common belief is the dish takes its name from the heroine of Vincenzo Bellini's opera by the same name. Supposedly, friends of the composer took to calling things they enjoyed *una vera Norma*, meaning "a real Norma."[13] The name stuck to the pasta dish.

This legend is disputed by the pasta scholar Oretta Zanini de Vita. According to Zanini de Vita, the name comes from two writers eating the pasta for lunch. Marietta Martoglio, wife of the poet Nino Martoglio, served pasta alla norma to their guest, the actor Angelo Musco. Musco loved it and declared the sauce a marvel.[14] In dialect, *marvel* is pronounced *norma*, and thus spaghetti alla norma is spaghetti in the way that is marvelous.

Another variation of this same story reversed the inventor. In this alternative telling, Musco and Martoglio were dining together around 1920 at a house on Via Etnea in Catania. In this version, it was not Martoglio's house but the house of Musco's family. The pasta dish was served. Martoglio burst out a compliment to Musco's sister-in-law declaring a vera norma (a real marvel).[15] This variation follows the same phrasing as the one supposedly used by Bellini's friends, although it is possible that Martoglio, as a writer, helped popularize the name spaghetti alla norma. Whether or not the pasta is named for being marvelous or for Bellini's opera, when *Norma* debuted in 1831, the opera featured a soprano by the name of Giuditta Pasta.[16] Unlike spaghetti alla puttanesca, pasta alla norma only grew popular in the United States well after red sauce cuisine had been displaced by a modern interpretation of Italian cuisine. The relentless pursuit of authentic regional cuisines led chefs back to southern cuisine, seeking new, classic recipes to introduce, offering norma as an authentic Sicilian pasta dish.

Puttanesca, however, spread outward from Italy in the 1960s. The *Observer of London* highlights the sauce in 1967 and notes that *putto* is a dialect word from Tuscany, meaning spicy or hot.[17] Hot peppers are often added to the dish, explaining the linguistic link. The arrival of puttanesca in the United States is slightly later. *Gourmet* magazine published a spaghetti alla Siracusa recipe in 1971. Puttanesca appears on menus at least as early as 1972, when the *New York Times* cited the dish in a review of Trattoria da Alfredo, a West Village eatery. New York's Channel 5 news broadcast a spaghetti puttanesca recipe in 1974, and it subsequently was published in the *News of Paterson*, a newspaper serving a New Jersey neighborhood with many ethnically Italian residents.[18] Puttanesca also appears as two distinct recipes in the 1983 book *Pasta and Rice Italian Style*, by Efrem Funghi Calingaert and Jacquelyn Days Serwer, the wives of American diplomats serving in Rome. The collection is described as a compilation from their friends, neighbors, and local restaurants. Like the New York–focused *Where to Dine in Thirty-Nine* or the Chicago guidebook featuring a carbonara recipe, the collection depicts a snapshot of Italian cuisine in a specific time and place.

Today, puttanesca regularly can be found on the menus of red sauce joints. The sauce represents a transitional phase in American dining between the old-style, southern-influenced restaurants of the first- and second-generation immigrants and more modern ideas of Italian food in America. It shows an attempt to modernize those older restaurants, even if only by refreshing the name of a traditional pasta preparation. Jarred versions of puttanesca are readily available in American grocery stores under a variety of brand names, competing alongside imported versions. Puttanesca, then, is a sauce with a noodle in both worlds: classic red sauce and authentic Italian. In either case, the legend of puttanesca as the sauce of prostitutes appears to be merely a gimmick.

During the same timeframe, penne alla vodka also emerged as a transitional dish, straddling the red sauce traditions of heavy, tomato-based sauces even while the conception of Italian food modernized in America. Penne is to vodka sauce what spaghetti is to meatballs—while frequently paired, any shape, especially circular rings, can convey the creamy, pink sauce. The origins of the sauce have been long disputed, even as the popularity of vodka sauce has grown. The sauce begins with a tomato base and combines onions, crushed red pepper, and garlic, along with the two essential ingredients—cream and vodka—creating a slightly sweet, often spicy or tangy flavor, and the color may vary from pink to orange, depending on the quantity of cream.

The inclusion of vodka in an Italian sauce might seem an odd addition given how rarely vodka plays into the culture generally. Vodka only first appeared in Italian discos in the 1970s.[19] The sudden presence of vodka and the view that it was a foreign spirit might have fueled conspiracies that the sauce's origin was sponsored by a Russian vodka company. The legend claims that a vodka company sponsored chefs to devise recipes including the alcohol as a way to normalize and promote the drink, but there seems little evidence that this is the case.

Although vodka was a new ingredient, grappa, the caustic alcohol produced from fermenting the skins of grapes, has been part of cooking long before the invention of pasta alla vodka. Grappa is a descendent of fig brandy,[20] likely another invention of Arab people who occupied parts of Italy. Although grappa varieties appear anywhere wine grapes are grown, it is consumed largely in the north.[21] Cooking with grappa to enhance flavors in some dishes is common. The stranger part of alla vodka sauce for Italians is the combination of tomatoes and cream. Tomatoes play a heavy role primarily in southern Italian cuisine, while cream and dairy products more generally are northern, and the combination of those ingredients is rare anywhere, with both northern and southern Italians believing in the purity of their ingredients. Tomatoes and cream should each remain unsullied by the addition of the other.[22] In this sense, penne alla vodka is truly Italian American, a fusion of the two halves of Italy created in the new world, and yet this assessment offers little to identify the creation.

The magic of vodka sauce stems from the vodka itself. Alcohol is added to foods to enhance flavor, and this is especially true with tomatoes. Very little of what we think of as flavor is actually owed to what we can taste. Some dishes, like puttanesca, load up on umami, which, like saltiness and sweetness, our tongues respond to directly. What we think of as food flavor though is often more of what we can smell, relying on aromatics to activate the sense. The compounds in foods—naturally occurring chemicals—that produce scents are not all equal. These compounds dissolve differently in fat and water. The presence of alcohol in a dish helps intensify flavors by dissolving compounds and transferring them to olfactory senses. In the case of vodka sauce, fat from the cream carries fat-soluble aromatics, and the alcohol carries water-soluble aromatics, creating twice as many vectors to double the impact of taste and enhancing the flavor of the tomato and the other ingredients. Vodka is particularly suited to the task, as it generally is flavorless, unlike grappa, an alcohol that has a strong and often unpleasant flavor.

Penne alla vodka has had numerous sightings in Italy, including Rome's Taverna Flavia,[23] known as a destination for celebrities and for serving the cast of Elizabeth Taylor's *Cleopatra* in the early 1960s. It has since closed. In Bologna, the restaurant Dante has been credited as serving the dish as a late-night offering for disco club partiers. Efrem Funghi Calingaert and Jacquelyn Days Serwer's *Pasta and Rice Italian Style* includes two vodka sauce recipes. A contemporary review notes some time had passed between when their husbands had been stationed in Italy and the completion of the book in 1983. In addition to a penne alla vodka *rosse*, with a presumably pinkish color, they included an all-white vodka cream sauce.[24] The book notes the white vodka recipe originates from a dear friend known for dinner parties, but it provides little else in the way of origins.

An American chef has long claimed authorship of penne alla vodka, insisting his variation, known as penne alla Russia, was the original vodka sauce pasta. The Italian-born Luigi Franzese prepared penne alla Russia tableside at Orsini's, a famed New York City restaurant, beginning around 1979.[25] Around this time, pasta with vodka sauce became the latest fad food to strike New York City, with copies of the dish proliferating at restaurants across the tri-state region. A 1981 review of Joanna, located on 18th Street in Manhattan, refers to the dish as penne alla vodka,[26] and reviews of restaurants on Long Island indicate it was a popular dish.[27]

The most compelling evidence supporting Luigi Franzese's claim may have been lost. Television host Joe Franklin had been a frequent diner at Orsini's and invited Luigi Franzese on television to discuss the dish's creation. Franklin hosted more than 300,000 guests in his career,[28] but the tape of Franzese appears lost forever. The owner of Orsini's, Armando Orsini, was a popular restauranteur, successful in his business, operating the 56th Street restaurant for four decades. While Armando's obituary doesn't mention penne alla vodka, it does note that Elizabeth Taylor dined at his restaurant.[29] This connection is likely a mere coincidence.

Despite all these claims, a dish named penne alla vodka can be tied to another midtown New York restaurant, Fontana di Trevi, more than a decade before Franzese is said to have added alla Russia to the menu at Orsini's. Armando Mei is credited in 1967 with creating a dish made with a sauce fortified with vodka, and unlike other versions, it was known as penne alla vodka.[30] Mei had been chef at Fontana di Trevi for more than a decade and was previously awarded a silver medal by the Italian government recognizing his resistance work during the Second World War.[31] He had been captured by the Germans and sentenced to death before the liberation by American soldiers. Fontana di Trevi was located on 57th Street in Manhattan, just a few blocks from Orsini's on 56th Street.

The great irony of penne alla Russia or penne alla vodka is that many Russians are unaware of the dish. Italian-style pastas have only recently taken off in the country. Not wanting to miss a marketing opportunity, the Italian industry group *Associazione delle Industrie del Dolce e della Pasta Italiane* hosted World Pasta Day in 2016 in Moscow, hoping to sell more Italian pasta to Russians. The organization even invited Russian celebrity chef Valentino Bontempi, who used the opportunity to introduce a version of vodka sauce garnished with caviar.[32]

The most common variation on the traditional vodka sauce includes salted pork like pancetta, guanciale, ham, or bacon tossed in with the pasta. In rarer variations, cream is excluded, leaving a darker sauce, although most recipes call for adding enough cream to lighten the sauce. Another frequent variation in the recipe is in the spice level, varying from mild sweet paprika to whole chili peppers. The sauce combination has proven so popular that it even now regularly tops pizzas.

The rapid spread of pasta alla vodka, first across New York–area restaurants and then throughout red sauce restaurants nationwide, shows consumers' desire for alternatives to the traditional red sauce menu. The era of the red sauce restaurant had already begun declining, losing out to newer-style restaurants promising northern Italian food. Penne alla vodka straddled the line between traditional, southern-style tomato sauce pastas and fresh, modern flavors arriving just as Americans started to have new ideas about Italian food and what it meant to be authentic.

16

❖ ❖

The Fall of Rome

Red sauce transitioned from the food of a foreign ethnic community into a symbol of the American empire during the latter half of the twentieth century. Recipes inspired by southern Italian tomato sauces had become "essentially classless parts of the national diet."[1] As this shift happened, a new conception of Italian food grew popular. Most Americans will recognize this shift as the rise of northern Italian recipes, although this term is as much a marketing tool than an accurate description of the shifting influences on Italian food in America.

Following the war, the patterns of Italian immigration changed significantly. Even before the war, immigration had begun to taper off as changes in laws made it more difficult. But in the years after it, Italian emigration shifted, with the postwar period seeing a decline of southern Italians, who had previously dominated since the 1880s. This change would eventually have a long-term impact on the perception of Italian cuisine in America.

Certainly, red sauce owes much of its legacy to southern cuisine and the direct link to the immigrants arriving from those regions, but it would be inaccurate to describe the changes that began in the 1970s as entirely a northern influence. A renewed interest in quality foods rather than convenience foods took hold in America. General food movements led by restaurateurs like Alice Waters, and a growing interest in local and organic foods, coincided with the shift away from red sauce. Consumers began to see those recipes as an old-fashioned way of eating. The qualities of richness and the celebration of wealth and luxury embraced by Italian immigrants also meant these foods contradicted an emerging ethos of lighter, fresher, seasonal, and local foods, all qualities that dovetailed with the push toward what became known as authentic Italian cuisine.

First, Marcella Hazan published her pair of influential cookbooks, beginning in 1973 with *The Classic Italian Cook Book.* Hazan is often compared to Julia Child, author of *Mastering the Art of French Cooking.* If Child introduced domestic American cooks to French cooking methods, Hazan introduced them to Italian cooking techniques. Both women introduced traditionally European cooking styles into a domestic setting at a time when American domestic cooks were rejecting the processed and precooked convenience foods of the immediate postwar period. Hazan followed up the 1973 book with *More Classic Italian Cooking*, later collecting the two into a single volume (*Essentials of Classic Italian Cooking*), which established her as a significant, influential food writer and cook. Both these books primarily focus on recipes from northern regions of Italy and are often credited as the introduction of northern cuisine to America.[2] Hazan, a native of Emilia-Romagna (a decidedly northern province), had never liked American food.

Hazan and her husband Victor moved to New York in the 1950s. She held a doctorate in biology but quit her job in the lab to teach cooking classes.[3] Victor attempted to publicize the classes by having them included in a list published by the *New York Times*. The list published without Hazan's class, but Craig Claiborne, the food writer, contacted Marcella. After a luncheon at Hazan's apartment, Claiborne published one of her recipes. That luncheon set in motion a major change for Marcella Hazan's career[4] and for the way Americans viewed Italian food.

Ironically, what Hazan is perhaps best known for is a simple tomato sauce, a smooth, red sauce equally at home in Italian American traditions as well as modern northern styles. Hazan Sauce, as it is colloquially known, consists merely of tomatoes, butter, and an onion and first appeared in *The Classic Italian Cook Book.* The original published version includes a quarter teaspoon of sugar missing in the later version, published in the current edition. The recipe manages to merge the tomatoes' acidic tang with buttery creaminess and sugars from the onion. Although Hazan gagged at ketchup,[5] her simple tomato sauce is remarkably similar to a Depression-era tomato sauce combination popularized in America. Ketchup and butter heated together provided many poorer Americans with their first taste of an Italian-inspired spaghetti sauce.

This ketchup-based sauce also gained renewed notoriety after being highlighted in the reality show *Here Comes Honey Boo Boo*. During a 2012 episode of the reality show, "Mama" June prepares a family meal she calls "sketti." The three-ingredient recipe of spaghetti, ketchup, and margarine took the blogsphere by storm. A food culture obsessed with authenticity found it hard to comprehend such base ingredients being combined into a spaghetti and pasta dish. Yet not only does Mama June explain that she was raised on sketti, but she also jokes that it is a family recipe.[6] Butter and ketchup sauce should not be dismissed out of hand as inauthentic—while it may have more added sugar and a tang of vinegar, the butter-ketchup sauce offered Americans a low-stakes and inexpensive way to participate in red sauce cuisine. And again, the ingredient list is not all that different from Hazan's simple and "authentic" Italian tomato sauce.

Hazan's tomato sauce isn't the only the only recipe that reimagines staples of the red sauce traditions, with her collection including recipes for Bolognese sauce, pizza Margherita, and lasagna. But she presented a new way of thinking about Italian food and encouraged eating local, in-season vegetables and fresh-made pasta. Her first book entered into American culture at the same time Italian American cuisine was beginning to evolve beyond red sauce. Consumers appreciated alternatives to heavy celebration dishes they had grown up knowing as Italian. By the late 1970s, many red sauce Italian trattorias were marketing themselves as "northern" Italian restaurants to distinguish their menus from the expected Italian American menus.

Lidia Bastianich, another early adopter of "northern" Italian cuisine, opened her first restaurant in Queens, New York, in 1971. Bastianich was born in Istria, in the region of Trieste, the northeastern area of Italy near Croatia, Slovenia, and Austria. The Italian foods from these areas show eastern and northern European influence. Bastianich experimented with Istrian recipes from her grandmother.[7] In 1981, she and her husband opened Felidia in Manhattan, embracing modern Italian dining. In 1979, Adi Giovanetti opened Il Nido, a Tuscan-inspired restaurant,[8] and soon New York City became the epicenter of anti-southern Italian cooking.

Bastianich's influence continued to grow, and in 1998 she launched a PBS cooking show, *Lidia's Italian Table*, promoting non–red sauce recipes from across Italy. Her son, Joe Bastianich, also entered into the family business, and together they have partnered with chef Mario Batali to open such famed restaurants as Babbo, Lupa, Esca, Otto, and Del Posto.[9] Batali has since been removed in name from these businesses following allegations of sexual harassment.[10] But Batali and Bastianich's partnerships have had a massive influence on the American consumer's understanding of modern Italian food, one where red sauce is relegated to antiquated status.

Both Hazan and Bastianich represent a shift in the latter half of the twentieth century. Overall, the number of Italian immigrants in the postwar period was relatively small in comparison to the great waves at the beginning of the twentieth century, but the people who came in the latter half represented a more varied and broader spectrum of the peninsula. The earlier waves of southern immigrants had also started to disperse beyond the immigrant enclaves they first lived in. They had grown wealthier in subsequent generations, and just as spaghetti and meatballs became American, so had ethnic Italians. They evolved from an insular, ethnic community into just another subset of White Americans. And like the other White Americans, the Italians left the urban centers during the period of White flight, many leaving behind the red sauce joints of their forefathers. Italians embraced their new status in the majority, fleeing for the suburbs and abandoning the urban neighborhoods they had once defined. Other ethnic minorities and immigrant groups replaced them in many places, often to the disappointment of older Italians who remained.

The abandonment of the city core changed the Little Italy neighborhoods profoundly. Instead of existing as living communities of multigenerational families with vibrant neighborhoods filled with essential services, they were distilled into the essence of ethnicity. Like the first Italian restaurants reflecting an invented image of the country the immigrant owners departed, now the Little Italy neighborhoods became a rarefied reflection of the neighborhoods they had once been. The districts commercialized their history, exploiting their connections to the past to sell cannoli and heaping plates of spaghetti. The neighborhood shops and services have been replaced by specialty food stores and restaurants.[11]

The last of the red sauce restaurants today exist in the shadow of the formerly lively communities, visited on weekends by elderly first- or second-generation immigrants. The restaurants in these neighborhoods continue to serve Italian American red sauce even while employing staff born in Italy and unfamiliar with American red sauce cuisine. These last outposts are being winnowed away year after year by higher rents driven by globalization and renewed interest in urban living. Gentrification is forcing out the old ethnic strongholds. Further hurting their financials is the modern bourgeois desire to seek out authentic Italian cuisine and an authentic Italy-Italian experience. Young and wealthy, the new bohemians shun the red sauce joint, believing, falsely, that the menus somehow betray an authentic Italian American experience. The remaining restaurants in places like Manhattan's Little Italy survive with an appeal to tourists, although they are scorned for it.

Also conspiring against red sauce cuisine was the publication of the Seven Countries study in 1978. The study began in the 1950s, tracking the diets and relative health of people from seven nations. The early results—follow-ups continued every five years—suggested that the diets associated with countries along the Mediterranean Sea might have health benefits leading to longevity. The study's results ended up regurgitated by the mainstream media as the Mediterranean Diet. The fad embraced olive oil, fish, and vegetables as panaceas for the growing American waistline.

The Seven Countries Study, by extolling the virtues of the Mediterranean diet, led Americans to seek out pasta dishes, but not necessarily heavy red sauce. Traditional red sauce restaurants tried to adapt. The postwar additions to menus of items like spaghetti alla puttanesca can be seen as a last-gasp effort by these restauranteurs, accustomed to serving stalwarts like spaghetti and meatballs and veal parmigiana, to change with the times. Despite these additions, restaurants featuring food branded as northern Italian or authentic Italian began replacing historically Italian American restaurants in the final decades of the twentieth century. After all, so many Italian American dishes were now readily available on grocery store shelves and in banal locations like mall food courts, airport waiting lounges, and highway rest areas; it became difficult to distinguish pizza or a meatball parmigiana sandwich as an ethnic food.

Authentic Italian food appeared to fit within the framework of a healthy Mediterranean Diet. These newly imported dishes embraced their humble origins, contrasting red sauce creations that aspired to replicate the food of the wealthy. And because chefs were often marketing these northern dishes to consumers concerned about health, they curated menus to reflect those desires. This shifting demand coincided with the rising interest in authentic cuisine, and restaurants latched onto "northern" Italian styles to take advantage of shifting consumer desires.

If there was a definitive end of the red sauce era, it was the invention of pasta primavera, a distinctly New York City original with an Italian name created for a French restaurant. Pasta primavera combines numerous vegetables, including broccoli, zucchini, asparagus, peas, mushrooms, fresh tomatoes, and garlic, along with chicken stock, butter, cream, and parmigiana cheese. The original pasta primavera premiered on the menu of Le Cirque, a famed upscale New York eatery that opened in 1974. The dish was a sensation. Restaurant owner Sirio Maccioni and chef Jean Vergnes served it to Craig Claiborne at his home in East Hampton,[12] and soon after

Claiborne featured it in the *New York Times Magazine*, the dish became a widely discussed conversation topic across New York City.[13]

The recipe for pasta primavera has its origins in New York, although several people are responsible for creating the final dish served at Le Cirque. In one version of the story, Ed Giobbi first cooked a version of the dish for Le Cirque's owner Sirio Maccioni and chef Jean Vergnes when the two visited Giobbi's kitchen in Katonah, New York. Giobbi claims the inspiration for the pasta came from his days as a student in Florence eating a pasta dish with fresh springtime vegetables.[14] Vergnes insists he reimagined the Giobbi's dish, adding French-influenced touches like cream. Maccioni's wife also is said to have invented the recipe by using the leftover vegetables remaining at the end of their vacation.[15] And like other fad foods that would follow in the years to come (cronuts come to mind), imitators began popping up on menus across the city. Imposter versions of Le Cirque's pasta dish permeated throughout the region, assuming an Italian identity in the process.

The decline of red sauce restaurants had already begun, but pasta primavera infiltrating Italian restaurant menus was the ultimate signal that the tomato sauce era was over. The primavera, an Italian-style pasta dish served at a predominantly French restaurant, helped awaken the idea of a different kind of Italian American cuisine, and—laden with fresh spring vegetables, including fresh tomatoes—it showed a new way.

In the final decades of the twentieth century, red sauce cuisine had started to look like a relic. The interiors with once-popular red-checked tablecloths and straw-wrapped Chianti bottles were being updated with modern design, and kitchens began serving food drawing on inspiration from other regions and provinces than the ones that had influenced red sauce over the previous century. The desire to reinvent ethnically Italian cuisine also coincided with the desire for authenticity, an arguably incompatible desire.

17

❖ ❖

The Search for Authenticity

The search for authenticity is linked directly to the commodification of Italian American identity as that ethnic identity melted into American mainstream culture. Pizzerias transitioned from serving ethnic enclaves into national fast-food chains. Lasagna moved from nonna's oven to supermarket freezers. And even the traditional red sauce joint ended up commodified and exploited by international restaurant groups. The desire for authentic markers of identity stems from the homogenization of Italian American culture and commercialization of identity largely created by marketing, from the perfect red tomato to red-checkered tablecloths. As Italian American food grew into a profitable enterprise, the quality of the food declined, further fueling a desire to seek out authentic experiences.

Early examples of commodification included Enrico Caruso lending his name to the spaghetti house chain and a full line of domestic products like olive oil. The Chef Boyardee brand made eating spaghetti and meatballs in the postwar era as simple as opening a can. But as spaghetti and tomato sauce became more widely available, Italian American ethnic identity faded. If everyone could have a little Italian spaghetti, then it wasn't something special.

The acquisition of Leone's by Restaurant Associates exemplifies this declining identity. The conglomerate ran coffee shops and airport restaurants before the acquisition, operating Newark Airport's The Newarker at the dawn of the jet age. The Newarker earned some credibility and fame for serving fine-dining fare at the burgeoning transportation hub, but Leone's proved the real financial winner. Leone's was earning the group almost $4 million a year at the time, and, along with the Four Seasons in the new Seagram building, it had become a company cash cow.[1] Leone's offered a multicourse meal at an affordable price,[2] taking advantage of the famous Leone's brand, appealing to customers in the same way earlier Italian American eateries did—by offering good value. Milking the cash cow cost the restaurant some of its charm. The restaurant continued its focus on providing large quantities of food at a good value, with seven-course prix fixe meals, but it eventually closed, citing the high rents.[3]

Restaurant Associates also embraced a new kind of Italian food with Trattoria. Trattoria joined two other Restaurant Associates properties in the Pan Am building constructed over Grand Central Terminal. They shared a common kitchen on the fifty-ninth floor of the tower, and although Trattoria promised Italian food, it rejected the traditional red sauce restaurant approach. The trattoria concept was intended to replicate the casual restaurants in actual Italian cities.[4] While Mamma Leone's represented the old-style red sauce joint, Trattoria showed the possibility of a different kind of Italian food.

As the American consumer grew wealthier and more suburban, the growth of what eventually became the fast-casual restaurant changed the perception of Italian cuisine forever. National chains would create a standard dining experience dictating how Americans perceived the one-time ethnic cuisine. In 1981, global restaurant chain Olive Garden opened its first store. It was soon followed by other competitors like Romano's Macaroni Grill, Johnny Carino's, Carrabba's, Bertucci's, and Buca di Beppo. These restaurants did not emerge from ethnic Little Italy neighborhoods, nor from immigrant Italian Americans, and yet they did alter Italian American cuisine by turning it into universal, middle-class dining experience with standardized recipes, and they did for Italian American food what McDonald's did for cheeseburgers.

The primary appeal of Olive Garden was cheap pasta, not necessarily good pasta. A regular promotion of the chain was some variation on the theme of "never-ending pasta." As promised, the promotion allowed customers unlimited servings on pasta dishes slathered in their trademarked sauces, often adulterations of traditional red sauce recipes. The success of the program even led the chain to offer never-ending pasta passes to encourage repeat offenders during the period of the promotion, and just in case that was not enough pasta, the chain also offered lifetime passes. Never-ending pasta paired well with the unlimited breadsticks, another marketing feature offering customers good value. Unlimited breadsticks helped make Olive Garden famous, and the Starboard Value presentation drew attention to the fact that these breadsticks often ended up wasted when consumers failed to finish them. Breadsticks were a major sticking point, actually, of the report, and headline-grabbing click-bait for news outlets writing about the presentation. Servers brought too many of the unlimited breadsticks to tables, leading to cold breadsticks, and since cold breadsticks were virtually inedible, the diners asked for even more baskets of bread. In many ways, this emphasis on value over quality was a hallmark of Italian American dining, since even early, independent red sauce restaurants were often known for the abundant portions and low prices.

Olive Garden launched during a period when Americans began eating out more, and formulaic restaurants satisfied a middle-class desire for a dining experience more formal than a fast-food chain or pizzeria but more casual than white-linen service. Italian American food easily fit that description, as it had always been a value-conscious cuisine. Olive Garden and competitors quickly blanketed the United States with outlets.

Authenticity became an increasingly important trait as commodified ethnic offerings saturated the market. Phil Romano, founder of Romano's Macaroni Grill, a major competitor of Olive Garden, focused on the concept of authenticity as a way of differentiating the brands. In his autobiography, Romano argues he believed that, as an Italian American, he could better replicate a more authentic Italian American experience than the Olive Garden, a corporation inventing a concept in a marketing lab.[5] And yet the idea of authenticity was relatively inauthentic. Romano built his career inventing restaurant concepts and selling them off as successful businesses. He's also responsible for enduring brands like Fuddruckers, the casual hamburger restaurant, as well as Spageddies, which would eventually become Johnny Carino's Italian Kitchen. The success Romano had with building an empire was less about the food, though, and more about the marketing. Rarely does he even describe serving the best food, instead bragging about unique and innovative promotional tools he invented.

Authenticity, then, was nothing more than another marketing ploy. When Romano developed the Mexican concept restaurant Nachomama, the approach was not to re-create anything specific to the Mexican experience. Instead, Romano wanted to create an experience more like the American idea of Mexico than the actual country of Mexico.[6] The same is true of his Macaroni Grill, emanating the vibes of authenticity as a manufactured product. Italian American red sauce was an invention of ethnic immigrants in America, now commodified into a national American food, and yet the same recipes were marketed as authentically Italian by Romano. According to Romano, when he launched the Macaroni Grill, his Italian mother didn't even like the food. By comparison, the first restaurant he opened decades earlier, the Gladiator, relied on his mother's, aunt's and uncle's old Italian recipes—offering spaghetti and meatball sandwiches. Romano failed to recognize the authenticity of these recipes, confusing Italian American food as simply American food. Macaroni Grill, like the other faux Italian, casual-dining restaurants of the era, mixed and matched regional Italian dishes alongside red-sauce recipes, eliminating any ethnic or regional distinction. This authenticity was not unlike Starboard Value's research team recommending a vegetarian Bolognese spaghetti as an authentic Italian dish for Olive Garden.

When places like Olive Garden and Macaroni Grill created commodity dining experiences, it only encouraged customers to seek authentic food, and at first this desire meant abandoning red sauce. Yet Olive Garden is not more or less authentic than family-operated Italian American red sauce joints. Olive Garden produced a series of commercials bragging about its "Culinary Institute of Tuscany," where employees trained to prepare their authentic Italian food. Since then, there have been accusations that the institute was nothing more than a hotel rented for the purposes of fulfilling the marketing department's claims, and employees essentially enjoyed a free vacation with very little actual kitchen time.[7]

Chain restaurants were not the only ones promising authentic Italian experiences. The call for authenticity was amplified by the introduction of TV Food Network, now branded as Food Network. Launched in 1993, the new cable channel reinvented the celebrity chef as not just a cook but also a television personality. At first, the network drew on a library of shows, including Julia Child's series from WGBH, but eventually it developed original programming and, in the process, created a new breed of celebrity chef. They extolled the virtues of "real" Italian food in contrast to the traditional Italian American red sauce. Mario Batali, among others like Giada De Laurentiis, instructed Americans on Italian alternatives to spaghetti and meatballs, veal parmigiana, and penne alla vodka. Batali (who is now discredited for his harassment of women) presented his menus as genuine Italian cooking learned in kitchens of northern Italy, and yet many of his popular dishes were actually inspired by southern recipes. For many of these projects, he was partnered with Joe Bastianich. The narrative reflects the same tenor of the Olive Garden's marketing of the Culinary Institute of Tuscany.

The idea of authentic Italian cuisine so saturated the American dining public that it spilled over into other cuisines. French restaurants reflected these changes in their menus by substituting olive oil for butter, using garlic instead of shallots, and adding tomatoes and basil.[8] Demand for Italian cuisine has grown, displacing traditional French restaurants, but also leaving behind Italian American cuisine.

The demand for authenticity persists. High-end, Michelin-starred Italian restaurants and fast-casual national chains share a common marketing narrative. Influencers further fuel the desire for the genuine by posting highly curated conceptions of authentic food to Instagram and other social media. Click-bait journalism feeds on artificial feuds like those created by the mayor of Amatrice defending the reputation of authentic amatriciana sauce. But does anyone need the Association of the True Neapolitan Pizza to tell us what is good, what is delicious, what is pizza? Perhaps the only problem with red sauce is the lack of champions for it as authentic, as a genuine example of ethnic, immigrant food.

Philip Romano did return to red sauce. He formed a partnership with Il Mulino, a family run, high-end red sauce restaurant based in New York City. The original restaurant opened in 1981 in the West Village,[9] a formerly ethnic immigrant neighborhood now known as the backyard of New York's celebrities. Il Mulino has attracted high-profile diners, including then-president Barack Obama, former president Bill Clinton,[10] A-Rod, and JLo. Romano partnered to open copies of Il Mulino across the country, in other high-profile locations, expanding in New York City, opening in WASPy destinations like the Hamptons, but also Las Vegas and Boca Raton. Perhaps the final chapter on red sauce still hasn't been written.

18

❖ ❖

The Red Sauce Renaissance

An Epilogue

I had just written a draft of the chapter on veal parmigiana when I discovered Trattoria Spaghetto had experienced the fate of so many red sauce joints in New York City. Brown paper covered the windows, and a small, typed sign on the door announced the closing. Writing the chapter had left me longing for a veal parmigiana, and I could think of no better place to order one. I was heartbroken.

Other classic New York red sauce restaurants, though, have seen a resurgence. Manhattan's Forlini's, a red sauce restaurant operating since 1956, hosted a *Vogue* magazine–sponsored Met Gala Party in 2018.[1] The hashtag #SpaghettiandMetballs trended, and the restaurant has been overwhelmed with influencers and trendsetters. The same has happened to Brooklyn red sauce stalwart Bamonte's. Located in the Little Italy of Williamsburg, Brooklyn, Bamonte's has operated since 1900, first as Liberty Hall before transitioning into the current restaurant.[2] It has seen an uptick in trendy young people with money seeking out a new kind of authenticity—the authentic flavors of red sauce cuisine they grew up with.

The renaissance of red sauce cuisine has started to unfold. Rich Torrisi, Jeff Zalaznick, and Mario Carbone lead with their flagship eatery, Carbone, offering modern versions of red sauce dishes including classics like lobster fra diavolo and veal "parmesan." They have locations in Miami, Hong Kong, and Las Vegas.[3] Their micro-chain, Parm, serves upscale parmigiana sandwiches. The expansion of Il Mulino across the country showed the demand for high-quality red sauce, and even Rao's, the East Harlem red sauce joint with impossible-to-obtain reservations, opened outposts in Las Vegas and Los Angeles.[4] Don Angie, another New York City restaurant, is mixing new American flavors with classics like lasagna, while the Meatball Shop chain is focusing on fast-casual pasta and meatballs.

Many of the traditional neighborhood red sauce joints have closed for a variety of reasons ranging from increasing rents to aging chefs to a shifting need for fresher concepts. Trattoria Spaghetto, for instance, was set to become the twenty-fifth location of Dig Inn,[5] a contemporary casual eatery promising real, authentic food devoid of any specific ethnicity or cultural influence. Cucina al Pesci, another neighborhood New York red sauce restaurant, closed after the landlord raised the rent.[6]

These changes happened in the years and months leading up to the global pandemic. The pandemic changed everything. It shuttered restaurants in New York, spawned new outposts in places like Miami, left millions unemployed, tanked commercial real estate prices, caused a shortage of bucatini pasta,[7] and upended restaurants around the world. Seven of Il Mulino's locations outside of New York filed for bankruptcy protection.[8] After 124 years of impossible-to-score reservations, Rao's began offering takeout.[9] The impact of the pandemic on red sauce cuisine and restaurants in general is yet to be seen. Even as the economy reopens and diners return to restaurants, things will be different.

The prepandemic resurgence of upscale, modernized red sauce menus suggests the cuisine will continue to thrive. A cuisine, like language, must continuously evolve if it is to survive. Red sauce is not a dead cuisine. It continues to adjust and adapt to the demands of restaurant patrons and pushes new limits and reinventions. Everything old will be new again, repackaged, reinvented, commodified, and modified to contemporary tastes.

Appendix

Historic Recipes

EARLY ITALIAN TOMATO SAUCE RECIPES

	Spanish Tomato Sauce	Vermicelli con lo Pommodoro	Salsa di Pomodoro
PUBLICATION	*Lo Scalco alla Moderna* Antonio Latini 1692	*Cucina Teorico-Practica* Ippolito Cavalcanti 1837	*La scienza in cucina e l'arte di mangiar bene* Pellegrino Artusi 1891
SERVING	Serve with anything boiled	12 oz vermicelli	Serve with boiled meat, pasta with cheese and butter, risotto
INGREDIENTS	6 tomatoes 1 onion Peppers Oil Vinegar	25 oz tomatoes Lard	7 or 8 tomatoes Basil leaves ¼ onion Parsley 1 clove garlic 1 stalk celery
INSTRUCTIONS	Roast tomatoes on a fire. Remove the skin with a knife. Add minced onions. Add minced peppers. Mix salt, oil and vinegar to taste. Served with anything boiled.	Slice tomatoes into quarters. Remove seeds. Boil tomatoes. Strain through a sieve. "Shrink" over fire and add lard. Add al dente vermicelli. Season with salt and pepper. Cook for a few minutes for pasta to absorb liquid.	Combine everything with oil, salt and pepper. Roast on a fire (presumably in a pot) until as thick as cream. Pass through a sieve. Serve.

Sources: Latini, *Lo Scalco All Moderna*, 444; Ortolani, *L'Italia della pasta*, 41; Artusi, *La scienza in cucina e l'arte di mangiar bene*, 62.

EARLY AMERICAN TOMATO SAUCE RECIPES

	Tomato Sauce	Macaroni with Tomato Sauce	Salsa di Pomodoro
PUBLICATION	*The Carolina Housewife* Sarah Rutledge 1847	*Simple Italian Cookery* Antonia Isola 1912	*The Italian Cookbook* Maria Gentile 1919
SERVING	No serving suggestions	12 oz macaroni	Serve with boiled meat, macaroni or spaghetti, or rice
INGREDIENTS	Tomatoes Butter 2 eggs Small handful of Breadcrumbs Teacup of milk 1 onion	2 tbsp tomato paste or 7 or 8 Tomatoes from a can Hot water Parmigiano-Reggiano Ham fat Onion Celery Parsley	¼ of onion Clove of garlic Piece of celery A few bay leaves Just enough parsley 7 or 8 tomatoes
INSTRUCTIONS	Scald tomatoes. Remove skins and sieve. Add butter, salt and pepper, beaten eggs, breadcrumbs soaked in milk, and thinly sliced onion. Stew over low heat for an hour or two.	Cook onion, celery and parsley in fat. Add tomato paste and water or tomatoes. Boil together for 15 minutes. Cook macaroni. Add cooked macaroni to sauce. Add grated cheese. Stir together and serve.	Combine ingredients over heat. Salt and pepper. Stir it from time to time. When juices have thickened, strain through sieve and serve.

Sources: Rutledge, *House and Home, or the Carolina Housewife,* 78; Isola, *Simple Italian Cookery,* 9; Gentile, *The Italian Cook Book,* 14.

MEATBALLS AND VARIATIONS

	Polpette	Savory Meat Balls	No. 282 Braised Meat Balls
PUBLICATION	*La scienza in cucina e l'arte di mangiar bene* Pellegrino Artusi 1891	*The New Macaroni Journal,* Oct 15, 1922 Rudy Valentino, film star 1922	U.S. Army War Department Technical Manual 1944
SERVING	Garnish with an egg.	Serve with parsley and potatoes.	Serves 100 with various sauces.
INGREDIENTS	Boiled Meat Parmesan Spices Raisins Pine Nuts Gruel (milk and bread) 1 or 2 eggs Garlic Parsley	1 lb ground top round Parsley 1 egg 1 cup grated bread ½ lb grated Parmigiana or Romano	5 lb dry bread 6.5 oz salt 45 lbs meat or carcass or ½ oz pepper 31 lbs ground meat 1 qt meat stock 10 eggs 5 lb onions
INSTRUCTIONS	Chop the meat. Combine with cheese, spices, raisins, nuts, gruel and egg. Form into balls the size of eggs. Fry in oil or lard with garlic and parsley. Garnish with an egg.	Combine meat, egg, bread, and cheese. Season with salt and pepper. Roll into balls. Flatten slightly. Fry in oil.	Soak bread in water; press and discard water. Cut meat into pieces. Grind meat. Mix all ingredients. Shape into 2 oz meat balls. Place in greased baking pans. Cook at 400 F until brown on all sides. Add small amount of stock. Cover and braise at 300 F about 30 minutes.

Sources: Artusi, *La scienza in cucina e l'arte di mangiar bene,* 120; National Pasta Association, "Test Macaroni Recipes," 38; War Department, *Army Recipes,* 99.

ORIGINS OF EGGPLANT PARMIGIANA

	Molignane alla parmisciana	Pumpkin "alla Parmegiana"	Eggplants in the Oven
PUBLICATION	*Cucina teorico-pratica* Ippolito Cavalcanti 1839	*Simple Italian Cookery* Antonia Isola 1912	*The Italian Cookbook* Maria Gentile 1919
SERVING	Serve after baking.	Serve after baking.	Serve after baking.
INGREDIENTS	Eggplants Grated Cheese Basil Leaves Tomato sauce or meat ragù	Pumpkin Allspice Parmesan or Gruyere Parsley	5 eggplants Oil 1 egg 2 teaspoons breadcrumbs Grated cheese Tomato sauce Flour
INSTRUCTIONS	Peel eggplants. Slice into medallions. Salt. Drain juices and squeeze dry. Layer with cheese, basil, sauce. Bake.	Peel pumpkin. Slice into medallions. Boil briefly in salted water. Fry in butter. Add salt and all-spice. Add thin-sliced cheese Brown in oven.	Peel eggplants. Salt and let sit for several hours. Dip eggplant in flour and oil. Layer in baking dish with cheese and sauce. Combine breadcrumbs, egg and teaspoon each of sauce and cheese. Top eggplant with mixture. Bake until cooked.

Sources: Calvacanti, *Cucina teorico-pratica*; Isola, *Simple Italian Cookery*, 43; Gentile, *The Italian Cook Book*, 76.

THE EVOLUTION OF FETTUCCINE ALFREDO

	Fettuccine Alfredo	Macaroni with Butter and Cheese	Fettuccine Alfredo	Noodles Alfredo
PUBLICATION	Alfredo di Lelio 1908	*Simple Italian Cookery* Antonia Isola 1912	*The Rector Cook Book* George Rector 1928	Pennsylvania Dutch Noodles 1966
SERVING	1 lb fresh egg fettuccine, serve with solid gold fork and spoon	1 lb spaghetti	Serve with noodles and alongside seared beef.	8 oz egg fettuccine
INGREDIENTS	½ lb butter ½ lb Parmigiano-Reggiano	4 tbsp butter 3 tbsp Parmesan	3 egg-sized butter lumps Parmesan cheese	½ cup butter ½ cup cream ½ cup Parmesan ¼ cup shredded Swiss cheese
INSTRUCTIONS	Beat the butter and cheese together. Cook the pasta. Drain pasta, but allow some of the starchy water to remain. Combine pasta with the butter and cheese.	Cook pasta. Drain. Add butter and cheese to saucepan. Toss with pasta over heat.	Cook pasta. Place in cold water. Separate noodles. Place in hot water. Drain after noodles are warmed. Place noodles on warm serving platter. Add "Parmesan" cheese to coat. Add butter. Toss until blended.	Cook pasta. Melt butter. Add cream. Heat cream through. Combine with pasta. Toss with cheese, salt, and pepper.

Sources: Coleman, "The Real Alfredo"; Isola, *Simple Italian Cookery,* 10; Rector, *The Rector Cook Book,* 70; Pennsylvania Dutch, "The Noodle People."

ORIGINS AND VARIATIONS ON PUTTANESCA

	Salsa del Papa	Spaghetti Syracuse Style	Spaghetti Hooker Style I
PUBLICATION	*La scienza in cucina e l'arte di mangiar bene* Pellegrino Artusi 1891	*The Talisman Italian Cook Book* Ada Boni, translated by Matilde La Rosa 1950	*Pasta and Rice Italian Style* Efrem Calingaert and Jacquelyn Days Serwer 1983
SERVING	Serve over fried cutlets.	1 lb spaghetti.	1 lb spaghetti.
INGREDIENTS	Small handful of capers Equal amount of sweetened olives Eggplant Onion Droplet of Vinegar Pinch of flour Anchovy Butter	1/2 oil 10 sicilian olives 2 cloves garlic 1 tablespoon capers 6 ripe tomatoes 1 tablespoon fresh basil 1 small eggplant 3 anchovy filets 2 roasted green peppers ½ teaspoon salt	1 cup tomato sauce 2 tablespoons black olives 4 ripe tomatoes 4 anchovy filets 5 tablespoons olive oil 1 red chili pepper 1 clove garlic 2 tablespoons basil leaves 1 tablespoon capers 1 lb sage
INSTRUCTIONS	Drain capers. Saute finely chopped onion in butter. Add a bit of water. Add minced capers, olives and eggplant. Simmer. Add vinegar. Add flour and more butter. Mince anchovies. Add anchovies serving without further cooking.	Brown garlic in oil. Remove garlic. Add tomatoes and eggplant. Cook 30 minutes. Add peppers, capers, basil, anchovies and season with salt and pepper. Simmer another 10 minutes. Serve over spaghetti.	Combine ingredients. Toss with hot pasta.

Sources: Artusi, La scienza in cucina e l'arte di mangiar bene, 64; Boni, The Talisman Italian Cookbook, 153; Calingaert and Serwer, Pasta and Rice Italian Style, 166.

Notes

CHAPTER 1

1. James Hoffmann, *The World Atlas of Coffee*, 2nd ed. (Richmond Hill, Ontario: Firefly Books, 2014), 50.

2. Hoffmann, *The World Atlas of Coffee*, 51.

3. Wendy Pojmann, *Espresso: The Art and Soul of Italy* (New York: Bordighera Press, 2021), 18.

4. Dixita Limbachia, "Pizza Hut Plans to Shut Down More Than 500 Dine-In Locations across US," *Detroit Free Press*, August 6, 2019, www.freep.com /story/money/business/2019/08/06/pizza-hut-close-500-dine-locations-across -us/1938667001.

5. Tim Forster, "Every Single Possible Combination of Pasta You Can Make with Olive Garden's Never Ending Pasta Pass," *Eater*, August 23, 2018, www.eater .com/2018/8/23/17769884/olive-garden-never-ending-pasta-pass-restaurant -menu-2018.

6. Robin Cherry, *Garlic: An Edible Biography* (Boston: Roost Books, 2014), 1.

7. Alison Griswold, "The Decline of Red Lobster Is the Decline of the Middle Class," *Slate*, August 1, 2014, https://slate.com/business/2014/08/red-lobster-olive -garden-the-decline-of-casual-dining-is-the-decline-of-the-middle-class.html.

8. Jordan Weissmann, "Olive Garden Has Been Committing a Culinary Crime against Humanity," *Slate*, September 12, 2014, https://slate.com/busi ness/2014/09/olive-garden-doesn-t-salt-its-pasta-water-investors-reveal-a-culinary -crime-against-humanity.html.

9. Emily Jane Fox, "How a Hedge Fund Saved Olive Garden by Making Its Breadsticks Better," *Vanity Fair*, April 6, 2016, www.vanityfair.com/news /2016/04/olive-garden-breadsticks-starboard.

10. U.S. Census Bureau, "Accommodation and Food Services: Subject Series— Misc Subjects: Principal Menu Type or Specialty 4 for the U.S. and States: 2012," 2012 Economic Census of the United States, accessed April 29, 2021, www.census .gov/data/tables/2012/econ/census/accommodation-food-services.html.

CHAPTER 2

1. Anthony P. Pizzo, "The Italian Heritage in Tampa," in *Little Italies in North America*, eds. Robert F. Harney and J. Vincenza Scarpaci (Toronto: The Multicultural Society of Ontario, 1981), 123.

2. Mort Rosenblum, *The Life and Lore of the Noble Fruit* (New York: North Point Press, 1996), 286.

3. Ted Merwin, *Pastrami on Rye: An Overstuffed History of the Jewish Deli* (New York: New York University Press, 2015), chap. 1, Kindle.

4. Paul Freedman, *Ten Restaurants That Changed America* (New York: Liverlight, 2018), 197.

5. Merwin, *Pastrami on Rye*, introduction.

6. Merwin, *Pastrami on Rye*, chap. 2.

7. John Mariani, *Encyclopedia of American Food and Drink* (New York: Bloomsbury, 1992), loc. 8500, Kindle.

8. John Mariani, *How Italian Food Conquered the World* (New York: Palgrave MacMillan, 2011), 46.

9. Vincenza J. Scarpaci, "Observations on an Ethnic Community: Baltimore's Little Italy," in *Little Italies in North America*, ed. Robert F. Harney and J. Vincenza Scarpaci (Toronto: The Multicultural Society of Ontario, 1981), 108.

10. Jane Ziegelman, *97 Orchard: An Edible History of Five Immigrant Families in One New York Tenement* (New York: Harper, 2010), 184.

11. U.S. Census Bureau, "Introduction," 1860 Census: Population of the United States, Country Where Born, accessed April 29, 2021, www.census.gov/library /publications/1864/dec/1860a.html.

12. John Dickie, *Delizia! The Epic History of the Italians and Their Food* (New York: Free Press, 2008), 218.

13. Fabio Parasecoli, *Al Dente: A History of the Food in Italy* (London: Reaktion Books, 2014), 225.

14. Nancy Verde Barr, *We Called It Macaroni: An American Heritage of Southern Italian Cooking* (New York: Knopf, 1996), 66.

15. Maddalena Tirabassi, "Making Space for Domesticity: Household Goods in Working-Class Italian American Homes, 1900–1940," in *Making Italian America:*

Consumer Culture and the Production of Ethnic Identities, ed. Cinotto Simone (New York: Fordham University Press, 2014), 58.

16. Danielle Battisti, "Italian Americans, Consumerism, and the Cold War in Transnational Perspective," in *Making Italian America: Consumer Culture and the Production of Ethnic Identities*, ed. Cinotto Simone (New York: Fordham University Press, 2014), 153.

17. Dickie, *Delizia!*, 224.

18. Ziegelman, *97 Orchard*, 189.

19. Andrew F. Smith, *New York City: A Food Biography* (Lanham, MD: Rowman & Littlefield, 2014), 56.

20. Tirabassi, "Making Space for Domesticity," 59.

21. Carol Helstosky, *Garlic and Oil: Food and Politics in Italy* (Oxford: Berg, 2004), 25.

22. Hasia R. Diner, *Hungering for America: Italian, Irish, & Jewish Foodways in the Age of Migration* (Cambridge, MA: Harvard University Press, 2001), 62–63.

23. Marlena Spieler, *A Taste of Naples: Neapolitan Culture, Cuisine, and Cooking* (Lanham, MD: Rowman & Littlefield, 2018), 35.

24. Helstosky, *Garlic and Oil*, 23.

25. Spieler, *A Taste of Naples*, 35.

26. Diner, *Hungering for America*, 49.

27. Simone Cinotto, *The Italian American Table: Food, Family, and Community in New York City* (Urbana: University of Illinois Press, 2013), 163.

28. Lou Di Palo, *Di Palo's Guide to the Essential Foods of Italy: 100 Years of Wisdom and Stories from Behind the Counter* (New York: Ballantine Books, 2014), xviii.

29. Di Palo, *Di Palo's Guide*, 7.

30. Di Palo, *Di Palo's Guide*, 7.

31. Diana Hubbell, "109-Year-Old Little Italy Cheese Shop di Palo's Now Has a Wine Bar Next Door," *Eater*, September 23, 2019, https://ny.eater.com/2019/9/23/20880026/c-di-palo-wine-bar-opens-little-italy-nyc.

32. Di Palo, *Di Palo's Guide*, xvii.

33. Harvey Levenstein, "The American Response to Italian Food, 1880–1930," in *Food in the USA*, ed. Carole M. Counihan (New York: Routledge, 1985), 76.

34. Diner, *Hungering for America*, 66.

35. Ziegelman, *97 Orchard*, 195.

36. Cinotto, *The Italian American Table*, 45.

37. Harvey Levenstein, *Revolution at the Table: The Transformation of the American Diet* (New York: Oxford University Press, 1998), 119.

38. Donna R. Gabaccia, *We Are What We Eat: Ethnic Food and the Making of Americans* (Cambridge, MA: Harvard University Press, 200), 138.

CHAPTER 3

1. National Pasta Association, "A Saga of Cathay," *The Macaroni Journal*, October 15, 1929, 32–34.

2. Vincenzo Buonassisi, *Pasta*, trans. Elisabeth Evans (Wilton, CT: Lyceum Books, 1976), 9.

3. Oretta Zanini de Vita and Maureen B. Fant, *Sauces & Shapes* (New York: Norton, 2013), 19.

4. Buonassisi, *Pasta*, 7.

5. Alberto Capatti and Massimo Montanari, *Italian Cuisine: A Cultural History* (New York: Columbia University Press, 1999), 51.

6. Fabio Parasecoli, *Al Dente: A History of the Food in Italy* (London: Reaktion Books, 2014), 94.

7. Buonassisi, *Pasta*, 7.

8. Oretta Zanini de Vita, *Encyclopedia of Pasta*, trans. Maureen B. Fant (Berkeley: University of California Press, 2009), 146.

9. Buonassisi, *Pasta*, 7.

10. Parasecoli, *Al Dente*, 94.

11. Capatti and Montanari, *Italian Cuisine*, 51.

12. Capatti and Montanari, *Italian Cuisine*, 51.

13. Julia Della Croce, *Pasta Classica: 125 Authentic Italian Recipes* (San Francisco: Chronicle Books, 1987), 13.

14. Silvano Serventi and Françoise Sabban, *Pasta: The Story of a Universal Food*, trans. Antony Shugaar (New York: Columbia University Press, 2000), 11.

15. John F. Mariani, *How Italian Food Conquered the World* (New York: Palgrave MacMillan, 2011), 14.

16. Zanini de Vita, *Encyclopedia of Pasta*, 107.

17. Parasecoli, *Al Dente*, 94.

18. Della Croce, *Pasta Classica*, 12.

19. Della Croce, *Pasta Classica*, 12.

20. Parasecoli, *Al Dente*, 94.

21. Mariani, *How Italian Food Conquered the World*, 14.

22. Mariani, *How Italian Food Conquered the World*, 14.

23. Giuseppe Prezzolini, *Spaghetti Dinner* (New York: Abbelards-Schumann, 1955), 18.

24. Serventi and Sabban, *Pasta*, 44.

25. Parasecoli, *Al Dente*, 94.

26. Massimo Montanari, *Italian Identity in the Kitchen, on Food and the Nation*, trans. Beth Archer Brombert (New York: Columbia University Press, 2010), 37–38.

27. John Dickie, *Delizia! The Epic History of Italians and Their Food* (New York: Free Press, 2008), 19.

28. Serventi and Sabban, *Pasta*, 261.

29. Buonassisi, *Pasta*, 8.

30. Della Croce, *Pasta Classica*, 14.

31. Serventi and Sabban, *Pasta*, 86.

32. Zanini de Vita, *Encyclopedia of Pasta*, 7.

33. Serventi and Sabban, *Pasta*, 86.

34. Zanini de Vita, *Encyclopedia of Pasta*, 7.

35. Massimo Montanari, *Italian Identity in the Kitchen, on Food and the Nation*, trans. Beth Archer Brombert (New York: Columbia University Press, 2010), 42.

36. Alberto Capatti and Massimo Montanari, *Italian Cuisine: A Cultural History* (New York: Columbia University Press, 1999), 57.

37. Good Housekeeping, "Macaroni," *Good Housekeeping* 9, no. 8 (August 17, 1889): 170, http://reader.library.cornell.edu/docviewer/digital?id=hearth6417403_1303_009#page/2/mode/1up.

38. Serventi and Sabban, *Pasta*, 111.

39. Serventi and Sabban, *Pasta*, 109.

40. Serventi and Sabban, *Pasta*, 110.

41. Zanini de Vita, *Encyclopedia of Pasta*, 9.

42. Zanini de Vita, *Encyclopedia of Pasta*, 9.

43. Zanini de Vita, *Encyclopedia of Pasta*, 19.

44. Serventi and Sabban, *Pasta*, 189.

45. Jane Ziegelman, *97 Orchard: An Edible History of Five Immigrant Families in One New York Tenement* (New York: Harper, 2010), 218.

46. Carol Helstosky, *Garlic and Oil: Food and Politics in Italy* (Oxford: Berg, 2004), 35.

47. Serventi and Sabban, *Pasta*, 158.

48. Helstosky, *Garlic and Oil* , 32.

49. Sheryll Bellman, *America's Little Italys* (South Portland, ME: Sellers, 2010), 21.

50. Della Croce, *Pasta Classica*, 17–18.

51. Zanini de Vita, *Encyclopedia of Pasta*, 260.

52. Simone Cinotto, *The Italian American Table: Food, Family, and Community in New York City* (Urbana: University of Illinois Press, 2013), 119.

53. Serventi and Sabban, *Pasta*, 119.

54. Maddalena Tirabassi, "Making Space for Domesticity: Household Goods in Working-Class Italian American Homes, 1900–1940," in *Making Italian America: Consumer Culture and the Production of Ethnic Identities*, ed. Cinotto Simone (New York: Fordham University Press, 2014), 61.

55. Donna R. Gabbacia, *We Are What We Eat: Ethnic Food and the Making of Americans* (Cambridge, MA: Harvard University Press, 2000), 132.

56. Aaron Bobrow-Strain, *White Bread: A Social History of the Store-Bought Loaf* (Boston: Beacon Press, 2012), loc. 843, Kindle.

57. "General Foods Corp. Will Acquire Spaghetti-Maker Ronzoni Corp.," UPI, January 10 1984, www.upi.com/Archives/1984/01/10/General-Foods-Corp-will-acquire-spaghetti-maker-Ronzoni-Corp-the/4268442558800.

58. Clare Transasso, "Ronzoni Founder's Great-Grandson Alfred Ronzoni Jr. Tells Family History," *Daily News*, May 16, 2011, www.nydailynews.com

/new-york/queens/ronzoni-founder-great-grandson-alfred-ronzoni-jr-tells-family
-history-article-1.145979.

59. Dustin Brown, "Ronzoni Family Dishes Out Memories of LIC Legacy," QNS,
October 9, 2002, https://qns.com/2002/10/ronzoni-family-dishes-out-memories
-of-lic-legacy.

60. Cinotto, *The Italian American Table*, 136.

61. Serventi and Sabban, *Pasta*, 192–93.

62. *Vincent De Luca v. Domenico Calandra, Andrew Cuneo, Frank A Zunino,
Charles Casazza, Emanuele Ronzoni, Atlantic Macaronic Company, New York
County National Bank, Basilea Calandra Co., Inc, and Bridge Café* (N Walton,
NY: Supreme Court, Appellate Division—Second Department, 1917), 22.

63. *Vincent De Luca v. Domenico Calandra*, 22.

64. Cinotto, *The Italian American Table*, 136.

65. "Emanuele Ronzoni, Macaroni Producer," *New York Times*, August 25,
1956, 15.

66. Clare Trapasso, "Ronzoni Founder's Great-Grandson Alfred Ronzoni Jr.
Tells Family History," *Daily News*, May 16, 2011, www.nydailynews.com/new
-york/queens/ronzoni-founder-great-grandson-alfred-ronzoni-jr-tells-family
-history-article-1.145979.

67. Serventi and Sabban, *Pasta*, 192.

68. National Pasta Association, "Who Is Buying Pasta," *The Macaroni Journal* 66, no. 8 (December 1984): 10, https://ilovepasta.org/wp-content/uploads
/macaroni/1984%2012%20DECEMBER%20-%20The%20New%20Macaroni%20
Journal.pdf.

69. Serventi and Sabban, *Pasta*, 171.

70. Harvey Levenstein, *Paradox of Plenty: A Social History of Eating in Modern
America* (Berkeley: University of California Press, 2003), 29.

71. Cinotto, *The Italian American Table*, 85.

72. Gabbacia, *We Are What We Eat*, 138.

73. Anne Milano Appel, *Why Italians Love to Talk about Food* (New York: Farrar, Straus, and Giroux, 2009), 353.

74. Helstocky, *Garlic and Oil*, 66.

75. Sophie Brickman, "The Food of the Future," *New Yorker*, September 1,
2014, www.newyorker.com/culture/culture-desk/food-future.

76. Brickman, "The Food of the Future."

77. Antony Shugaar, "Introduction," in *The Duke's Table: The Complete Book
of Vegetarian Italian Cooking* (Brooklyn, NY: Melville House, 2013), 11.

78. Enrico Alliata, "Author's Forward," in *The Duke's Table: The Complete
Book of Vegetarian Italian Cooking*, trans. Anthony Shugaar (Brooklyn, NY: Melville House, 2013), 19.

79. Karen Pinchin, "An Italian Vegetarian Cookbook That Was Ahead of Its
Time," *The Globe and Mail*, June 4, 2013.

80. Fabio Parasecoli, *Al Dente: A History of the Food in Italy* (London: Reaktion
Books, 2014), 175.

81. Gabbacia, *We Are What We Eat*, 150.

82. UPI, "Hector Boiardi Is Dead: Began Chef Boy-ar-dee," *New York Times*, June 23, 1985, www.nytimes.com/1985/06/23/us/hector-boiardi-is-dead-began-chef-boy-ar-dee.html.

83. Anna Boiardi, *Delicious Memories: Recipes and Stories from the Chef Boyardee Family* (New York: Stewart, Tabori, & Chang, 2011), 10.

84. UPI, "Hector Boiardi Is Dead."

85. Arthur Allen, *Ripe: The Search for the Perfect Tomato* (Berkeley, CA: Counterpoint, 2010), 182.

86. Boiardi, *Delicious Memories*, 13.

87. UPI, "Hector Boiardi Is Dead."

88. Boiardi, *Delicious Memories*, 12.

89. Boiardi, *Delicious Memories*, 13.

90. Gabbacia, *We Are What We Eat*, 150.

91. Levenstein, *Paradox of Plenty*, 122.

92. "About Us," National Pasta Association, https://ilovepasta.org/about-us.

93. Dickie, *Delizia!*, 154.

94. "Pasta at a Glance," Associazione Italiana Industrie Prodotti Alimentari, accessed June 6, 2019, www.aidepi.it/en/pasta.html.

95. Zanini de Vita, *Encyclopedia of Pasta*, 214.

CHAPTER 4

1. Fabio Parasecoli, *Al Dente: A History of Food in Italy* (London: Reaktion Books, 2014), 98.

2. David Gentilcore, *Pomodoro! A History of the Tomato in Italy* (New York: Columbia University Press, 2010), 52–53.

3. Nany Harmon Jenkins, *Cucina del Sole: A Celebration of Southern Italian Cooking* (New York: William Morrow Cookbooks, 2007), 7.

4. Michael Krondl, *Sweet Invention: A History of Dessert* (Chicago: Chicago Review Press, 2011), 159.

5. Henry Notaker, *A History of Cookbooks: From Kitchen to Page Over Seven Centuries* (Oakland: University of California Press, 2017), 121.

6. Oretta Zanini de Vita, *Encyclopedia of Pasta*, trans. Maureen B. Fant (Berkeley: University of California Press, 2009), 5.

7. Zanini de Vita, *Encyclopedia of Pasta*, 70.

8. Fred Potkin, "Eating Well in the Italian Kitchen," *Gastronomica* 5, no. 2 (Spring 2005): 100–102, www.jstor.org/stable/10.1525/gfc.2005.5.2.100.

9. Potkin, "Eating Well in the Italian Kitchen."

10. Notaker, *A History of Cookbooks*, 41.

11. Potkin, "Eating Well in the Italian Kitchen."

12. Potkin, "Eating Well in the Italian Kitchen."

13. Hearst Corporation, "Simple Italian Cookery," *Harper's Bazar* 46 (January 1912): 362.

14. Ken Albala, "Italianità in America: The Cultural Politics of Representing 'Authentic' Italian Cuisine in the US," in *Representing Italy through Food*, eds. Peter Naccarato, Zachary Nowak, and Elgin K. Eckert (New York: Bloomsbury, 2017), 206.

15. Maria Lo Pinto, *New York Cookbook* (New York: A.A. Wyn, 1952), 7.

16. Bill Daley, "Culinary Giant: Ada Boni," *Chicago Tribune*, May 13, 2013, www.chicagotribune.com/dining/ct-xpm-2013-05-15-sc-food-0510-giants-boni -20130515-story.html.

17. Mark Kurlansky, *Cod: A Biography of the Fish That Changed the World* (New York: Penguin, 1998), 264.

18. A&P, "Ann Page Macaroni Pie," *Life* 42, no. 9 (March 4, 1957): 53.

19. Mark Bittman, "Remembering Marcella," *New York Times*, November 6, 2013, www.nytimes.com/2013/11/10/magazine/remembering-marcella.html.

20. Dulcy Braindard, "Marcella Hazan: Education America's Palate," *Publisher's Weekly* 244, no. 45 (November 3, 1997): 62–63.

21. Braindard, "Marcella Hazan."

22. Braindard, "Marcella Hazan."

23. Braindard, "Marcella Hazan."

24. John Mariani, *How Italian Food Conquered the World* (New York: Palgrave, 2011), 177–78.

25. James F. Clarity, "BRIEFING; Split over Radio Marti," *New York Times*, September 19, 1983, www.nytimes.com/1983/09/19/us/briefing-split-over-radio -marti.html.

26. "The Silver Spoon," *Publishers Weekly*, October 3, 2005, www.publishers weekly.com/978-0-7148-4531-9.

CHAPTER 5

1. William Grimes, *Appetite City: A Culinary History of New York* (New York: North Point Press, 2009), 96.

2. Jane Ziegelman, *97 Orchard: An Edible History of Five Immigrant Families in One New York Tenement* (New York: Harper, 2010), 220.

3. John F. Mariani, *How Italian Food Conquered the World* (New York: Palgrave MacMillan, 2011), 51.

4. *Oxford-Paravia Italian Dictionary*, 3rd ed (Oxford: Oxford University Press, 2010), 1039.

5. Giuseppe Corra, *Sicily: Culinary Crossroads*, trans. Gaetano Cipolla (New York: Oronzo Editions, 2008), 163.

6. Marcella Hazan, *The Classic Italian Cook Book* (New York: Alfred A. Knopf, 1980), 6.

7. Mary Tebben, *Sauces: A Global History* (London: Reaktion Books, 2014), 86.

8. Andrew Smith, *The Tomato in America: Early History, Culture, and Cookery* (Columbia: University of South Carolina Press, 1994), 73.

9. John Russell, *House and Home, or the Carolina Housewife* (Charleston, SC: John Russell, 1855), 4.

10. Smith, *The Tomato in America*, 78.

11. Waverly Root, *The Food of Italy* (New York: Vintage Books, 1992), 502.

12. Arthur Schwartz, *Naples at the Table* (New York: HarperCollins, 1998), 44.

13. Francesa Romina, *Mangia, Little Italy! Secrets from a Sicilian Family Kitchen* (San Francisco: Chronicle Books, 1998), 112.

14. Romina, *Mangia, Little Italy!*, 112.

15. Schwartz, *Naples at the Table*, 45.

16. Schwartz, *Naples at the Table*, 45.

17. Mariani, *How Italian Food Conquered the World*, 38.

18. Rian James, *Dining in New York* (New York: John Day Company, 1931), 197.

CHAPTER 6

1. Barry Estabrook, *Tomatoland: How the Modern Industrial Agriculture Destroyed Our Most Alluring Fruit* (Kansas City, MO: Andrews McMeel, 2011), loc. 203, Kindle.

2. Estabrook, *Tomatoland*, loc. 203.

3. Sylvia Johnson, *Tomatoes, Potatoes, Corn and Beans: How the Foods of the Americas Changed Eating around the World* (New York: Atheneum Books for Young Readers, 1997), 85.

4. Estabrook, *Tomatoland*, loc. 225.

5. Wolf D. Storle, *A Curious History of Vegetables* (Berkeley, CA: North Atlantic Books, 2016), 262.

6. Johnson, *Tomatoes, Potatoes, Corn and Beans*, 85.

7. Storle, *A Curious History of Vegetables*, 262.

8. Johnson, *Tomatoes, Potatoes, Corn and Beans*, 85.

9. Anne Milano Appel, *Why Italians Love to Talk about Food* (New York: Farrar, Straus, and Giroux, 2009), 121.

10. Cristina Ortolani, *L'Italia della pasta* (Milano, Italy: Club Italiano, 2003), 41.

11. John Dickie, *Delizia! The Epic History of Italians and Their Food* (New York: Free Press, 2008), 162.

12. Arthur Allen, *Ripe: The Search for the Perfect Tomato* (Berkeley, CA: Counterpoint, 2010), 44.

13. Storle, *A Curious History of Vegetables*, 264.

14. Allen George McCue, "The History of the Use of the Tomato: An Annotated Bibliography," *Annals of the Missouri Botanical* 39, no. 4 (November 1952): 289–348, www.jstor.org/stable/2399094?seq=1.

15. Allen, *Ripe*, 14.

16. David Gentilcore, *Pomodoro! A History of the Tomato in Italy* (New York: Columbia University Press, 2010), 16.

17. Gentilcore, *Pomodoro!*, 16.

18. Gentilcore, *Pomodoro!*, 18.

19. Storle, *A Curious History of Vegetables*, 262.

20. Anthony John Carter, "Myths and Mandrakes," *Journal of the Royal Society of Medicine* (March 2003): 144–147, www.ncbi.nlm.nih.gov/pmc/articles/PMC539425.

21. Carter, "Myths and Mandrakes," 144–47.

22. Storle, *A Curious History of Vegetables*, 261.

23. Richard Cavendish, ed., *Man Myth & Magic: The Illustrated Encyclopedia of Mythology, Religion, and the Unknown* (New York: Marshall Cavendish, 1995), 1,560.

24. Nachman Ben-Yehuda, "The European Witch Craze of the 14th to 17th Centuries: A Sociologist's Perspective," *American Journal of Sociology* 86, no. 1 (July 1980): 1–31, www.journals.uchicago.edu/doi/abs/10.1086/227200.

25. Marlena Spieler, *A Taste of Naples: Neapolitan Culture, Cuisine, and Cooking* (New York: Rowman & Littlefield, 2018), 43.

26. Andrew F. Smith, *Super Tomatoes: The Story of America's Favorite Food* (New Brunswick, NJ: Rutgers University Press, 1946), 29.

27. Spieler, *A Taste of Naples*, 65.

28. Fabio Parasecoli, *Al Dente: A History of the Food in Italy* (London: Reaktion Books, 2014), 128.

29. Appel, *Why Italians Love to Talk about Food*, 122.

30. Gentilcore, *Pomodoro!*, 25.

31. *Flowers, Fruit, Vegetables and Two Lizards*, Web Gallery of Art, accessed September 2, 2021, www.wga.hu/html_m/m/master/hartford/2flowers.html.

32. Smith, *Super Tomatoes*, 75.

33. Dickie, *Delizia!*, 163.

34. Gentilcore, *Pomodoro!*, 76.

35. Francesa Romina Mangia, *Little Italy! Secrets from a Sicilian Family Kitchen* (San Francisco: Chronicle Books, 1998), 104.

36. Jerre Mangione and Ben Morreale, *La Storia: Five Centuries of the Italian American Experience* (New York: Harper Perennial, 1993), 136.

37. Mangione and Morreale, *La Storia*, 136.

38. Nancy Verde Barr, *We Called It Macaroni: An American Heritage of Southern Italian Cooking* (New York: Knopf, 1996), 60.

39. Waverly Root, *The Food of Italy* (New York: Vintage Books, 1992), 235.

40. Andrew Smith, *The Tomato in America: Early History, Culture and Cookery* (Columbia: University of South Carolina Press, 1994), 17.

41. Smith, *The Tomato in America*, 25.

42. Johnson, *Tomatoes, Potatoes, Corn and Beans*, 91.

43. Johnson, *Tomatoes, Potatoes, Corn and Beans*, 93.

44. Sarah Lohman, *Eight Flavors: The Untold Story of American Cuisine* (New York: Simon & Schuster, 2016), 124.

45. Smith, *The Tomato in America*, 29.

46. Smith, *Super Tomatoes*, 39.

47. Smith, *Super Tomatoes*, 35.

48. Christopher Martin Cuomo, *Encyclopedia of Cultivated Plants: From Acacia to Zinnia*, 3 vols. (Santa Barbara, CA: ABC-CLIO, 2013).

49. John Hoenig, *Garden Variety: The American Tomato from Corporate to Heirloom* (New York: Columbia University Press, 2018), 19.

50. Smith, *Super Tomatoes*, 33.

51. Smith, *The Tomato in America*, 109.

52. Hoenig, *Garden Variety*, 33.

53. Robert Chambers, "The Tomato," Texas Agricultural Experiment Station, 1903.

54. Estabrook, *Tomatoland*, loc. 291.

55. Estabrook, *Tomatoland*, loc. 52.

56. Estabrook, *Tomatoland*, loc. 142.

57. Smith, *Super Tomatoes*, 2–3.

58. Hoenig, *Garden Variety*, 62.

59. Marion Stevens, "The Tomato," *Journal of Education* 78, no. 1 (July 3, 1913): 21, www.jstor.org/stable/i40107305.

60. Simone Cinotto, *The Italian American Table: Food, Family, and Community in New York City* (Urbana: University of Illinois Press, 2013), 143.

61. Smith, *Super Tomatoes*, 56.

62. Allen, *Ripe*, 181.

63. Alberto Capatti and Massimo Montanari, *Italian Cuisine: A Cultural History* (New York: Columbia University Press, 1999), 256.

64. Hoenig, *Garden Variety*, 66.

65. Allen, *Ripe*, 195.

66. Sheryll Bellman, *America's Little Italys* (South Portland, ME: Sellers Publisher, 2010), 19.

67. Allen, *Ripe*, 46.

CHAPTER 7

1. "Enrico Fasani, Set Up Italian Cuisine Here," *New York Times,* February 26, 1949, 15.

2. "News of Food: For a Teen-Age Celebration," *New York Times*, June 24, 1946, 34.

3. "News of Food," 34.

4. Simone Cinotto, *The Italian American Table: Food, Family, and Community in New York City* (Urbana: University of Illinois Press, 2013), 185.

5. John Mariani, *Encyclopedia of American Food and Drink* (New York: Bloomsbury, 1992), 187.

6. Florence Fabricant, "Origin of Popular Lobster Fra Diavolo Bedevils the Experts," *New York Times*, May 29, 1996, C3.

7. Mimi Sheraton, *1,000 Foods to Eat before You Die: A Food Lover's Life List* (New York: Workman, 2013), 202–3.

8. Diana Ashley, *Where to Dine in Thirty-Nine* (New York: Crown Publishers, 1939), 233.

9. Fabricant, "Origin of Popular Lobster Fra Diavolo," C3.

10. Andrew P. Haley, *Turning the Tables: Restaurants and the Rise of the American Middle Class, 1880–1920* (Chapel Hill: University of North Carolina Press, 2011), 211.

11. Nina Wallace, "Interview with Angel Marinaccio," *Community Oral History Project*, New York Public Library, 15:13, http://oralhistory.nypl.org/interviews /angel-marinaccio-i54jb0.

12. Hasia R. Diner, *Hungering for America: Italian, Irish, & Jewish Foodways in the Age of Migration* (Cambridge, MA: Harvard University Press, 2001), 204.

13. Arthur Schwartz, *Arthur Schwartz's New York City Food* (New York: Stewart, Tabori & Chang, 2004), 158–59.

14. Schwartz, *Arthur Schwartz's New York City Food*, 158–59.

15. Harvey Levenstein, *Revolution at the Table: The Transformation of the American Diet* (New York: Oxford University Press, 1988), 190–91.

16. Haley, *Turning the Tables*, 2.

17. Haley, *Turning the Tables*, 103.

18. Haley, *Turning the Tables*, 94.

19. William Grimes, *Appetite City: A Culinary History of New York* (New York: North Point Press, 2009), 125.

20. "Caruso Dies in Naples Following Operation," *Oakland Tribune* (Oakland, California), August 2, 1921, 2.

21. Michael Scott, *The Great Caruso: A Biography* (New York: Knopf, 1988), 69.

22. Scott, *The Great Caruso*, 91.

23. Maria Laurino, *The Italian Americans: A History* (New York: W.W. Norton, 2015), 198.

24. "Caruso Says Suing Chef Failed to Fill Major Role," *New-York Tribune* (New York, New York), December 16, 1920.

25. Scott, *The Great Caruso*, 94.

26. "Several Miles of Good Spaghetti with Caruso," *The Paducah Sun-Democrat* (Paducah, Kentucky), May 27, 1921, 3.

27. Giuseppe Prezzolini, *Spaghetti Dinner* (New York: Abelard-Schuman, 1955), 45.

28. John Kobler, "Bravo Caruso!" *American Heritage* 35, no. 2 (February/March 1984).

29. Douglas Martin, "About New York; Mamma Leone's Spicy Tales of Sweet Success," *New York Times*, September 19, 1987.

30. Mark Rotella, *The Story of Italian American Song: Amore* (New York: Macmillan, 2019), 13.

31. Paul Freedman, *Ten Restaurants That Changed America* (New York: Liverlight, 2018), 183.

32. Ken Bloom, *Broadway: Its History, People, and Places, An Encyclopedia* (London: Routledge, 2003), 330.

33. Gene Leone, *Leone's Italian Cookbook* (New York: Harper & Row, 1967), 5.

34. Freedman, *Ten Restaurants That Changed America*, 190.

35. Leone, *Leone's Italian Cookbook*, 7.

36. Douglas Martin, "About New York; Mamma Leone's: Spicy Tales of Sweet Success," *New York Times*, September 19, 1987.

37. Diane Darrow and Tom Mebesca, *The Seasons of the Italian Kitchen* (New York: Grove Atlantic, 2012), 464.

38. Kobler, "Bravo Caruso!"

39. Edward L. Bernays, *The Biography of an Idea: The Founding Principles of Public Relations* (New York: Open Road Media, 2015), ch. 9, Google Books.

40. Bernays, *The Biography of an Idea*, ch. 9.

41. Scott, *The Great Caruso*, 109.

42. Jean Anderson, *The American Century Cookbook* (New York: Clarkson Potter, 1997), 186–87.

43. Anderson, *The American Century Cookbook*, 186–87.

44. Craig Claiborne, *Craig Claiborne's* The New York Times *Food Encyclopedia* (New York: Wings Books, 1985), 448.

45. Anderson, *The American Century Cookbook*, 188.

46. James Beard, *American Cookery* (New York: Little, Brown, 1972), 202.

47. Anderson, *The American Century Cookbook*, 188.

48. Sam Sifton, "Chicken Terazzini, the Casserole Even Snobs Love," *New York Times Magazine*, September 26, 2016.

CHAPTER 8

1. Carol Helstosky, *Garlic and Oil: Food and Politics in Italy* (Oxford: Berg, 2004), 23.

2. Waverly Root, *The Food of Italy* (New York: Vintage Books, 1992), 198.

3. Saveur, *The New Comfort Food: Home Cooking from around the World*, ed. James Oseland (San Francisco: Chronicle Books, 2011), 84.

4. Mary Taylor Simeti, *Pomp and Sustenance: Twenty-Five Centuries of Sicilian Food* (New York: Knopf, 1989), 160.

5. Danielle Battisti, "Italian Americans, Consumerism, and the Cold War Perspective," *Making Italian America: Consumer Culture and the Product of Ethnic Identities*, ed. Cinotto Simone (New York: Fordham University Press, 2014), 153.

6. Gabriella Romani, *Postal Culture: Writing and Reading Letters in Post-Unification Italy* (Toronto: University of Toronto Press, 2013), 28.

7. Simeti, *Pomp and Sustenance*, 161.

8. "The Italian Way of Cooking It," *Good Housekeeping* 3, no. 13 (October 30, 1886): 319.

9. Linda Civitello, *Cuisine and Culture: A History of Food and People* (Hoboken, NJ: Wiley, 2004), 234.

10. Clifford Wright, *A Mediterranean Feast: The Story of the Birth of the Celebrated Cuisines of the Mediterranean from the Merchants of Venice to the Barbary Corsairs, with More Than 500 Recipes* (New York: HarperCollins, 1999), 78.

11. Craig Clairborne and Pierre Franey, "Meat Rolls by Many Other Names: FOOD," *New York Times*, January 23, 1983, SM46.

12. Antonia Isola, *Simple Italian Cookery* (New York: Harper & Brothers, 1912), 54–55.

13. Arthur Schwartz, *Naples at the Table* (New York: HarperCollins, 1998), 52.

14. Schwartz, *Naples at the Table*, 52.

15. Root, *The Food of Italy*, 292.

16. Marlena Spieler, *A Taste of Naples: Neapolitan Culture, Cuisine, and Cooking* (Lanham, MD: Rowman & Littlefield, 2018), 170.

17. Alice Gitchell Kirk, "Domestic Science," *South Bend Tribune*, April 9, 1913, 18, www.newspapers.com/image/514067995.

18. "Test Macaroni Recipes," *New Macaroni Journal*, October 15, 1922, 38.

19. American Beauty Macaroni Products, "Meatballs and Spaghetti," *The Daily Sentinel* (Grand Junction, Colorado), October 19, 1923, 12, https://newscomwc.newspapers.com/image/535895823.

20. Fabio Parasecoli, *Al Dente: A History of Food in Italy* (London: Reaktion Books, 2014), 234.

21. War Department. *Army Recipes: War Department Technical Manual TM 10-412* (Washington, DC: U.S. Government Printing Office, 1944), 99.

CHAPTER 9

1. Harvey Levenstein, *Paradox of Plenty: A Social History of Eating in Modern America* (Berkeley: University of California Press, 2003), 51.

2. Oretta Zanini de Vita, *Encyclopedia of Pasta*, trans. Maureen B. Fant (Berkeley: University of California Press, 2009), 105.

3. Henry Russell, *The Passing Show* (Boston: Little, Brown, 1926), 116, Google Books.

4. Rian James, *Dining in New York* (New York: John Day Company, 1931), 33.

5. Mary Frost Mabon, "Fare Thee Well," *Town & Country*, 91, no. 4161 (February 1936): 82–85.

6. Waverly Root, *The Food of Italy* (New York: Vintage Books, 1992), 19.

7. Zanini de Vita, *Encyclopedia of Pasta*, 150.

8. Anne Milano Appel, *Why Italians Love to Talk about Food* (New York: Farrar, Straus, and Giroux, 2009), 120.

9. Anna Del Conte, *The Concise Gastronomy of Italy* (London: Pavilion, 2004), 30.

10. Appel, *Why Italians Love to Talk about Food*, 320.

11. Spieler, *A Taste of Naples*, 189.

12. Appel, *Why Italians Love to Talk about Food*, 320.

13. Mary Taylor Simeti, *Pomp and Sustenance: Twenty-Five Centuries of Sicilian Food* (New York: Knopf, 1989), 82.

14. Spieler, *A Taste of Naples*, 190.

15. David Gentilcore, *Pomodoro! A History of the Tomato in Italy* (New York: Columbia University Press, 2010), 61.

16. Melissa Clark, "Parmigiana Dishes to Warm Weary Souls," *New York Times*, January 30, 2015, www.nytimes.com/2015/02/04/dining/parm-dishes-to-warm-weary-souls.html.

17. Alan Davidson, *The Oxford Companion to Food* (Oxford: Oxford University Press, 1999), 153.

18. Lucy M. Long, *Ethnic American Food Today: A Cultural Encyclopedia* (New York: Rowman & Littlefield, 2015), 321.

19. Davidson, *The Oxford Companion to Food*, 848.

20. Anna Del Conte, *The Concise Gastronomy of Italy* (London: Pavilion, 2004), 298.

21. John Ayto, *The Diner's Dictionary: Word Origins of Food and Drink* (Oxford: Oxford University Press, 2012), 328.

22. Molly O'Neill, "Food; Pressing the Flesh," *New York Times*, April 4, 1999, www.nytimes.com/1999/04/04/magazine/food-pressing-the-flesh.html.

23. Andrew P. Haley, *Turning the Tables: Restaurants and the Rise of the American Middle Class, 1880–1920* (Chapel Hill: University Press of North Carolina, 2011), 99.

24. Craig Clairborne and Pierre Franey, "Food; Italian American-Style," *New York Times*, April 26, 1981, www.nytimes.com/1981/04/26/magazine/food-Italian American-style.html.

25. Robert Sedlac, "Die Wahrheit über das Wiener Schnitzel," *Wiener Zeitung*, July 3, 2007, www.wienerzeitung.at/meinung/glossen/99743_Die-Wahrheit-ueber-das-Wiener-Schnitzel.html.

26. Alan Davidson, *The Oxford Companion to Food*, 848.

27. Robert Sedlac, "Das wiener schnitzel—zweiter tail," *Wiener Zeitung*, November 25, 2008, www.wienerzeitung.at/meinung/glossen/250616_Das-Wiener-Schnitzel-zweiter-Teil.html.

28. Kristberg Kristbergsson and Jorge Oliveira, ed., *Traditional Foods: General and Consumer Aspects* (New York: Springer, 2016), 252.

29. Andrew Z. Galarneau, "The Story behind Spaghetti Parm, Buffalo's Favorite Pasta," *Buffalo News*, August 21, 2018, https://buffalonews.com/entertainment/dining/the-story-behind-spaghetti-parm-buffalos-favorite-pasta/article_9e8fc606-2078-5a6f-af7d-83be2574c95f.html.

30. Sarah Lohman, *Eight Flavors: The Untold Story of American Cuisine* (New York: Simon & Schuster, 2016), 163.

31. Robin Cherry, *Garlic: An Edible Biography* (Boston: Roost Books, 2014), 1.

CHAPTER 10

1. Il Vero Alfredo Emperor of Fettuccine, "Our History," accessed September 3, 2021, www.ilveroalfredo.it/en/history.

2. Mark Kurlansky, *Milk: A 10,000-Year Fracas* (New York: Bloomsbury, 2018), 38.

3. Katia Amore, "Fettuccinne al Burro or Fettuccine Alfredo," *Italy Magazine*, October 13, 2014.

4. "Armando 'Alfredo' Di Lelio, Son of Creator . . . ," UPI, April 6, 1982, www.upi.com/Archives/1982/04/06/Armando-Alfredo-Di-Lelio-son-of-the-creator-of/3187386917200.

5. Todd Coleman, "The Real Alfredo," *Saveur*, April 13, 2009, www.saveur.com/article/Kitchen/The-Real-Alfredo.

6. "Rector Buys Churchill's," *New York Times*, August 16, 1909, 14.

7. "George Rector, 69, Noted Host, Dead," *New York Times*, November 27, 1947, 31.

8. "Sailor's Fight at Rector's," *New York Times*, May 24, 1917, 10.

9. William Grimes, *Appetite City* (New York: North Point Press, 2009), 136.

10. George Rector, "A Cook's Tour," *Saturday Evening Post*, November 19, 1927, 14.

11. George Rector, *The Rector Cook Book* (Chicago: Rector, 1928), 70.

12. Henry McLemore, "Rome's 'King of the Noodles' Climbs Ladder of Success," *Spokane Chronicle*, February 28, 1951, 12.

13. Paul Hofmann, "Fettuccine—a Dish Fit for a Duchess," *New York Times*, November 1, 1981, XX9.

14. Hofmann, "Fettuccine," XX9.

15. Todd Coleman, "The Real Alfredo," *Saveur*, April 13, 2009.

16. Marcella Hazan, *The Classic Italian Cook Book* (New York: Knopf, 1980), 150.

17. WFMY News 2 Digital Team, "The Secrets to Olive Garden's Alfredo Sauce," *Good Morning Show*, October 9, 2019, www.wfmynews2.com/article/news/local/good-morning-show/olive-garden-pasta-bar-alfredo-sauce/83-ef0f6dfb-c6cf-4dea-bc9f-46578d5b72e5.

CHAPTER 11

1. Rosario Buonassisi, *Pizza: From Its Italian Origins to the Modern Table* (Buffalo: Firefly Books, 2000), 32.

2. Marlena Spieler, *A Taste of Naples: Neapolitan Culture, Cuisine, and Cooking* (Lanham, MD: Rowman & Littlefield, 2018), 138.

3. John Dickie, *Delizia! The Epic History of Italians and Their Food* (New York: Free Press, 2008), 188.

4. Buonassisi, *Pizza*, 32.

5. Antonio Mattozzi, *Inventing the Pizzeria: A History of Pizza Making in Naples*, trans. Zacharty Nowak (London: Bloomsbury Academic, 2009), 6.

6. Dickie, *Delizia!*, 186.

7. Buonassisi, *Pizza*, 40.

8. Buonassisi, *Pizza*, 40.

9. Mattozzi, *Inventing the Pizzeria*, 11.

10. Carlo Middione, *The Food of Southern Italy* (New York: William Morrow, 1987), 59.

11. Waverly Root, *The Food of Italy* (New York: Vintage Books, 1992), 501–2.

12. Buonassisi, *Pizza*, 48.

13. Carol Helstosky, *Pizza: A Global History* (London: Reaktion Books, 2014), 23.

14. Buonassisi, *Pizza*, 42.

15. Mark Cirillo, *Pizza Culture: The Story of the World's Most Popular Dish* (Toronto: Mansfield Press, 2017), 28.

16. Buonassisi, *Pizza*, 23.

17. Mattozzi, *Inventing the Pizzeria*, 78–79.

18. Mattozzi, *Inventing the Pizzeria*, 85.

19. Mattozzi, *Inventing the Pizzeria*, 32.

20. Brad Cohen, ed., "The Untold Story of How My Grandfather Brought Pizza to America," *Vice*, February 19, 2017, www.vice.com/en/article/3d4nb9/the -untold-story-of-how-my-grandfather-brought-pizza-to-america.

21. Penny Pollack and Jeff Ruby, *Everybody Loves Pizza* (Cincinnati: Emmis Books, 2005), 21.

22. Mike Pomranz, "New York's Pizza History May Need a Major Rewrite, According to an Upcoming Book," *Food and Wine*, February 6, 2019, www.foodand wine.com/news/nyc-pizza-history-book-filippo-milone.

23. Pollack and Ruby, *Everybody Loves Pizza*, 21.

24. Cirillo, *Pizza Culture*, 32.

25. Jill P. Capuzzo, "The Original," *New Jersey Monthly*, January 12, 2010.

26. Peter Genovese, "Nation's Oldest Pizzeria in Trenton, Claims Owner," NJ.com, July 27, 2011, www.nj.com/entertainment/dining/2011/07/nations_oldest _pizzeria_in_tre.html.

27. Genovese, "Nation's Oldest Pizzeria in Trenton, Claims Owner."

28. Jane Black, "How Patsy Grimaldi, the 81-Year-Old New York Pizza Legend, Is Getting His Good Name Back," *Grub Street*, October 21, 2012, www.grub street.com/2012/10/pizza-legend-patsy-grimaldi-gets-his-good-name-back.html.

29. Gayle Turim, "Who Invented Pizza," History.com, July 27, 2012, www.his tory.com/author/gayle-turim.

30. Marian Burros, "In New Haven, Pizza Is Serious," *New York Times*, July 18, 1987, 52.

31. Kristin Hussey, "Uncertain Future for Pizzeria That Gave New Haven a Special Flavor," *New York Times*, January 14, 2016, A24.

32. Helstosky, *Pizza*, 55.

33. "The Definitive Guide to New Haven Pizza," *Eater*, March 18, 2014, www .eater.com/2014/3/18/6264277/the-definitive-guide-to-new-haven-pizza.

34. Burros, "In New Haven, Pizza Is Serious," 52.

35. Burros, "In New Haven, Pizza Is Serious," 52.

36. Donna R. Gabaccia, *We Are What We Eat: Ethnic Food and the Making of Americans* (Cambridge, MA: Harvard University Press, 2000), 197.

37. Buonassisi, *Pizza*, 50.

38. Max Read, "The Pizza Belt: The Most Important Pizza Theory You'll Read," *Gawker*, July 12, 2013, www.gawker.com/the-pizza-belt-the-most-important -pizza-theory-youll-r-743629037.

39. Carol Brock and Katherine Fisher, "It's Tomato Time," *Good Housekeeping* 125, no. 3 (September 1947): 122–23, 160, 162.

40. Malcom La Prade, "Meals by Men," *Ladies Home Journal* 165, no. 4 (April 1948): 286–88.

41. Eric Martone, ed., *Italian Americans: The History and Culture of a People* (Santa Barbara, CA: ABC-CLIO, 2017), 167.

42. Peter Hogness, "Obituary of Ira Nevins," *New York Times*, January 25, 1995, section C.

43. Hogness, "Obituary of Ira Nevins," section C.

44. Hunt's, "Ten Minute Pizza," *Redbook* 104, no. 6 (April 1955): 64.

45. Harvey Levenstein, *Paradox of Plenty: A Social History of Eating in Modern America* (Berkeley: University of California Press, 2003), 122.

46. Pollack and Ruby, *Everybody Loves Pizza*, 55.

47. Levenstein, *Paradox of Plenty*, 230.

48. Helstosky, *Pizza*, 14.

49. Liz Barret, *Pizza: A Slice of American History* (Minneapolis: Quarto, 2014), 142.

50. Helstosky, *Pizza*, 88.

51. Pollack and Ruby, *Everybody Loves Pizza*, 50.

52. Anthony Ramirez, "Soviet Pizza Huts Have Local Flavor," *New York Times*, September 11, 1990, D5.

53. "Who Invented Deep Dish?" *Chicago Tribune*, February 18, 2009, www .chicagotribune.com/news/ct-xpm-2009-02-18-0902180055-story.html.

54. Pollack and Ruby, *Everybody Loves Pizza*, 30.

55. Patricia Tennison, "Revealed: Secret Behind Pizzas at Gino's East," *Chicago Tribune*, April 13, 1989, www.chicagotribune.com/news/ct-xpm-1989-04-13-8904030809-story.html.

56. Cirillo, *Pizza Culture*, 98.

57. Barret, *Pizza*, 92.

58. Barret, *Pizza*, 67.

59. Erica Marcus, "Grandma Pizza: The Full Story," *Newsday*, September 10, 2008, www.newsday.com/lifestyle/restaurants/grandma-pizza-the-full-story-1.825269.

60. Barret, *Pizza*, 63.

61. Fabio Parasecoli, *Al Dente: A History of Food in Italy* (London: Reaktion Books, 2014), 243.

62. Nell Casey, "LES Group Calls for an End to Invasive Dollar Slice Joints," *Gothamist*, February 14, 2014, https://gothamist.com/food/les-group-calls-for-an-end-to-invasive-dollar-slice-joints.

63. Liz Robbins, "A Dash of Drama in the Pizza World," *New York Daily News*, November 29, 2011, https://cityroom.blogs.nytimes.com/2011/11/29/a-dash-of-drama-in-the-pizza-world.

64. Liz Robbins, "Close to Fetching Coal and Making Pizza," *New York Times City Room*, December 16, 2011, https://cityroom.blogs.nytimes.com/2011/12/16/close-to-fetching-coal-and-making-pizza.

65. Julia Moskin, "The Kings of the Dollar Slice Build a Better Pizza," *New York Times*, February 19, 2019, www.nytimes.com/2019/02/19/dining/nyc-pizza-upside-dollar-slice.html.

CHAPTER 12

1. Mark Fahey, "Americans Have an Insatiable Demand for Pizza Cheese," *CNBC.com*. October 4, 2016, www.cnbc.com/2016/10/04/best-cheeses-americans-have-an-insatiable-demand-for-pizza-cheese.html.

2. Fahey, "Americans Have an Insatiable Demand for Pizza Cheese."

3. Paul S. Kindstedt, *Cheese and Culture: A History of Cheese and Its Place in Western Civilization* (White River Junction, VT: Chelsea Green, 2012), 209.

4. David L. Thurmond and Sandra P. Thurmond, *The Great History of Mozzarella* (Ogliastro Cilento, Italy: Licosia Italiacs, 2017), 88.

5. Thurmond and Thurmond, *The Great History of Mozzarella*, 63.

6. Thurmond and Thurmond, *The Great History of Mozzarella*, 63.

7. Sam Anderson, "Go Ahead, Milk My Day," *New York Times*, October 11, 2012, SM75.

8. Anderson, "Go Ahead, Milk My Day," SM75.

9. Thurmond and Thurmond, *The Great History of Mozzarella*, 38.

10. Thurmond and Thurmond, *The Great History of Mozzarella*, 62.

11. Thurmond and Thurmond, *The Great History of Mozzarella*, 63.

12. Thurmond and Thurmond, *The Great History of Mozzarella*, 63.

13. Peter Sardo, Gigi Piumatti, and Roberto Rubino, eds., *Italian Cheese: A Guide to Their Discovery and Appreciation* (Bra, Italy: Slow Food Arcigola Editore, 1999), 84.

14. Thurmond and Thurmond, *The Great History of Mozzarella*, 100.

15. Thurmond and Thurmond, *The Great History of Mozzarella*, 109.

16. Kindstedt, *Cheese and Culture*, 204.

17. Kindstedt, *Cheese and Culture*, 209.

18. Gabriella Ganugi, *Cheese: An Italian Pantry* (San Francisco: Wine Appreciation Guild, 2004), 39.

19. Ganugi, *Cheese*, 48.

20. Ganugi, *Cheese*, 17.

21. Ganugi, *Cheese*, 39.

22. Marian Burros, "To Every Parmigiano, a Season," *New York Times*, July 26, 2000, F1.

23. Max Calman and David Gibbons, *Cheese: A Connoisseur's Guide in the World's Best* (New York: Clarkson Potter, 2005), 193.

24. Calman and Gibbons, *Cheese*, 193.

25. Burros, "To Every Parmigiano, a Season," F1.

26. Hannah Crowley, "The Great Parm Debate," *Cooks Illustrated*, July 1, 2016, www.cooksillustrated.com/articles/263-the-great-parm-debate.

27. Florence Fabricant, "Food: Parmesan Cheese Has Many Uses but Seek the Real Thing," *New York Times*, November 25, 1984, CN23.

28. Sardo and Piumatti, *Italian Cheese*, 66.

29. Kindstedt, *Cheese and Culture*, 84.

30. Sandy Carr, *Cheese: A Complete Guide to the Cheeses of the World* (New York: Simon & Schuster, 1992), 108.

31. Sardo and Piumatti, *Italian Cheese*, 228.

32. "Do You Know These Cheeses?" *Women's Day* 1 (October 1949): 64–65.

33. "Do you Know These Cheeses?"

34. Elena Kostioukovitch, *Why Italians Love to Talk about Food: A Journey through Italy's Great Regional Cuisines, from the Alps to Sicily* (New York: Farrar, Straus and Giroux, 2009), 52.

35. Julie Owen, "Food: Italian Cheese," *New York Times*, April 9, 1956, 24.

36. Katie Lobosco, "Trump's Other Trade War Could Hit Cheeses and Olive Oil," *CNN*, September 7, 2019, www.cnn.com/2019/09/07/politics/trade-war -europe-cheese-wine-trump.

CHAPTER 13

1. Alberto Capatti and Massimo Montanari, *Italian Cuisine: A Cultural History* (New York: Columbia University Press, 1999), 51.

2. Anthony F. Buccini, "Lasagna: A Layered History," in *Wrapped & Stuffed Foods*, ed. Mark McWilliams (Devon, UK: Prospect Books, 2013), 98.

3. Buccini, "Lasagna," 98.

4. Alberto Capatti and Massimo Montanari, *Italian Cuisine: A Cultural History* (New York: Columbia University Press, 1999), 52.

5. Silvano Servenitt and Françoise Sabban, *Pasta: The Story of a Universal Food*, trans. Antony Shugaar (New York: Columbia University Press, 2000), 75.

6. Servenitt and Sabban, *Pasta*, 54.

7. Buccini, "Lasagna," 95.

8. Marlena Spieler, *A Taste of Naples: Neapolitan Culture, Cuisine, and Cooking* (Lanham, MD: Rowman & Littlefield, 2018), 170.

9. Anna Boiardi and Stephanie Lyness, *Delicious Memories: Recipes and Stories from the Chef Boyardee Family* (New York: Stewart, Tabori & Chang, 2011), 95.

10. Oretta Zanini de Vita, *Encyclopedia of Pasta*, trans. Maureen B. Fant (Berkeley: University of California Press, 2009), 150.

11. Evan Kleiman, "Lasagne, Not Lasagna: Why a Pan of Béchamel Lasagna Is Just the Kind of Comfort Food You May Need," *Los Angeles Times*, January 5, 2018, www.latimes.com/food/dailydish/la-fo-co-lasagne-bechamel-evan-kleiman-20171208-story.html.

12. Jean Anderson, *The American Century Cookbook: The Most Popular Recipes of the 20th Century* (New York: Clarkson Potter, 1997), 164.

13. Anderson, *The American Century Cookbook*, 164.

14. Diana Ashley, *Where to Dine in Thirty-Nine* (New York: Crown, 1939), 36.

15. Pasquale Bruno Jr., *Pasta Tecnica* (Chicago: Contemporary Books, 1981), 55.

16. Elena Kostiloukovitch, *Why Italians Love to Talk about Food* (New York: Farrar, Straus, and Giroux, 2009), 137.

17. Michael Ruhlman, *Grocery: The Buying and Selling of Food in America* (New York: Harry N Abrams, 2017), 301.

18. Caz Hildebrand and Jacob Kenedy, *The Geometry of Pasta* (Philadelphia: Quirk Books, 2010), 208.

19. Bruno, *Pasta Tecnica*, 68.

20. Zanini de Vita, *Encyclopedia of Pasta*, 226.

21. Tony May, *Italian Cuisine* (New York: St. Martin's Press, 2005), 156.

22. Arthur Schwartz, *Arthur Schwartz's New York City Food* (New York: Stewart, Tabori, & Chang, 2004), 176.

23. Louella G. Shouer, "Thrifty Meals Italian Style," *Ladies Home Journal* 68, no. 2 (February 1951): 148–49, 155.

24. Candy Sagon, "The Americanization of Lasagna," *Washington Post*, February 16, 2000, www.washingtonpost.com/wp-srv/WPcap/2000-02/16/001r-021600-idx.html.

CHAPTER 14

1. Douglas Martin, "About New York; Mamma Leone's: Spicy Tales of Sweet Success," *New York Times*, September 19, 1987, 33.

2. Paul Freedman, *Ten Restaurants That Changed America* (New York: Liverlight, 2018), 157.

3. "Pet Elephant Dies," *New York Dispatch*, December 27, 1952, www.news papers.com/image/614082860.

4. David Gentilcore, *Pomodoro! A History of the Tomato in Italy* (New York: Columbia University Press, 2010), 184.

5. Amy Gulick, "Recipe of the Week: Pasta alla Gricia," *Italy Magazine*, May 15, 2015, www.italymagazine.com/recipe/recipe-week-pasta-alla-gricia.

6. Gulick, "Recipe of the Week."

7. Mary Taylor Simeti, *Pomp and Sustenance: Twenty-Five Centuries of Sicilian* (New York: Knopf, 1989), 170.

8. Anthony F. Buccini, "On Spaghetti alla Carbonara and Related Dishes of Central and Southern Italy," in *Eggs in Cookery*, ed. Richard Hosking (London: Prospect Books, 2007), 41–42.

9. Susan McKenna Grant, "What's for Dinner: Cart Driver's Spaghetti," *Post Gazette*, June 17, 2009, www.post-gazette.com/life/food/2009/06/17/What-s-for -dinner-Cart-Driver-s-Spaghetti/stories/200906170241.

10. Florence Fabricant, "The Meet of the Matter in a Pasta Debate," *New York Times*, January 16, 2008, F1, www.nytimes.com/2008/01/16/dining/16ital.html.

11. "Bucatini (O Spaghetti) All 'Matriciana," *Accademia Italiana della Cucina*, www.accademiaitalianadellacucina.it/it/ricette/ricetta/bucatini-o-spaghetti-alla -%E2%80%9Cmatriciana%E2%80%9D.

12. Corby Kummer, "Mangia, Mangia, in the Mountains," Corby's Table, *The Atlantic Online—Atlantic Unbound*, October 7, 1998, www.theatlantic.com/past /docs/unbound/corby/ct981007.htm.

13. Stephanie Kirchgaessner, "Italian Birthplace of Amatriciana Denounces Chef's 'Secret Ingredient,'" *The Guardian*, February 9, 2015, www.theguardian .com/lifeandstyle/2015/feb/09/italian-chef-cracco-ridiculed-amatriciana-secret -ingredient-garlic.

14. Maria Luisa Taglienti, *The Italian Cookbook* (New York: Random House, 1955), 60.

15. Thrillist, "The 101 Dishes That Changed America," *Thrillist*, March 20, 2018, www.thrillist.com/eat/nation/most-important-dishes-food-that-changed -america.

16. Luca Cesari, "Carbonara: History, Origins and Anecdotes of a Legendary Recipe," *Gambero Rosso*, April 2, 2019, www.gamberorossointernational.com /uncategorised/carbonara-history-origins-and-anecdotes-of-a-legendary-recipe-2.

17. Obituary of Maria Grodzicki, Angel Valley Funeral Home, November 2017, https://angelvalleyfuneralhome.com/tribute/details/19011/Maria-Grodzicki/obitu ary.html.

18. Maryann Tebben, *Sauces: A Global History* (London: Reaktion Books, 2014), 89.

19. Adam Gopnik, "Carbonara Purists Can't Stop the Pasta Revolution," *New Yorker*, April 15, 2016, www.newyorker.com/culture/cultural-comment/carbonara -purists-cant-stop-the-pasta-revolution.

20. La Cucina Italiana, "L'enigma della carbonara," *La Cucina Italiana*, April 6, 2018, www.lacucinaitaliana.it/news/in-primo-piano/lenigma-della-carbonara.

21. Buccini, "On Spaghetti alla Carbonara," 43.

22. Anna Del Conte, *Italian Kitchen: La Pastasciutta* (New York: Simon & Schuster, 1993), 37.

23. Buccini, "On Spaghetti alla Carbonara," 39.

24. Marlena Spieler, *A Taste of Naples: Neapolitan Culture, Cuisine, and Cooking* (Lanham, MD: Rowman & Littlefield, 2018), 26.

25. Encyclopedia Britannica, "Carbonari," *Encyclopedia Britannica*, www.britannica.com/topic/Carbonari.

26. "22 settembre 1944—Nasce a Riccione la pasta alla carbonara," Almanacco quotidiano, *Chiamanicitta.it*, www.chiamamicitta.it/22-settembre-1944-nasce -riccione-la-pasta-alla-carbonara.

27. Buccini, "On Spaghetti alla Carbonara," 44.

28. Buccini, "On Spaghetti alla Carbonara," 43.

29. Karim Moyer-Nocchi, "From Half Baked to Homogenized: Risorgimento— Unita—Fascismo and the Rise of the Borghese Cookbook," *Dublin Gastronomy Symposium*, 2016 Food and Revolution, May 31–June 1, 2016.

30. Maurizio Bertera, "Carbonara: Nascita e gloria del piatto più amato (e falsificato) d'Italia," *Vanity Fair*, April 6, 2019, www.vanityfair.it/vanityfood /ricette/2019/04/06/carbonara-storia-curiosita-ricette-originale-ristorante.

31. Marjorie Schaffer, *Pepper: A History of the World's Most Influential Spice* (New York: Thomas Dunne Books: 2013), 2.

32. Schaffer, *Pepper*, 47.

33. Jean Andrews, *Peppers: The Domesticated Capsiums* (Austin: University of Texas Press, 1984), 4.

34. Schaffer, *Pepper*, 116.

35. Sarah Lohman, *Eight Flavors: The Untold Story of American Cuisine* (New York: Simon & Schuster, 2016), 6.

36. Lohman, *Eight Flavors*, 16.

37. Pete Wells, "At Momofuku Nishi, David Chang's Magic Shows a Little Wear," *New York Times*, May 17, 2016, www.nytimes.com/2016/05/18/dining /momofuku-nishi-review.html.

38. Robin Raisfeld and Rob Patronite, "How the Humble Cacio e Pepe Transcended Its Roots," *New York Magazine*, January 25, 2016, www.grubstreet.com /2016/01/how-cacio-e-pepe-transcended-its-roots.html.

39. Dave DeWitt and Janie Lamson, *The Field Guide to Peppers* (Portland, OR: Timber Press, 2015), 22.

40. Andrews, *Peppers*, 4.

41. DeWitt and Lamson, *The Field Guide to Peppers*, 172.

42. DeWitt and Lamson, *The Field Guide to Peppers*, 172.

43. Sara Moulton, "Of All the Ways Chicken and Sausage Can Be Cobbled Together, This Might Be the Tastiest," *Washington Post Magazine*, September 27, 2018, www.washingtonpost.com/lifestyle/magazine/of-all-the-ways-chicken-and-sausage-can-be-cobbled-together-this-might-be-the-tastiest/2018/09/24/c037d0f4-ad3c-11e8-b1da-ff7faa680710_story.html.

44. Arthur Schwartz, "Chicken Scarpariello," *The Three Tomatoes*, June 15, 2014, http://thethreetomatoes.com/chicken-scarpariello.

45. "Chicken Scarpariello," *Lidia's Italy*, https://lidiasitaly.com/recipes/chicken-scarpariello-2.

46. Craig Claiborne and Pierre Franey, "Food; Italian, American-Style," *New York Times*, April 26, 1981, SM128.

47. "Sweetwaters," *New York Magazine*, June 30–July 7, 1986; "Monte's Venetian Room," *New York Magazine*, March 23, 1987; "Ponte's," *New York Magazine*, December 24–31, 1984; "The Old Reliables: Nanni," *New York Magazine*, August 13, 1984.

48. Alfred E. Clark, "San Gennaro Fete Opens 9-Day Run," *New York Times*, September 13, 1964, 41.

49. John F. Mariani, *How Italian Food Conquered the World* (New York: Palgrave, 2011), 37.

50. April L. Goldman, "Grand Old Festa of Mulberry St. Is On," *New York Times*, September 12, 1980, C24.

51. Linda Civitello, *Cuisine and Culture: A History of Food and People* (Hoboken, NJ: Wiley, 2004), 234.

52. Craig Claiborne, "Street Festival Begins Wednesday; Gastronomic Delights Await Visitors," *New York Times*, September 10, 1959, 38.

53. Andrews, *Peppers*, 54.

54. Marcella Hazan and Victor Hazan, *Ingredienti: Marcella's Guide to the Market* (New York: Scribner, 2016), 48.

55. Schaffer, *Pepper*, 10.

56. "Penne triangolari all'arrabbiata," *La Rustichella*, October 17, 2016, www.larustichella.it/penne-triangolari-allarrabbiata.

57. Oretta Zanini de Vita and Maureen B. Fant, *Sauces & Shapes* (New York: Norton, 2013), 92.

CHAPTER 15

1. Oretta Zanini de Vita and Maureen B. Fant, *Sauces & Shapes* (New York: Norton, 2013), 68.

2. Diane Seed, *The Top One Hundred Pasta Sauces* (London: Rosendale Press, 1987), 20.

3. Seed, *The Top One Hundred Pasta Sauces*, 20.

4. Mary Gibson, *Gender, Family, and Sexuality: The Private Sphere in Italy, 1860–1945*, ed. Perry Willson (New York: Palgrave MacMillan, 2004), 99.

5. *Oxford-Paravia Italian Dictionary*, 3rd ed. (Oxford: Oxford University Press, 2010).

6. Annarita Cuomo, "Il sugo 'alla puttanesca' nacque per caso ad Ischia, dall'estro culinario di Sandro Petti," *Il Golfo*, February 17, 2005, https://web .archive.org/web/20080209143520/www.ilgolfo.it/t/storehtm/htm19/17Feb0501f.

7. Cuomo, "Il sugo 'alla puttanesca.'"

8. Luciano Pignataro, *La Cucina Napoletana* (Milan: Hoepli, 2016), Google Books.

9. "Diocese of Ischia—Past and Present Ordinaries," *Catholic Hierarchy*, accessed September 3, 2021, www.catholic-hierarchy.org/diocese/disch.html.

10. Raffaele La Capria, *Ferito a morte* (Milan: Oscar Mondadori, 1984), 156.

11. Pellegrino Artusi, *Exciting Food for Southern Types*, trans. Marsilio Publishers (London: Penguin/University of Toronto Press, 2003), 24.

12. Zanini de Vita and Fant, *Sauces & Shapes*, 130.

13. Jennifer V. Cole, "How a Simple Pasta Dish Set One Writer on a Life-Changing Journey," *Food and Wine*, September 10, 2018, www.foodandwine.com /cooking-techniques/sicily-pasta-alla-norma.

14. Zanini de Vita and Fant, *Sauces & Shapes*, 130.

15. Giuseppina Siotto, *Vegetaliana: note di cucina italiana vegetale* (Modena, Italy: Edizioni del Loggione, 2014), 162.

16. Roger Parker, ed., *The Oxford Illustrated History of Opera* (Oxford: Oxford University Press, 2001), 187–89.

17. "Hot Stuff from Tuscany," *The Observer* (London), October 29, 1967, 29, www.newspapers.com/image/258895165.

18. "What's the Story on Pasta? Ask Richard Castellano," *The News* (Paterson, New Jersey), August 8, 1974, 27, www.newspapers.com/image/532134206.

19. Hannah Norwick, "The 8 Dishes That Made My Career: Cesare Casella," *First We Feast*, February 11, 2013, https://firstwefeast.com/eat/2013/02/cesare -casella-8-career-changing-dishes.

20. Waverly Root, *The Food of Italy* (New York: Vintage Books, 1992), 5.

21. Dian Darrow and Tom Maresca, *The Seasons of the Italian Kitchen* (New York: Grove/Atlantic, 2012), 454.

22. Robin Raisfeld and Rob Patronite, "The Truth about Vodka Sauce," *New York Magazine*, October 3, 2017, www.grubstreet.com/2017/10/truth-about-vodka -sauce-carbone.html.

23. Nigella Lawson, "At My Table; Pasta That Adds Bite to Vodka," *New York Times*, October 29, 2003, F3.

24. Efram Funghi Calingaert and Jacquelyn Days Serwer, *Pasta and Rice Italian Style* (New York: Scribners, 1983), 185.

25. Susan Selasky, "In Good Taste: Pasta alla Vodka Sauce," *Detroit Free Press*, April 2, 2016, www.freep.com/story/life/food/recipes/2016/04/02/pasta-alla-vodka-sauce/82497814.

26. Florence Fabricant, "Dining Out; Italian Fare with Emphasized Décor," *New York Times*, June 30, 1981, L123.

27. Florence Fabricant, "Dining Out; Italian Fare in a Pleasant Setting," *New York Times*, August, 2 1981, L119.

28. James Barron, "Joe Franklin, a Talk Show Institution in New York, Dies at 88," *New York Times*, January 24, 2015, www.nytimes.com/2015/01/25/nyregion/joe-franklin-local-talk-show-pioneer-dies-at-88.html.

29. Paul Vitello, "Armando Orsini, a New York Restauranteur, Dies at 88," *New York Times*, July 20, 2011, www.nytimes.com/2011/07/21/nyregion/armando-orsini-a-new-york-restaurateur-dies-at-88.html.

30. *The Daily News* (New York), November 6, 1967, 579, www.newspapers.com/image/463950910.

31. *The Cincinnati Enquirer*, July 20, 1957, 8, www.newspapers.com/image/100934017.

32. "World Pasta Day a Mosca: Si celebra con le penne alla vodka," *L'Espresso Food & Wine*, Espresso.rupubblica.it, October 25, 2016, http://espresso.repubblica.it/food/dettaglio/world-pasta-day-a-mosca_-si-celebra-con-le-penne-alla-vodka/2231016.html.

CHAPTER 16

1. Harvey Levenstein, *Paradox of Plenty: A Social History of Eating in Modern America* (Berkeley: University of California Press, 2003), 223.

2. Mark Bittman, "Remembering Marcella," *New York Times*, November 10, 2013, SM46.

3. Brainard Dulcy, "Marcella Hazan: Educating America's Palate," *Publisher's Weekly* 244, no. 45 (November 3, 1997): 62–63, www.publishersweekly.com/pw/by-topic/authors/interviews/article/26571-pw-marcella-hazan-educating-america-s-palate.html.

4. Dulcy, "Marcella Hazan," 62–63.

5. Kim Severson, "For Better, for Worse, for Richer, for Pasta," *New York Times*, September 9, 2008, F1.

6. "Time for a Sketti!" *Here Comes Honey Boo Boo*, Season 1, Episode 8, original airdate October 12, 2012.

7. John F. Mariani, *How Italian Food Conquered the World* (New York: Palgrave Macmillan, 2011), 166.

8. Mariani, *How Italian Food Conquered the World*, 166.

9. William Grimes, *Appetite City: A Culinary History of New York* (New York: North Point Press, 2009), 306.

10. Tara Law, "Mario Batali Relinquishes His Restaurants Following Sexual Harassment and Assault Allegations," *TIME*, March 7, 2019, https://time.com/5546290/mario-batali-sells-restaurants.

11. Ervin Kosta, "The Immigrant Enclave as Theme Park," in *Making Italian America: Consumer Culture and the Production of Ethnic Identities*, ed. Cinotto Simone (New York: Fordham University Press, 2014), 233–34.

12. Craig Claiborne with Pierre Franey, "Spaghetti with a French Accent," *New York Times*, October 2, 1977, SM20.

13. Sherri Liberman, ed., *American Food by the Decades* (Santa Barbara, CA: Greenwood, 2011), 191.

14. David Kamp, *The United States of Arugula* (New York: Broadway Books, 2006), 223.

15. Amanda Hesser, *The Essential New York Times Cook Book: Classic Recipes for a New Century* (New York: W.W. Norton, 2010), Google Books.

CHAPTER 17

1. Geofrey T. Hellman, "Profiles: Directed to the Product," *New Yorker*, October 17, 1964, 75.

2. Hellman, "Profiles," 59.

3. Associated Press, "Mamma Leone Shuts Doors in Manhattan," *New York Times*, January 11, 1994, www.nytimes.com/1994/01/11/nyregion/mamma-leone-shuts-doors-in-manhattan.html.

4. Marcia Biderman, *Popovers and Candlelight: Patricia Murphy and the Rise and Fall of a Restaurant Empire* (Albany: State University of New York Press, 2018), 170–71.

5. Philip J. Romano, *Food for Thought* (Chicago: Dearborn Trade, 2005), x.

6. Romano, *Food for Thought*, 114.

7. Michele Travierso, "What Actually Goes on at Olive Garden's 'Culinary Institute' in Tuscany?" *TIME*, April 5, 2011, https://newsfeed.time.com/2011/04/15/what-actually-goes-on-at-olive-gardens-culinary-institute-in-tuscany.

8. Molly O'Neil, "Quel Shock! The Italianization of French Cuisine," *New York Times*, October 5, 1994, C1.

9. Frank Bruni, "An Act You've Known All These Years," *New York Times—Diner's Journal*, February 20, 2006, https://dinersjournal.blogs.nytimes.com/2006/02/20/an-act-youve-known-for-all-these-years.

10. Jeff Zeleny and Sewell Chan, "Obama and Bill Clinton Have Lunch in the Village," *New York Times*, September 14, 2009, https://cityroom.blogs.nytimes.com/2009/09/14/obama-and-clinton-have-lunch-in-the-village.

CHAPTER 18

1. Alex Vadukul, "How Forlini's Survives the Instagram Horde," *New York Times*, September 14, 2018, www.nytimes.com/2018/09/14/nyregion/forlinis -instagram.html.

2. Kevin Kessler, "Bamonte's Is the Best of Old Brooklyn," *Village Voice*, September 25, 2014, www.villagevoice.com/2014/09/25/bamontes-is-the-best-of -old-brooklyn.

3. Helen Rosner, "How to Get a Table at Carbone," *New Yorker*, May 19, 2021, www.newyorker.com/culture/annals-of-gastronomy/how-to-get-a-table-at-carbone.

4. Adam Nagourney, "Red Sauce and Rivalry at New Rao's: A Storied New York Restaurant Makes a Move on Los Angeles," *New York Times*, January 22, 2014, D1.

5. Anthony Noto, "Mom-and-Pop Italian Restaurant to Become a 'Dig Inn,'" *New York Business Journal*, April 22, 2019, www.bizjournals.com/newyork /news/2019/04/22/mom-and-pop-italian-restaurant-to-become-a-dig-inn.html.

6. "After 32 Years on 4th Street, Cucina di Pesce Will Close after Service on Sunday," *EV Grieve*, September 21, 2018, https://evgrieve.com/2018/09/after -32-years-on-4th-street-cucina-di.html.

7. Rachel Handler, "What the Hole Is Going On? The Very Real, Totally Bizarre Bucatini Shortage of 2020," *Grub Street*, December 28, 2020, www.grubstreet .com/2020/12/2020-bucatini-shortage-investigation.html.

8. Steve Cuozzo, "Hamptons Il Mulino, Six Other Non-NYC Locations File for Bankruptcy," *New York Post*, July 29, 2020, https://nypost.com/2020/07/29 /hamptons-il-mulino-six-other-non-nyc-locations-file-for-bankruptcy.

9. Tae Yoon, "Legendary Rao's in East Harlem Is Offering Takeout for the First Time in Its 124-Year History," *Thrillist*, December 8, 2020, www.thrillist.com/eat /new-york/raos-to-go-takeout-east-harlem-nyc.

Bibliography

A&P. "Ann Page Macaroni Pie." *Life* 42, no. 9 (March 4, 1957): 53.

"After 32 Years on 4th Street, Cucina di Pesce Will Close after Service on Sunday." *EV Grieve*, September 21, 2018. https://evgrieve.com/2018/09/after-32-years-on-4th-street-cucina-di.html.

Albala, Ken. "Italianità in America: The Cultural Politics of Representing 'Authentic' Italian Cuisine in the US." In *Representing Italy Through Food*, edited by Peter Naccarato, Zachary Nowak, and Elgin K. Eckert. New York: Boomsbury, 2017.

Allen, Arthur. *Ripe: The Search for the Perfect Tomato*. Berkeley: Counterpoint, 2010.

Alliata, Enrico. "Author's Forward." *The Duke's Table: The Complete Book of Vegetarian Italian Cooking*. Translated by Anthony Shugaar. Brooklyn: Melville House, 2013.

American Beauty Macaroni Products. "Meatballs and Spaghetti." *The Daily Sentinel* (Grand Junction, Colorado), October 19, 1923. https://newscomwc.newspapers.com/image/535895823.

Amore, Katia. "Fettuccinne al Burro or Fettuccine Alfredo." *Italy Magazine*, October 13, 2014.

Anderson, Jean. *The American Century Cookbook: The Most Popular Recipes of the 20th Century*. New York: Clarkson Potter, 1997.

Anderson, Sam. "Go Ahead, Milk My Day." *New York Times*, October 11, 2012, SM75.

Andrews, Jean. *Peppers: The Domesticated Capsiums*. Austin: University of Texas Press, 1984.

Appel, Anne Milano. *Why Italians Love to Talk about Food.* New York: Farrar, Straus, and Giroux, 2009.

"Armando 'Alfredo' Di Lelio, Son of Creator. . . ." UPI, April 6, 1982. www .upi.com/Archives/1982/04/06/Armando-Alfredo-Di-Lelio-son-of-the-creator -of/3187386917200.

Artusi, Pellegrino. *Exciting Food for Southern Types.* Translated by Marsilio Publishers. London: Penguin/University of Toronto Press, 2003.

———. *La scienza in cucina e l'arte di mangiar bene: Manuale pratico per le famiglie compilato da.* 1999. http://www.livrosgratis.com.br/ler-livro-online-121084 /la-scienza-in-cucina-e-le039arte-di-mangiar-bene.

Ashley, Diana. *Where to Dine in Thirty-Nine.* New York: Crown Publishers, 1939.

Associated Press. "Mamma Leone Shuts Doors in Manhattan." *New York Times,* January 11, 1994. www.nytimes.com/1994/01/11/nyregion/mamma-leone-shuts -doors-in-manhattan.html.

Associazione Italiana Industrie Prodotti Alimentari. "Pasta at a Glance." AIDEPI, June 6, 2019. www.aidepi.it/en/pasta.html.

Ayto, John. *The Diner's Dictionary: Word Origins of Food and Drink.* Oxford: Oxford University Press, 2012.

Barr, Nancy Verde. *We Called It Macaroni: An American Heritage of Southern Italian Cooking.* New York: Knopf, 1996.

Barret, Liz. *Pizza: A Slice of American History.* Minneapolis: Quarto Publishing Group, 2014.

Barron, James. "Joe Franklin, a Talk Show Institution in New York, Dies at 88." *New York Times,* January 24, 2015. www.nytimes.com/2015/01/25/nyregion/joe -franklin-local-talk-show-pioneer-dies-at-88.html.

Battisti, Danielle. "Italian Americans, Consumerism, and the Cold War in Transnational Perspective." In *Making Italian America: Consumer Culture and the production of Ethnic Identities,* edited by Cinotto Simone. New York: Fordham University Press, 2014.

Beard, James. *American Cookery.* New York: Little, Brown and Company, 1972.

Bellman, Sheryll. *America's Little Italys.* South Portland, ME: Sellers Publisher, 2010.

Ben-Yehuda, Nachman. "The European Witch Craze of the 14th to 17th Centuries: A Sociologist's Perspective." *American Journal of Sociology* 86, no. 1 (July 1980): 1–31. www.journals.uchicago.edu/doi/abs/10.1086/227200.

Bernays, Edward L. *The Biography of an Idea: The Founding Principles of Public Relations.* New York: Open Road Media, 2015.

Bertera, Maurizio. "Carbonara: nascita e gloria del piatto più amato (e falsificato) d'Italia." *Vanity Fair,* April 6, 2019. www.vanityfair.it/vanityfood/ricette /2019/04/06/carbonara-storia-curiosita-ricette-originale-ristorante.

Biderman, Marcia. *Popovers and Candlelight: Patricia Murphy and the Rise and Fall of a Restaurant Empire.* Albany: State University of New York Press, 2018.

Bittman, Mark. "Remembering Marcella." *New York Times,* November 10, 2013, SM46. www.nytimes.com/2013/11/10/magazine/remembering-marcella.html.

Black, Jane. "How Patsy Grimaldi, the 81-Year-Old New York Pizza Legend, Is Getting His Good Name Back." *Grub Street*, October 21, 2012. www.grubstreet .com/2012/10/pizza-legend-patsy-grimaldi-gets-his-good-name-back.html.

Bloom, Ken. *Broadway: Its History, People, and Places, An Encyclopedia.* London: Routledge, 2003.

Bobrow-Strain, Aaron. *White Bread: A Social History of the Store-Bought Loaf.* Boston: Beacon Press, 2012. Kindle.

Boiardi, Anna, and Stephanie Lyness. *Delicious Memories: Recipes and Stories from the Chef Boyardee Family.* New York: Stewart, Tabori & Chang, 2011.

Boni, Ada. *The Talisman Italian Cookbook.* Translated by Matilde la Rosa. New York: Crown Publishers, 1950.

Braindard, Dulcy. "Marcella Hazan: Education America's Palate." *Publisher's Weekly* 244, no. 45 (November 3, 1997): 62–63.

Brickman, Sophie. "The Food of the Future." *New Yorker*, September 1, 2014. www.newyorker.com/culture/culture-desk/food-future.

Brock, Carol, and Katherine Fisher. "It's Tomato Time." *Good Housekeeping* 125, no. 3 (September 1947): 122–23, 160, 162.

Brown, Dustin. "Ronzoni Family Dishes Out Memories of LIC Legacy." *QNS*, October 9, 2002. https://qns.com/2002/10/ronzoni-family-dishes-out-memories -of-lic-legacy.

Bruni, Frank. "An Act You've Known All These Years." *New York Times—Diner's Journal—New York Times Blog on Dining Out*, February 20, 2006. https://diners journal.blogs.nytimes.com/2006/02/20/an-act-youve-known-for-all-these-years.

Bruno, Pasquale, Jr. *Pasta Tecnica*. Chicago: Contemporary Books, 1981.

"Bucatini (O Spaghetti) All 'Matriciana.'" *Accademia Italiana della Cucina*. www .accademiaitalianadellacucina.it/it/ricette/ricetta/bucatini-o-spaghetti-alla-%E2% 80%9Cmatriciana%E2%80%9D.

Buccini, Anthony F. "Lasagna: A Layered History." In *Wrapped and Stuffed Foods*, edited by Mark McWilliams. Devon, UK: Prospect Books, 2013.

———. "On Spaghetti alla Carbonara and Related Dishes of Central and Southern Italy." In *Eggs in Cookery*, edited by Richard Hosking. London: Prospect Books, 2007.

Buonassisi, Rosario. *Pizza: From Its Italian Origins to the Modern Table*. Buffalo: Firefly Books, 2000.

Buonassisi, Vincenzo. *Pasta*. Translated by Elisabeth Evans. Wilton, CT: Lyceum Books, 1976.

Burros, Marian. "In New Haven, Pizza Is Serious." *New York Times*, July 18, 1987, 52.

———. "To Every Parmigiano, a Season." *New York Times*, July 26, 2000, F1.

Calingaert, Efram Funghi, and Jacquelyn Days Serwer. *Pasta and Rice Italian Style*. New York: Scribners, 1983.

Calman, Max, and David Gibbons. *Cheese: A Connoisseur's Guide in the World's Best*. New York: Clarkson Potter, 2005.

Calvacanti, Ippolito. *Cucina teorico-pratica.* Napoli, Italy: G. Capasso, 1852. Google Books.

Capatti, Alberto, and Massimo Montanari. *Italian Cuisine: A Cultural History.* New York: Columbia University Press, 1999.

Capuzzo, Jill P. "The Original." *New Jersey Monthly,* January 12, 2010.

Carr, Sandy. *Cheese: A Complete Guide to the Cheeses of the World.* New York: Simon & Schuster, 1992.

Carter, Anthony John. "Myths and Mandrakes." *Journal of the Royal Society of Medicine,* March 2003, 144–47. www.ncbi.nlm.nih.gov/pmc/articles/PMC 539425.

"Caruso Says Suing Chef Failed to Fill Major Role." *New-York Tribune* (New York, New York), December 16, 1920.

Casey, Nell. "LES Group Calls for an End to Invasive Dollar Slice Joints." *Gothamist,* February 14, 2014. https://gothamist.com/food/les-group-calls-for -an-end-to-invasive-dollar-slice-joints.

Catholic Hierarchy. "Diocese of Ischia—Past and Present Ordinaries." Accessed August 30, 2021. www.catholic-hierarchy.org/diocese/disch.html.

Cavendish, Richard, ed. *Man Myth & Magic: The Illustrated Encyclopedia of Mythology, Religion, and the Unknown.* New York: Marshall Cavendish, 1995.

Cesari, Luca. "Carbonara: History, Origins and Anecdotes of a Legendary Recipe." *Gambero Rosso,* April 2, 2019. www.gamberorossointernational.com/uncatego rised/carbonara-history-origins-and-anecdotes-of-a-legendary-recipe-2.

Chambers, Robert. "The Tomato." Texas Agricultural Experiment Station, 1903.

Cherry, Robin. *Garlic: An Edible Biography.* Boston: Roost Books, 2014.

Chiamanicitta.it. "22 settembre 1944—Nasce a Riccione la pasta alla carbonara." *Almanacco quotidiano,* September 22, 2020. www.chiamamicitta.it/22-settem bre-1944-nasce-riccione-la-pasta-alla-carbonara.

Chicago Tribune. "Who Invented Deep Dish?" *Chicago Tribune,* February 18, 2009. www.chicagotribune.com/news/ct-xpm-2009-02-18-0902180055-story.html.

"Chicken Scarpariello." *Lidia's Italy.* Accessed August 30, 2021. https://lidiasitaly .com/recipes/chicken-scarpariello-2.

The Cincinnati Enquirer, July 20, 1957, 8. www.newspapers.com/image/100934017.

Cinotto, Simone. *The Italian American Table: Food, Family, and Community in New York City.* Urbana: University of Illinois Press, 2013.

Cirillo, Mark. *Pizza Culture: The Story of the World's Most Popular Dish.* Toronto: Mansfield Press, 2017.

Civitello, Linda. *Cuisine and Culture: A History of Food and People.* Hoboken, NJ: Wiley, 2004.

Claiborne, Craig. *Craig Claiborne's the New York Times Food Encyclopedia.* New York: Wings Books, 1985.

———. "Street Festival Begins Wednesday; Gastronomic Delights Await Visitors." *New York Times,* September 10, 1959, 38.

Claiborne, Craig, and Pierre Franey. "Food; Italian, American-Style." *New York Times,* April 26, 1981, SM128.

———. "Meat Rolls by Many Other Names: FOOD." *New York Times*, January 23, 1983, SM46.

———. "Spaghetti with a French Accent." *New York Times*, October 2, 1977, SM20.

Clarity, James F. "BRIEFING; Split over Radio Marti." *New York Times*, September 19, 1983. www.nytimes.com/1983/09/19/us/briefing-split-over-radio-marti.html.

Clark, Alfred E. Clark. "San Gennaro Fete Opens 9-Day Run." *New York Times*, September 13, 1964, 41.

Clark, Melissa. "Parmigiana Dishes to Warm Weary Souls." *New York Times*, January 30, 2015. www.nytimes.com/2015/02/04/dining/parm-dishes-to-warm -weary-souls.html.

Cohen, Brad, ed. "The Untold Story of How My Grandfather Brought Pizza to America." *Vice*, February 19, 2017. www.vice.com/en/article/3d4nb9/the-untold -story-of-how-my-grandfather-brought-pizza-to-america.

Cole, Jennifer V. "How a Simple Pasta Dish Set One Writer on a Life-Changing Journey." *Food and Wine*, September 10, 2018. www.foodandwine.com/cooking -techniques/sicily-pasta-alla-norma.

Coleman, Todd. "The Real Alfredo." *Saveur*, April 13, 2009. www.saveur.com /article/Kitchen/The-Real-Alfredo.

Corra, Giuseppe. *Sicily: Culinary Crossroads*. Translated by Gaetano Cipolla. New York: Oronzo Editions, 2008.

Corrado, Vincenzo Il. *Il Cuoco Galante*. Napoli, 1773. Google Books.

Crowley, Hannah. "The Great Parm Debate." *Cooks Illustrated*, July 1, 2016. www .cooksillustrated.com/articles/263-the-great-parm-debate.

Cuomo, Annarita. "Il sugo 'alla puttanesca' nacque per caso ad Ischia, dall'estro culinario di Sandro Petti." *Il Golfo*, February 17, 2005. https://web.archive.org /web/20080209143520/www.ilgolfo.it/t/storehtm/htm19/17Feb0501f.

Cuomo, Christopher Martin. *Encyclopedia of Cultivated Plants: From Acacia to Zinnia*. 3 vols. Santa Barbara, CA: ABC-CLIO, 2013.

Cuozzo, Steve. "Hamptons Il Mulino, Six Other Non-NYC Locations File for Bankruptcy." *New York Post*, July 29, 2020. https://nypost.com/2020/07/29 /hamptons-il-mulino-six-other-non-nyc-locations-file-for-bankruptcy.

The Daily News (New York), November 6, 1967, 579. www.newspapers.com/image /463950910.

Daley, Bill. "Culinary Giant: Ada Boni." *Chicago Tribune*, May 13, 2013. www.chicagotribune.com/dining/ct-xpm-2013-05-15-sc-food-0510-giants-boni -20130515-story.html.

Darrow, Dian, and Tom Maresca. *The Seasons of the Italian Kitchen*. New York: Grove/Atlantic, 2012.

Davidson, Alan. *The Oxford Companion to Food*. Oxford: Oxford University Press, 1999.

"The Definitive Guide to New Haven Pizza." *Eater*, March 18, 2014. www.eater .com/2014/3/18/6264277/the-definitive-guide-to-new-haven-pizza.

Del Conte, Anna. *The Concise Gastronomy of Italy*. London: Pavilion, 2004.

————. *Italian Kitchen: La Pastasciutta.* New York: Simon & Schuster, 1993.

Della Croce, Julia. *Pasta Classica: 125 Authentic Italian Recipes.* San Francisco: Chronicle Books, 1987.

DeWitt, Dave, and Janie Lamson. *The Field Guide to Peppers.* Portland, OR: Timber Press, 2015.

Di Palo, Lou. *Di Palo's Guide to the Essential Foods of Italy: 100 Years of Wisdom and Stories from Behind the Counter.* New York: Ballantine Books, 2014.

Dickie, John. *Delizia! The Epic History of Italians and Their Food.* New York: Free Press, 2008.

Diner, Hasia R. *Hungering for America: Italian, Irish, & Jewish Foodways in the Age of Migration.* Cambridge, MA: Harvard University Press, 2001.

"Do You Know These Cheeses?" *Women's Day*, no. 1 (October 1949): 64–65.

Dulcy, Brainard. "Marcella Hazan: Educating America's Palate." *Publisher's Weekly* 244, no. 45 (November 3, 1997): 62–63. www.publishersweekly.com /pw/by-topic/authors/interviews/article/26571-pw-marcella-hazan-educating -america-s-palate.html.

"Emanuele Ronzoni, Macaroni Producer." *New York Times*, August 25, 1956, 15.

Encyclopedia Britannica. "Carbonari." *Encyclopedia Britannica.* www.britannica .com/topic/Carbonari.

"Enrico Fasani, Set Up Italian Cuisine Here." *New York Times*, February 26, 1949, 15.

Estabrook, Barry. *Tomatoland: How the Modern Industrial Agriculture Destroyed Our Most Alluring Fruit.* Kansas City, MO: Andrews McMeel, 2011. Kindle.

Fabricant, Florence. "Dining Out; Italian Fare in a Pleasant Setting." *New York Times*, August 2, 1981, LI19.

————. "Dining Out; Italian Fare with Emphasized Décor." *New York Times*, June 30, 1981, LI23.

————. "Food: Parmesan Cheese Has Many Uses but Seek the Real Thing." *New York Times*, November 25, 1984, CN23.

————. "The Meet of the Matter in a Pasta Debate." *New York Times*, January 16, 2008, F1. www.nytimes.com/2008/01/16/dining/16ital.html.

————. "Origin of Popular Lobster Fra Diavolo Bedevils the Experts." *New York Times*, May 29, 1996, C3.

Fahey, Mark. "Americans Have an Insatiable Demand for Pizza Cheese." *CNBC. com*, Tuesday, October 4, 2016. www.cnbc.com/2016/10/04/best-cheeses-ameri cans-have-an-insatiable-demand-for-pizza-cheese.html.

Flowers, Fruit, Vegetables and Two Lizards. Web Gallery of Art. www.wga.hu /html_m/m/master/hartford/2flowers.html.

Forster, Tim. "Every Single Possible Combination of Pasta You Can Make with Olive Garden's Never Ending Pasta Pass." *Eater*, August 23, 2018. www.eater .com/2018/8/23/17769884/olive-garden-never-ending-pasta-pass-restaurant -menu-2018.

Fox, Emily Jane. "How a Hedge Fund Saved Olive Garden by Making Its Breadsticks Better." *Vanity Fair*, April 6, 2016. www.vanityfair.com/news/2016/04 /olive-garden-breadsticks-starboard.

Freedman, Paul. *Ten Restaurants That Changed America.* New York: Liverlight, 2018.

Gabaccia, Donna R. *We Are What We Eat: Ethnic Food and the Making of Americans.* Cambridge, MA: Harvard University Press, 2000.

Galarneau, Andrew Z. "The Story Behind Spaghetti Parm, Buffalo's Favorite Pasta." *The Buffalo News,* August 21, 2018. https://buffalonews.com/entertain ment/dining/the-story-behind-spaghetti-parm-buffalos-favorite-pasta/article _9e8fc606-2078-5a6f-af7d-83be2574c95f.html.

Ganugi, Gabriella. *Cheese: An Italian Pantry.* San Francisco: Wine Appreciation Guild, 2004.

"General Foods Corp. Will Acquire Spaghetti-Maker Ronzoni Corp." UPI, January 10, 1984. www.upi.com/Archives/1984/01/10/General-Foods-Corp-will-acquire -spaghetti-maker-Ronzoni-Corp-the/4268442558800.

Genovese, Peter. "Nation's Oldest Pizzeria in Trenton, Claims Owner." NJ.com, July 27, 2011. www.nj.com/entertainment/dining/2011/07/nations_oldest_piz zeria_in_tre.html.

Gentilcore, David. *Pomodoro! A History of the Tomato in Italy.* New York: Columbia University Press, 2010.

Gentile, Maria. *The Italian Cook Book: The Art of Eating Well.* New York: Italian Book Co., 1919. Google Books.

"George Rector, 69, Noted Host, Dead." *New York Times,* November 27, 1947, 31.

Gibson, Mary. *Gender, Family, and Sexuality: The Private Sphere in Italy, 1860–1945.* Edited by Perry Willson. New York: Palgrave Macmillan, 2004.

Goldman, April L. "Grand Old Festa of Mulberry St. Is On." *New York Times,* September 12, 1980, C24.

Gopnik, Adam. "Carbonara Purists Can't Stop the Pasta Revolution." *New Yorker,* April 15, 2016. www.newyorker.com/culture/cultural-comment/carbonara-purists -cant-stop-the-pasta-revolution.

Grant, Susan McKenna. "What's for Finner: Cart Driver's Spaghetti." *Post Gazette,* June 17, 2009. www.post-gazette.com/life/food/2009/06/17/What-s-for-dinner -Cart-Driver-s-Spaghetti/stories/200906170241.

Grimes, William. *Appetite City: A Culinary History of New York.* New York: North Point Press, 2009.

Griswold, Alison. "The Decline of Red Lobster Is the Decline of the Middle Class." *Slate,* August 1, 2014. https://slate.com/business/2014/08/red-lobster-olive -garden-the-decline-of-casual-dining-is-the-decline-of-the-middle-class.html.

Gulick Amy. "Recipe of the Week: Pasta alla Gricia." *Italy Magazine,* May 15, 2015. www.italymagazine.com/recipe/recipe-week-pasta-alla-gricia.

Haley, Andrew P. *Turning the Tables: Restaurants and the Rise of the American Middle Class, 1880–1920.* Chapel Hill: University of North Carolina Press, 2011.

Handler, Rachel. "What the Hole Is Going On? The Very Real, Totally Bizarre Bucatini Shortage of 2020." *Grub Street,* December 28, 2020. www.grubstreet .com/2020/12/2020-bucatini-shortage-investigation.html.

Hazan, Marcella. *The Classic Italian Cook Book*. New York: Alfred A. Knopf, 1980.

———. *More Classic Italian Cooking*. New York: Alfred A. Knopf, 1978.

Hazan, Marcella, and Victor Hazan. *Ingredienti: Marcella's Guide to the Market*. New York: Scribner, 2016.

Hearst Corporation. "Simple Italian Cookery." *Harper's Bazar* 46 (January 1912): 362.

"Hector Boiardi Is Dead: Began Chef Boy-ar-dee." UPI, *New York Times*, June 23, 1985.

Hellman, Geofrey T. "Profiles: Directed to the Product." *New Yorker*, October 17, 1964.

Helstosky, Carol. *Garlic and Oil: Food and Politics in Italy*. Oxford: Berg, 2004.

———. *Pizza: A Global History*. London: Reaktion Books, 2014.

Here Comes Honey Boo Boo. "Time for a Sketti!" Season 1, episode 8, original airdate October 12, 2012.

Hesser, Amanda. *The Essential New York Times Cook Book: Classic Recipes for a New Century*. New York: W.W. Norton, 2010. Google Books.

Hildebrand, Caz, and Jacob Kenedy. *The Geometry of Pasta*. Philadelphia: Quirk Books, 2010.

Hoenig, John. *Garden Variety: The American Tomato from Corporate to Heirloom*. New York: Columbia University Press, 2018.

Hoffmann, James. *The World Atlas of Coffee*, 2nd ed. Richmond Hill, Ontario: Firefly Books, 2014.

Hofmann, Paul. "Fettuccine—a Dish Fit for a Duchess." *New York Times*, November 1, 1981, XX9.

Hogness, Peter. "Obituary of Ira Nevins." *New York Times*, January 25, 1995, Section C.

"Hot Stuff from Tuscany." *The Observer* (London), October 29, 1967, 29. www.newspapers.com/image/258895165.

Hubbell, Diana. "109-Year-Old Little Italy Cheese Shop di Palo's Now Has a Wine Bar Next Door." *Eater*, September 23, 2019. https://ny.eater.com/2019/9/23/20880026/c-di-palo-wine-bar-opens-little-italy-nyc.

Hunt's. "Ten Minute Pizza." *Redbook* 104, no. 6 (April 1955): 64.

Hussey, Kristin. "Uncertain Future for Pizzeria That Gave New Haven a Special Flavor." *New York Times*, January 14, 2016, A24.

Il Vero Alfredo, Emperor of Fettuccine. "Our History." Accessed August 30, 2021. www.ilveroalfredo.it/en/history.

Isola, Antonia. *Simple Italian Cookery*. New York: Harper & Brothers, 1912.

"The Italian Way of Cooking It." *Good Housekeeping* 3, no. 13 (October 30, 1886): 319.

James, Rian. *Dining in New York*. New York: John Day, 1931.

Jenkins, Nany Harmon. *Cucina del Sole: A Celebration of Southern Italian Cooking*. New York: William Morrow Cookbooks, 2007.

Johnson, Sylvia. *Tomatoes, Potatoes, Corn and Beans: How the Foods of the Americas Changed Eating around the World*. New York: Atheneum Books for Young Readers, 1997.

Kamp, David. *The United States of Arugula*. New York: Broadway Books, 2006.

Kessler, Kevin. "Bamonte's Is the Best of Old Brooklyn." *Village Voice*, September 25, 2014. www.villagevoice.com/2014/09/25/bamontes-is-the-best-of-old-brooklyn/%20.

Kindstedt, Paul S. *Cheese and Culture: A History of Cheese and Its Place in Western Civilization*. White River Junction, VT: Chelsea Green Publishing, 2012.

Kirchgaessner, Stephanie. "Italian Birthplace of Amatriciana Denounces Chef's 'Secret Ingredient.'" *The Guardian*, February 9, 2015. www.theguardian.com/lifeandstyle/2015/feb/09/italian-chef-cracco-ridiculed-amatriciana-secret-ingredient-garlic.

Kirk, Alice Gitchell. "Domestic Science." *South Bend Tribune*, April 9, 1913, 18. www.newspapers.com/image/514067995.

Kleiman, Evan. "Lasagne, not Lasagna: Why a Pan of Béchamel Lasagna Is Just the Kind of Comfort Food You May Need." *Los Angeles Times*, January 5, 2018. www.latimes.com/food/dailydish/la-fo-co-lasagne-bechamel-evan-kleiman-20171208-story.html.

Kobler, John. "Bravo Caruso!" *American Heritage* 35, no. 2 (February/March 1984).

Kosta, Ervin. "The Immigrant Enclave as Theme Park." In *Making Italian America: Consumer Culture and the Production of Ethnic Identities*, edited by Cinotto Simone, 233–34. New York: Fordham University Press, 2014.

Kostioukovitch, Elena. *Why Italians Love to Talk about Food: A Journey through Italy's Great Regional Cuisines, from the Alps to Sicily*. New York: Farrar, Straus and Giroux, 2009.

Kristbergsson, Kristberg, and Jorge Oliveira, eds. *Traditional Foods: General and Consumer Aspects*. New York: Springer, 2016.

Krondl, Michael. *Sweet Invention: A History of Dessert*. Chicago: Chicago Review Press, 2011.

Kummer, Corby. "Mangia, Mangia, in the Mountains." Corby's Table, *The Atlantic Online—Atlantic Unbound*, October 7, 1998. www.theatlantic.com/past/docs/unbound/corby/ct981007.htm.

Kurlansky, Mark. *Cod: A Biography of the Fish That Changed the World*. New York: Penguin, 1998.

———. *Milk: A 10,000-Year Fracas*. New York: Bloomsbury, 2018.

La Capria, Raffaele. *Ferito a morte*. Milan: Oscar Mondadori, 1984.

La Cucina Italiana. "L'enigma della carbonara." *La Cucina Italiana*, April 6, 2018. www.lacucinaitaliana.it/news/in-primo-piano/lenigma-della-carbonara.

La Prade, Malcom. "Meals by Men." *Ladies Home Journal* 165, no. 4 (April 1948): 286–88.

Latini, Antonio. *Lo Scalco All Moderna*. Naples, 1694. Google Books.

Laurino, Maria. *The Italian Americans: A History*. New York: W.W. Norton, 2015.

Law, Tara. "Mario Batali Relinquishes His Restaurants Following Sexual Harassment and Assault Allegations." *TIME*, March 7, 2019. https://time.com/5546290/mario-batali-sells-restaurants.

Lawson, Nigella. "At My Table; Pasta That Adds Bite to Vodka." *New York Times*, October 29, 2003, F3.

Leone, Gene. *Leone's Italian Cookbook*. New York: Harper & Row, 1967.

Levenstein, Harvey. "The American Response to Italian Food, 1880–1930." In *Food in the USA*, edited by Carole M. Counihan. New York: Routledge, 1985.

———. *Paradox of Plenty: A Social History of Eating in Modern America*. Berkeley: University of California Press, 2003.

Liberman, Sherri, ed. *American Food by the Decades*. Santa Barbara, CA: Greenwood, 2011.

Limbachia, Dixita. "Pizza Hut Plans to Shut Down More Than 500 Dine-in Locations across US." *Detroit Free Press*, August 6, 2019. www.freep.com/story/money/business/2019/08/06/pizza-hut-close-500-dine-locations-across-us/1938667001.

Lo Pinto, Maria. *New York Cookbook*. New York: A.A. Wyn, 1952.

Lo Pinto, Maria, and Milo Miloradovich. *The Art of Italian Cooking*. Garden City, NY: Doubleday & Company, 1948.

Lobosco, Katie. "Trump's Other Trade War Could Hit Cheeses and Olive Oil." CNN, September 7, 2019. www.cnn.com/2019/09/07/politics/trade-war-europe-cheese-wine-trump.

Lohman, Sarah. *Eight Flavors: The Untold Story of American Cuisine*. New York: Simon & Schuster, 2016.

Long, Lucy M. *Ethnic American Food Today: A Cultural Encyclopedia*. Lanham, MD: Rowman & Littlefield, 2015.

Mabon, Mary Frost. "Fare Thee Well." *Town & Country* 91, no. 4161 (February 1936).

"Macaroni." *Good Housekeeping* 9, no. 8 (August 17, 1889): 170. http://reader.library.cornell.edu/docviewer/digital?id=hearth6417403_1303_009#page/2/mode/1up.

Mangione, Jerre, and Ben Morreale. *La Storia: Five Centuries of the Italian American Experience*. New York: Harper Perennial, 1993.

Marcus, Erica. "Grandma Pizza: The Full Story." *Newsday*, September 10, 2008. www.newsday.com/lifestyle/restaurants/grandma-pizza-the-full-story-1.825269.

Mariani, John. *Encyclopedia of American Food and Drink*. New York: Bloomsbury, 1992. Kindle.

Mariani, John F. *How Italian Food Conquered the World*. New York: Palgrave MacMillan, 2011.

Marinetti, Filippo Tommaso. *The Futurist Cookbook*. Translated by Suzanne Brill. New York: Penguin, 1989.

Martin, Douglas. "About New York; Mamma Leone's: Spicy Tales of Sweet Success." *New York Times*, September 19, 1987, 33.

Martone, Eric, ed., *Italian Americans: The History and Culture of a People.* Santa Barbara, CA: ABC-CLIO, 2017.

Mattozzi, Antonio. *Inventing the Pizzeria: A History of Pizza Making in Naples.* Translated by Zacharty Nowak. London: Bloomsbury Academic, 2009.

May, Tony. *Italian Cuisine.* New York: St. Martin's Press, 2005.

McCue, Allen George. "The History of the Use of the Tomato: An Annotated Bibliography." *Annals of the Missouri Botanical* 39, no. 4 (November 1952): 289–348. www.jstor.org/stable/2399094?seq=1.

McLemore, Henry. "Rome's 'King of the Noodles' Climbs Ladder of Success." *Spokane Chronicle*, February 28, 1951, 12.

Merwin, Ted. *Pastrami on Rye: An Overstuffed History of the Jewish Deli.* New York: New York University Press, 2015. Kindle.

Middione, Carlo. *The Food of Southern Italy.* New York: William Morrow, 1987.

Montanari, Massimo. *Italian Identity in the Kitchen, on Food and the Nation.* Translated by Beth Archer Brombert. New York: Columbia University Press, 2010.

"Monte's Venetian Room." *New York Magazine*, March 23, 1987.

Moskin, Julia. "The Kings of the Dollar Slice Build a Better Pizza." *New York Times*, February 19, 2019. www.nytimes.com/2019/02/19/dining/nyc-pizza-upside-dollar-slice.html.

Moulton, Sara. "Of All the Ways Chicken and Sausage Can Be Cobbled Together, This Might Be the Tastiest." *Washington Post Magazine*, September 27, 2018. www.washingtonpost.com/lifestyle/magazine/of-all-the-ways-chicken-and-sausage-can-be-cobbled-together-this-might-be-the-tastiest/2018/09/24/c037d0f4-ad3c-11e8-b1da-ff7faa680710_story.html.

Moyer-Nocchi, Karim. "From Half Baked to Homogenized: Risorgimento—Unita—Fascismo and the Rise of the Borghese Cookbook." *Dublin Gastronomy Symposium*, May 31–June 1, 2016.

Nagourney, Adam. "Red Sauce and Rivalry at New Rao's a Storied New York Restaurant Makes a Move on Lose Angeles." *New York Times*, January 22, 2014, D1.

National Pasta Association. "About Us." Accessed August 30, 2021. https://ilovepasta.org/about-us.

———. "A Saga of Cathay." *The Macaroni Journal*, October 15, 1929, 32–34.

———. "Who Is Buying Pasta." *The Macaroni Journal* 66, no. 8 (December 1984): 10. https://ilovepasta.org/wp-content/uploads/macaroni/1984%2012%20DECEMBER%20-%20The%20New%20Macaroni%20Journal.pdf.

"News of Food: For a Teen-Age Celebration." *New York Times*, June 24, 1946, 34.

Norwick, Hannah. "The 8 Dishes That Made My Career: Cesare Casella." *First We Feast*, February 11, 2013. https://firstwefeast.com/eat/2013/02/cesare-casella-8-career-changing-dishes.

Notaker, Henry. *A History of Cookbooks: From Kitchen to Page Over Seven Centuries.* Oakland: University of California Press, 2017.

Noto, Anthony. "Mom-and-Pop Italian Restaurant to Become a 'Dig Inn.'" *New York Business Journal*, April 22, 2019. www.bizjournals.com/newyork /news/2019/04/22/mom-and-pop-italian-restaurant-to-become-a-dig-inn.html.

Oakland Tribune (Oakland, California). "Caruso Dies in Naples Following Operation." August 2, 1921, 2.

Obituary of Maria Grodzicki. *Angel Valley Funeral Home*, November 2017. https:// angelvalleyfuneralhome.com/tribute/details/19011/Maria-Grodzicki/obituary. html.

"The Old Reliables: Nanni." *New York Magazine*, August 13, 1984.

O'Neill, Molly. "Food; Pressing the Flesh." *New York Times*, April 4, 1999. www .nytimes.com/1999/04/04/magazine/food-pressing-the-flesh.html.

———. "Quel Shock! The Italianization of French Cuisine." *New York Times*, October 5, 1994, C1.

Ortolani, Cristina. *L'Italia della Pasta*. Milano, Italy: Club Italiano, 2003.

Owen, Julie. "Food: Italian Cheese." *New York Times*, April 9, 1956, 24.

Oxford-Paravia Italian Dictionary, 3rd ed. Oxford: Oxford University Press, 2010.

Parasecoli, Fabio. *Al Dente: A History of Food in Italy*. London: Reaktion Books, 2014.

Parker, Roger, ed. *The Oxford Illustrated History of Opera*. Oxford: Oxford University Press, 2001.

"Penne triangolari all'arrabbiata." *La Rustichella*, October 17, 2016. www.larus tichella.it/penne-triangolari-allarrabbiata.

Pennsylvania Dutch. "The Noodle People." Magazine clipping (1970).

"Pet Elephant Dies." *New York Dispatch*, December 27, 1952. www.newspapers .com/image/614082860.

Pignataro, Luciano. *La Cucina Napoletana*. Milan: Hoepli, 2016. Google Books.

Pinchin, Karen. "An Italian Vegetarian Cookbook That Was Ahead of Its Time." *The Globe and Mail*, June 4, 2013.

Pizzo, Anthony P. "The Italian Heritage in Tampa." In *Little Italies in North America*, edited by Robert F. Harney and J. Vincenza Scarpaci. Toronto: Multicultural History Society of Ontario, 1981.

Pojmann, Wendy. *Espresso: The Art and Soul of Italy*. New York: Bordighera Press, 2021.

Pollack, Penny, and Jeff Ruby. *Everybody Loves Pizza*. Cincinnati: Emmis Books, 2005.

Pomranz, Mike. "New York's Pizza History May Need a Major Rewrite, According to an Upcoming Book." *Food and Wine*, February 6, 2019. www.foodandwine .com/news/nyc-pizza-history-book-filippo-milone.

"Ponte's." *New York Magazine*, December 24–31, 1984.

Potkin, Fred. "Eating Well in the Italian Kitchen." *Gastronomica* 5, no. 2 (Spring 2005): 100–102. www.jstor.org/stable/10.1525/gfc.2005.5.2.100.

Prezzolini, Giuseppe. *Spaghetti Dinner*. New York: Abbelards-Schumann, 1955.

Publishers Weekly. "The Silver Spoon." *Publishers Weekly*, October 3, 2005. www.publishersweekly.com/978-0-7148-4531-9.

Raisfeld, Robin, and Rob Patronite. "How the Humble Cacio e Pepe Transcended Its Roots." *New York Magazine*, January 25, 2016. www.grubstreet.com/2016/01/how-cacio-e-pepe-transcended-its-roots.html.

———. "The Truth about Vodka Sauce." *New York Magazine*, October 3, 2017. www.grubstreet.com/2017/10/truth-about-vodka-sauce-carbone.html.

Ramirez, Anthony. "Soviet Pizza Huts Have Local Flavor." *New York Times*, September 11, 1990, D5.

Read, Max. "The Pizza Belt: The Most Important Pizza Theory You'll Read." *Gawker*, July 12, 2013. www.gawker.com/the-pizza-belt-the-most-important-pizza-theory-youll-r-743629037.

Rector, George. "A Cook's Tour." *Saturday Evening Post*, November 19, 1927, 14.

———. *The Rector Cook Book*. Chicago: Rector, 1928.

"Rector Buys Churchill's." *New York Times*, August 16, 1909, 14.

Robbins, Liz. "Close to Fetching Coal and Making Pizza." *New York Times City Room*, December 16, 2011. https://cityroom.blogs.nytimes.com/2011/12/16/close-to-fetching-coal-and-making-pizza.

———. "A Dash of Drama in the Pizza World." *New York Daily News*, November 29, 2011. https://cityroom.blogs.nytimes.com/2011/11/29/a-dash-of-drama-in-the-pizza-world.

Romani, Gabriella. *Postal Culture: Writing and Reading Letters in Post-Unification Italy*. Toronto: University of Toronto Press, 2013.

Romano, Philip J. *Food for Thought*. Chicago: Dearborn Trade, 2005.

Romina, Francesa. *Mangia, Little Italy! Secrets from a Sicilian Family Kitchen*. San Francisco: Chronicle Books, 1998.

Root, Waverly. *The Food of Italy*. New York: Vintage Books, 1992.

Rosenblum, Mort. *The Life and Lore of the Noble Fruit*. New York: North Point Press, 1996.

Rosner, Helen. "How to Get a Table at Carbone." *New Yorker*, May 19, 2021. www.newyorker.com/culture/annals-of-gastronomy/how-to-get-a-table-at-carbone.

Rotella, Mark. *The Story of Italian American Song: Amore*. New York: Macmillan, 2019.

Ruhlman, Michael. *Grocery: The Buying and Selling of Food in America*. New York: Harry N Abrams, 2017.

Russell, Henry. *The Passing Show*. Boston: Little, Brown, 1926.

Rutledge, Sarah. *House and Home, or the Carolina Housewife*. Charleston, SC: John Russell, 1855.

Sagon, Candy. "The Americanization of Lasagna." *Washington Post*, February 16, 2000. www.washingtonpost.com/wp-srv/WPcap/2000-02/16/001r-021600-idx.html.

"Sailor's Fight at Rector's." *New York Times*, May 24, 1917, 10.

Sardo, Peter, Gigi Piumatti, and Roberto Rubino, eds. *Italian Cheese: A Guide to Their Discovery and Appreciation*. Bra, Italy: Slow Food Arcigola Editore, 1999.

Saveur. *The New Comfort Food: Home Cooking from around the World*. Edited by James Oseland. San Francisco: Chronicle Books, 2011.

Scarpaci, Vincenza J. "Observations on an Ethnic Community: Baltimore's Little Italy." In *Little Italies in North America*, edited by Robert F. Harney and J. Vincenza Scarpaci. Toronto: The Multicultural Society of Ontario, 1981.

Schaffer, Marjorie. *Pepper: A History of the World's Most Influential Spice*. New York: Thomas Dunne Books, 2013.

Schwartz, Arthur. *Arthur Schwartz's New York City Food*. New York: Stewart, Tabori, & Chang, 2004.

———. "Chicken Scarpariello." *The Three Tomatoes*, June 15, 2014. http://thethree tomatoes.com/chicken-scarpariello.

———. *Naples at the Table*. New York: Harper Collins, 1998.

Scott, Michael. *The Great Caruso: A Biography*. New York: Knopf, 1988.

Sedlac, Robert. "Das wiener schnitzel—zweiter tail." *Wiener Zeitung*, November 25, 2008. www.wienerzeitung.at/meinung/glossen/250616_Das-Wiener-Schnitzel -zweiter-Teil.html.

———. "Die wahrheit über das wiener schnitzel." *Wiener Zeitung*, July 3, 2007. www.wienerzeitung.at/meinung/glossen/99743_Die-Wahrheit-ueber-das -Wiener-Schnitzel.html.

Seed, Diane. *The Top One Hundred Pasta Sauces*. London: Rosendale Press, 1987.

Selasky, Susan. "In Good Taste: Pasta Alla Vodka Sauce." *Detroit Free Press*, April 2, 2016. www.freep.com/story/life/food/recipes/2016/04/02/pasta-alla -vodka-sauce/82497814.

Serventi, Silvano, and Françoise Sabban. *Pasta: The Story of a Universal Food*. Translated by Antony Shugaar. New York: Columbia University Press, 2000.

"Several Miles of Good Spaghetti with Caruso." *The Paducah Sun-Democrat* (Paducah, Kentucky), May 27, 1921, 3.

Severson, Kim. "For Better, for Worse, for Richer, for Pasta." *New York Times*, September 9, 2008, F1.

Sheraton, Mimi. *1,000 Foods to Eat before You Die: A Food Lover's Life List*. New York: Workman, 2013.

Shouer, Louella G. "Thrifty Meals Italian Style." *Ladies Home Journal* 68, no. 2 (February 1951): 148–49, 155.

Shugaar, Antony. "Introduction." In *The Duke's Table: The Complete Book of Vegetarian Italian Cooking*. Brooklyn: Melville House, 2013.

Sifton, Sam. "Chicken Terazzini, the Casserole Even Snobs Love." *New York Times Magazine*, September 26, 2016.

The Silver Spoon. New York: Phaidon Press, 2005.

Simeti, Mary Taylor. *Pomp and Sustenance: Twenty-Five Centuries of Sicilian Food*. New York: Knopf, 1989.

Siotto, Giuseppina. *Vegetaliana: Note di cucina italiana vegetale*. Modena: Edizioni del Loggione, 2014.

Smith, Andrew F. *New York City: A Food Biography*. Lanham, MD: Rowman & Littlefield, 2014.

———. *Super Tomatoes: The Story of America's Favorite Food*. New Brunswick, NJ: Rutgers University Press, 1946.

———. *The Tomato in America: Early History, Culture and Cookery*. Columbia: University of South Carolina Press, 1994.

Spieler, Marlena. *A Taste of Naples: Neapolitan Culture, Cuisine, and Cooking*. New York: Rowman & Littlefield, 2018.

Stevens, Marion. "The Tomato." *Journal of Education* 78, no. 1 (July 3 1913), 21. www.jstor.org/stable/i40107305.

Storle, Wolf D. *A Curious History of Vegetables*. Berkeley, CA: North Atlantic Books, 2016.

"Sweetwaters." *New York Magazine*, June 30–July 7, 1986.

Taglienti, Maria Luisa. *The Italian Cookbook*. New York: Random House, 1955.

Tebben, Maryann. *Sauces: A Global History*. London: Reaktion Books, 2014.

Tennison, Patricia. "Revealed: Secret Behind Pizzas at Gino's East." *Chicago Tribune*, April 13, 1989. www.chicagotribune.com/news/ct-xpm-1989-04-13 -8904030809-story.html.

"Test Macaroni Recipes." *New Macaroni Journal*, October 15, 1922, 38.

Thrillist. "The 101 Dishes That Changed America." *Thrillist*, March 20, 2018. www.thrillist.com/eat/nation/most-important-dishes-food-that-changed-america.

Thurmond, David L., and Sandra P. Thurmond. *The Great History of Mozzarella*. Ogliastro Cilento, Italy: Licosia Italiacs, 2017.

Tirabassi, Maddalena. "Making Space for Domesticity: Household Goods in Working-Class Italian American Homes, 1900–1940." In *Making Italian America: Consumer Culture and the Production of Ethnic Identities*, edited by Cinotto Simone. New York: Fordham University Press, 2014.

Transasso, Clare. "Ronzoni Founder's Great-Grandson Alfred Ronzoni Jr. Tells Family History." *Daily News*, May 16, 2011. www.nydailynews.com/new-york /queens/ronzoni-founder-great-grandson-alfred-ronzoni-jr-tells-family-history -article-1.145979.

Travierso, Michele. "What Actually Goes on at Olive Garden's 'Culinary Institute' in Tuscany?" *TIME*, April 5, 2011. https://newsfeed.time.com/2011/04/15/what -actually-goes-on-at-olive-gardens-culinary-institute-in-tuscany.

Turim, Gayle. "Who Invented Pizza." History.com, July 27, 2012. www.history .com/author/gayle-turim.

U.S. Census Bureau. "Accommodation and Food Services: Subject Series—Misc Subjects: Principal Menu Type or Specialty 4 for the U.S. and States: 2012." 2012 Economic Census of the United States. Accessed April 29, 2021. www .census.gov/data/tables/2012/econ/census/accommodation-food-services.html.

———. "Introduction." *1860 Census: Population of the United States, Country Where Born*. Accessed April 29, 2021. www.census.gov/library/publications /1864/dec/1860a.html.

Urban, Raymond A. "Mama Leone's Restaurants." *Harvard Crimson*, December 2, 1972. www.thecrimson.com/article/1972/12/2/mama-leones-pbmbama-leones -restaurant-opened.

Vadukul, Alex. "How Forlini's Survives the Instagram Horde." *New York Times*, September 14, 2018. www.nytimes.com/2018/09/14/nyregion/forlinis-instagram .html.

Vincent De Luca v. Domenico Calandra, Andrew Cuneo, Frank A Zunino, Charles Casazza, Emanuele Ronzoni, Atlantic Macaronic Company, New York County National Bank, Basilea Calandra Co., Inc, and Bridge Café. N Walton, NY: Supreme Court, Appellate Division—Second Department, 1917.

Vitello, Paul. "Armando Orsini, a New York Restauranteur, Dies at 88." *New York Times,* July 20, 2011. www.nytimes.com/2011/07/21/nyregion/armando-orsini -a-new-york-restaurateur-dies-at-88.html.

Wallace, Nina. "Interview with Angel Marinaccio." *Community Oral History Project,* New York Public Library, 15:13. http://oralhistory.nypl.org/interviews /angel-marinaccio-i54jb0.

War Department. *Army Recipes: War Department Technical Manual TM 10-412.* Washington, DC: U.S. Government Printing Office, 1944.

Weissmann, Jordan. "Olive Garden Has Been Committing a Culinary Crime against Humanity." *Slate,* September 12, 2014. https://slate.com/business/2014/09/olive -garden-doesn-t-salt-its-pasta-water-investors-reveal-a-culinary-crime-against -humanity.html.

Wells, Pete. "At Momofuku Nishi, David Chang's Magic Shows a Little Wear." *New York Times,* May 17, 2016. www.nytimes.com/2016/05/18/dining/momo fuku-nishi-review.html.

WFMY News 2 Digital Team. "The Secrets to Olive Garden's Alfredo Sauce." *Good Morning Show,* October 9, 2019. www.wfmynews2.com/article/news /local/good-morning-show/olive-garden-pasta-bar-alfredo-sauce/83-ef0f6dfb -c6cf-4dea-bc9f-46578d5b72e5.

"What's the Story on Pasta? Ask Richard Castellano." *The News* (Paterson, New Jersey), August 8, 1974, 27. www.newspapers.com/image/532134206.

"World Pasta Day a Mosca: Si celebra con le penne alla vodka." *L'Espresso Food & Wine,* October 25, 2016. http://espresso.repubblica.it/food/dettaglio/world -pasta-day-a-mosca_-si-celebra-con-le-penne-alla-vodka/2231016.html.

Wright, Clifford. *A Mediterranean Feast: The Story of the Birth of the Celebrated Cuisines of the Mediterranean from the Merchants of Venice to the Barbary Corsairs, with More than 500 Recipes.* New York: Harper Collins, 1999.

Yoon, Tae. "Legendary Rao's in East Harlem Is Offering Takeout for the First Time in Its 124-Year History." *Thrillist,* December 8, 2020. www.thrillist.com /eat/new-york/raos-to-go-takeout-east-harlem-nyc.

Zanini de Vita, Oretta. *Encyclopedia of Pasta.* Translated by Maureen B. Fant. Berkeley: University of California Press, 2009.

Zanini de Vita, Oretta, and Maureen B. Fant. *Sauces & Shapes.* New York: Norton, 2013.

Zeleny, Jeff, and Sewell Chan. "Obama and Bill Clinton Have Lunch in the Village." *New York Times,* September 14, 2009. https://cityroom.blogs.nytimes .com/2009/09/14/obama-and-clinton-have-lunch-in-the-village.

Ziegelman, Jane. *97 Orchard: An Edible History of Five Immigrant Families in One New York Tenement.* New York: Harper, 2010.

Index

About the Author

Ian MacAllen is a writer and book critic. His maternal grandfather was born in Bagnoli del Trigno in Molise, Italy, and his maternal grandmother's family was from Naples and Sicily. He is descended from a line of Sicilian strega. He lives in Brooklyn, New York, with his wife and son.

CPSIA information can be obtained
at www.ICGtesting.com
Printed in the USA
BVHW042236090422
633650BV00001B/1